Advanced GNVQ
BUSINESS AND THE LAW

Advanced GNVQ
BUSINESS AND THE LAW

Ewan MacIntyre LLB Cert Ed.

Lecturer in Law,
Clarendon College, Nottingham

PITMAN PUBLISHING

Published in association with

PITMAN PUBLISHING
128 Long Acre, London WC2 9AN
Tel: +44 (0)171 447 2000
Fax: +44 (0)171 240 5771

A Division of Pearson Professional Limited

First published in Great Britain in 1995

ISBN 0 273 61239 5

British Library Cataloguing in Publication Data
A CIP catalogue record for this book can be obtained from the British Library

10 9 8 7 6 5 4 3 2

Typeset by M Rules
Printed and bound in Great Britain by Clays Ltd, St Ives plc

The Publishers' policy is to use paper manufactured from sustainable forests.

Contents

Element 15.2
THE LEGAL STATUS OF BUSINESSES

Element 15.3
LEGAL RELATIONSHIPS ARISING FROM BUSINESS OPERATIONS AND ACTIVITIES

Preface

This book has been written specifically for Unit 15, the *Business and the Law* option of the BTEC GNVQ course in Advanced Business. All of BTEC's performance criteria are covered in appropriate depth and detail.

The full unit specification is reproduced on pages 375–81, but the three elements are:

Element 15.1 Investigate the effect of law on business operations and activities

Element 15.2 Examine the legal status of businesses

Element 15.3 Investigate legal relationships arising from business operations and activities

This book differs from most legal textbooks in that it contains a very large number of student activity questions. All law books written for this level of qualification paraphrase the law, and most pose a few questions at the end of each chapter. I too have tried to paraphrase the law, and I hope that I have done this in a way which makes it interesting and comprehensible. But in addition, about 20 per cent of the text is given over to different types of student activity questions.

There are two reasons for my having adopted this approach. First, I have always thought that texts aimed at this level should include as many questions as possible. Students tend to enjoy problem solving, and as a lecturer it is not always easy to think of appropriate questions on every aspect of a topic as broad as *Business and the Law*. Second, and more important, students on GNVQ courses must put together a portfolio of evidence to show that they have achieved all of the performance criteria required in a particular unit. I hope that the large number of student activity questions will ensure that all students using this book have plenty of material to provide the necessary portfolio evidence.

The *Business and the Law* option is divided into three elements, and BTEC have listed evidence indicators for each element. I have included assignments to cover the first two of these elements. Students who completed these assignments would produce evidence of all the necessary performance criteria. But this book also contains three other types of questions: Activity Questions, Further Activity Questions and Tasks.

The Activity Questions run throughout each chapter and are designed to check that the students have grasped the essentials of each of the performance criteria. The answers to these questions are included at the back of the book.

The Further Activity Questions are more demanding, challenging the students to apply the law to a variety of problems. In an Instructor's Manual, available free of charge to lecturers who adopt the book, I have attempted to explain both the answers to these questions and the ways in which they could provide portfolio evidence. However, it must be stated that the students have no need to consider the Further Activity Questions, and that many students using the book might not do so. I have included the questions because my experience as a lecturer has shown that some students are particularly interested in law. They like to think about the subject in depth, and they like the challenge which legal problems provide. I hope that such students will enjoy the Further Activity Questions.

Finally, there are the Tasks, one at the end of each chapter. I have included these as alternative evidence indicators, recognising that many lecturers have their own favourite assignments and that such assignments might cover some parts of an element but not others. The Tasks are designed to complement lecturers' own assignments, ensuring that the students always have portfolio evidence for all the performance criteria.

Element 15.3 is very much larger than Elements 15.1 and 15.2. I have not written an assignment for Element 15.3 because it covers so many different types of business liability. However, ten of the Tasks, and almost 100 sets of activity questions relate to this element. These will give the students ample opportunity to produce portfolio evidence.

An evidence indicator table is shown on page xi, and this shows how the different types of questions might be used as portfolio evidence.

In some ways this is a new type of law book. If anyone, lecturer, student or other reader, has any comments on the book, or suggestions as to how it might be improved, I would be more than pleased to hear from them.

Acknowledgements

I would like to thank all those at Pitman for their help in producing this book in the face of changing BTEC specifications. Particular thanks to Pat Bond, for his confidence that things would work out in the end, and to Lisa Howard, for making sense of my instructions for change.

I would also like to thank Hire Association Europe for their permission to use their standard form contract.

Evidence indicator table

Performance Criteria		Evidence	Alternative Evidence
15.1.1	Outline the types of law which may affect a business.		
15.1.2	Describe and give examples of the types of legal duties arising from business operations and activities.	Assignment 1	AQs 1.1–2.1
15.1.3	Identify and give examples of legal rights of groups affected by business operations and activities.		Tasks 1 and 2
15.1.4	Explain the types of legal processes and procedures which may result from the bringing of legal actions against a business.		
15.2.1	Describe the legal characteristics of different types of businesses.		AQs 3.1–3.7 FAQs 3.1–3.7 Task 3
15.2.2	Explain factors that can affect the choice of legal status for a business.	Assignments 2(a) and 2(b)	AQs 4.1–4.2 FAQs 4.1–4.2 Task 4
15.2.3	Outline the legal process of formation of different types of businesses.		AQs 5.1–5.6 FAQs 5.1–5.5 Task 5
15.3.1	Identify the specific legal responsibilities of businesses towards key external parties to the organisation.		AQs 6.1–9.4 FAQs 6.1–9.4
15.3.2	Summarise the specific legal responsibilities of businesses towards key internal parties.	Tasks 6–15	AQs 10.1–12.4 FAQs 10.1–12.4
15.3.3	Describe the ways in which a business's legal liability for civil and criminal wrongs committed can be reduced.		AQs 13.1–15.5 FAQs 13.1–15.5

AQs = Activity Questions
FAQs = Further Activity Questions

Table of cases

Table of statutes

Introduction

This introduction covers matters which are not contained in the Advanced GNVQ specifications. Consequently it does not contain any Activity Questions. It would be possible for students to study the rest of this book without reading the introduction. However, a knowledge of the matters dealt with in the introduction would enhance a student's understanding of the rest of the book.

An English trial is a peculiar process. The achievement of justice is not the main aim of the lawyers or of the judge. The lawyers are adversaries, arguing with every means at their disposal to win the case for the client they represent. If they exchanged clients they would argue the opposing case with equal enthusiasm. The judge is not an inquisitor searching for truth and justice. He is there to apply the law, regardless of whether or not this leads to the fairest outcome. His job is to obey the rules and see that everyone else does the same.

Despite its adversarial nature, the English legal system seems to achieve justice as effectively as any other. Indeed English business law, the subject of this book, is one of the UK's invisible exports. When two foreign businesses make a contract with each other, perhaps a German company buys goods from a Japanese company, it is common for a term of the contract to state that in the event of a dispute English law should apply.

Most people have little idea of how lawyers argue their case. It is commonly assumed that they try to persuade a court to decide in favour of their client on the grounds that this would be just and fair. In English law this is far from true. First the lawyers try to establish the facts of the case, what actually happened. But once the facts have been established (and in many cases they are not even in dispute) the lawyers politely order the judge to decide for their client, whether this is fair or not. The judge is of course in a superior position to the lawyers. He is in charge of the proceedings. But what is often not realised is that he is bound by very strict rules which he will be compelled to apply, no matter how much he might wish not to do so.

These rules might well be contained in a statute, an Act of Parliament. Alternatively they might be found in the growing body of European Community law. But England (and those countries upon which it imposed its legal system in the days of Empire) uses a system of judicial precedent. As we shall see, this means that the courts are arranged in a hierarchical structure and that a judge in a lower court is **bound** to follow legal principles which were previously formulated in higher courts.

About half of the law which this book covers was made by statute. The other half was made by precedent. This is not representative of English law as a whole. Far more has been made by precedent than by statute. Furthermore, much of the law contained in statutes was originally made by precedents. The Sale of Goods Act 1979, which we consider in detail in Chapter 2, provides an example. It is one of the most important statutes in English law. But although Parliament enacted this law it did not really create it. The law contained in the Sale of Goods Act 1979 was made by the precedents of countless nineteenth-century judges. When Parliament passed the original Sale of Goods Act, in 1893, it merely decided to codify all the existing precedents into one comprehensible piece of legislation.

Sources of law

Statutes

How is a statute passed?

The Government of the day is formed by the political party which wins a majority of the seats in the House of Commons. Government Departments, such as the Ministry of Defence, propose legislation for approval. Parliamentary draftsmen (civil service lawyers who specialise in drafting legislation) then draw up a Bill and the Bill starts its parliamentary journey.

To become a statute the Bill must pass through both Houses of Parliament and then gain the Royal Assent. Many Bills achieve this without significant alterations. Others have to be amended to gain parliamentary approval, and some Bills fail to become statutes at all.

Bills usually start in the House of Commons. The initial stage is the **First Reading**. This merely gives the title of the Bill and announces the date of the **Second Reading**. At the Second Reading the principles of the Bill are debated. If the Bill passes this stage, that is more MPs vote for it than against it, it is referred to a Standing Committee which considers the details of the Bill. The Bill then proceeds to the **Third Reading**. Like the First Reading, this is a short stage where amendments are not usually allowed.

The Bill is then sent to the House of Lords, where the whole process is repeated. The wording of the Bill must be the same for both Houses. If the House of Lords disagrees with the wording, or refuses to pass the Bill, the Parliament Act 1949 will be invoked. The effect of this will be that the Bill will go ahead without House of Lords approval, after a delay of one year.

After passing through both Houses of Parliament, the Bill will then receive the Royal Assent. It is a convention that the Queen does not withhold consent and no monarch has done so since 1707.

Once the Bill has received the Royal Assent it becomes a statute which the courts must enforce.

Effect of a statute

A statute is the ultimate source of law. It will overrule any other rules of law which conflict with it, including earlier statutes. Judges may not consider the validity of statutes, and they are compelled to apply them.

In *British Railways Board* v *Pickin*, for example, a person whose land had been compulsorily purchased under the British Railways Act 1968 tried to argue that the statute was invalid, on the grounds that Parliament had been fraudulently misled into passing it. The House of Lords, the highest court in the land, ruled that such an argument could not be raised in any court.

Furthermore, statutes remain in force indefinitely or until they are repealed. A statute loses none of its authority merely because it lies dormant for many years. In *R* v *Duncan* (1944), for example, a defendant was convicted of fortune telling under the Witchcraft Act 1735, even though the statute had long since fallen into disuse.

A judge then must apply a statute, and in the vast majority of cases he will find no difficulty in doing so. However, some statutes are ambiguous, in which case the judge must decide which of the two or more possible interpretations he should apply.

Literal approach to statutory interpretation

Judges who believe in the **literal approach** give words in a statute their ordinary, literal meaning, no matter how absurd the result. An example of this approach can be seen in *IRC* v *Hinchy*, in which the House of Lords was considering the effect of the Income Tax Act 1952. Section 25 of the Act stated that any tax avoider should pay a £20 fine and *'treble the tax which he ought to be charged under this Act'*. Hinchy's lawyers argued that this meant a £20 fine and treble the amount of tax which had been avoided. Unfortunately for Hinchy, the House of Lords decided that the literal meaning of *'treble the tax which he ought to be charged under this Act'* was that a tax avoider should pay a £20 fine and treble his whole tax bill for the year.

The outcome of the case was that Hinchy had to pay £438 even though the amount he had avoided was only £14. This was obviously a severe blow for Hinchy. (In 1960, £438 could be a year's pay for an unskilled worker.) But the implications for other tax avoiders were terrifying. Under the system of precedent, all other courts are absolutely bound to follow House of Lords decisions. So other tax avoiders appearing before the courts would have to be fined on the same basis as Hinchy had been fined. A court hearing the case of a wealthy businessman, who rightly paid £1,000,000 tax in the year but avoided paying £5, would have no alternative but to fine him £3,000,035!

It is almost certain that the meaning applied by the House of Lords was not what Parliament had in mind when the Income Tax Act 1952 was passed. The statute was badly worded. The blame for this must lie with the parliamentary draftsmen. But at the same time it must be realised that they have a near impossible task. Skilled lawyers though these draftsmen are, they cannot possibly foresee every interpretation of the statutes they prepare. But once the statute has become law, every lawyer in the land might be looking for an interpretation which would suit his client. In Hinchy's case the Revenue lawyers, with typical ingenuity, spotted a literal meaning that had not been apparent before. They then managed to persuade the House of Lords judges that it was their duty to apply this meaning.

The Civil War, 350 years ago, established the principle that an elected Parliament makes the law. Judges who adhere to the literal approach do so on the grounds of parliamentary sovereignty. They believe that less harm is done by allowing a statute to operate unfairly for a short time (until Parliament has time to pass another amending statute) than would be done by allowing the judges to take over the law-making role altogether (as they would be in danger of doing if they interpreted statutes in any way they saw fit).

The purposive approach to statutory interpretation

Other judges though, perhaps the majority, believe in the **purposive approach**. Using this approach judges will give the words in a statute their ordinary, literal meaning as far as possible, but only to the extent that this would not produce an absurd result.

In *R v Allen*, for example, the defendant's lawyer's argued that although Allen had married two different women he could not be guilty of bigamy because the crime, as described in the Offences Against the Person Act 1862, was impossible to commit. Section 57 of the Act provides that *'whosoever, being married, shall marry any other person during the life of the former husband or wife,'* shall be guilty of bigamy. Allen's lawyers argued that this crime was impossible to commit. They were not saying that it did not take account of divorce, which later sections of the Act do, but that it just was not possible to do what was described in section 57. Their argument was that one of the qualifications for getting married is that you are not already married. Therefore *'whosoever, being married, shall marry...'* has already defined the impossible. They contended that the section should have read, 'whosoever, being married, shall *go through a ceremony of marriage* during the life of the former husband or wife' shall be guilty of bigamy.

If the judges in this case had used the literal approach they might well have acquitted. Unfortunately for Allen, they used the purposive approach and convicted him. They decided that the literal approach would have produced an absurd result, that they had not the slightest doubt what Parliament had meant when it passed the statute, and that Allen was therefore plainly guilty.

It is never possible to say in advance which approach a court will adopt, although the purposive approach is currently more in favour than the literal.

Whichever approach the judges go for, there is no doubt that a statute is the strongest source of law. A lawyer who has a statute on his side holds the most powerful card in the game. He may appear to be inviting the judge to apply the statute, but in effect he is ordering him to do so.

Rules of statutory interpretation

Other, less important, rules of statutory interpretation are applied by all judges. The **mischief rule** says that the judge can take into account what 'mischief' the statute set out to remedy. In *Smith* v *Hughes*, the Lord Chief Justice, Lord Parker, had to consider whether prostitutes who were soliciting from balconies and from behind windows were soliciting 'in the street' within the meaning of section 1 of the Street Offences Act 1959. Using the mischief rule, he had little difficulty in deciding that they were. The prostitutes were not literally soliciting 'in the street', but their behaviour was just the kind which the Act sought to prevent.

The *ejusdem generis* **rule** (of the same kind rule) means that general words which follow specific words must be given the same type of meaning as the specific words. For example, the Betting Act 1853 prohibited betting in any 'house, office, room or other place'. In *Powell* v *Kempton Racecourse Company*, the court held that the Act did not apply to a racecourse. The specific words 'house, office, room' were all indoor places, and so the general words 'or other place' had to be interpreted as applying only to indoor places.

The rule *expressio unius est exclusio alterius* (to express one thing is to exclude another) means that if there is a list of specific words, not followed by any general words, then the statute applies only to the specific words mentioned. For example, in *R* v *Inhabitants of Sedgeley*, a statute which raised taxes on 'lands, houses, tithes and coal mines' did not apply to other types of mines.

Until recently, a judge interpreting a statute was not allowed to consider the speeches which MPs made when the statute was being debated. However, in *Pepper* v *Hart* (1993), a landmark decision, the House of Lords held that *Hansard* could be consulted if this was the only way to solve an ambiguity.

Judicial precedent

As already mentioned, the doctrine of judicial precedent holds that judges in lower courts are absolutely bound to follow decisions previously made in higher courts. As so much of the law in this book is derived from precedent, it seems important to examine the system in some detail.

The hierarchy of the courts

In Chapter 2 we shall examine the court structure in more depth. For the purposes of understanding precedent, we only need to know that the courts are arranged in an hierarchical structure and that there are four levels in the hierarchy.

The House of Lords

This is the highest level of all. The 13 judges in the House of Lords, five of whom sit in any one case, are not bound by any previous precedents. Furthermore, their decisions are absolutely binding on all courts beneath them. (In practice the House of Lords judges do tend to follow their own previous decisions unless there is a good reason not to.) These same House of Lords judges also hear appeals from some Commonwealth countries. When the Law Lords sit in this capacity they are known as the Privy Council. Technically, decisions of the Privy Council are not binding on English courts, but in practice they are usually regarded as having the same authority as House of Lords decisions.

The Court of Appeal

The Court of Appeal is the next rung down the ladder. Its decisions are binding on all lower courts. They are also binding on future Court of Appeal judges. In terms of precedent, the Court of Appeal is the most important court. The House of Lords hears only about a hundred cases a year; the Court of Appeal hears several thousand. However, the House of Lords hears cases of greater public importance, and there is no doubt that its decisions have the greatest authority.

The High Court

Judges in the High Court are bound by decisions of the House of Lords and the Court of Appeal. High Court decisions are binding upon all lower courts. If there is only one judge sitting in a High Court case his decision is not binding on other High Court judges. In a Divisional Court of the High Court more than one judge sits. The decisions of Divisional Courts are therefore binding on other High Court judges.

Inferior courts

The decisions of inferior courts (the Crown Court, the County Court and the Magistrates' Court) are not binding on any other courts. Judges sitting in these courts do not make precedents.

The binding part of cases

In the Appendix at the back of this book a Divisional Court case, *Partridge* v *Crittenden*, is included. The decision in this case is typically lengthy. The lawyer's task is to sort out the important part of the case, known as the *ratio decidendi* (often abbreviated to the *ratio*).

The **ratio decidendi**, loosely translated from the Latin as 'the reason for the decision,' is the part of the case which is binding on other judges. It is the statement of law which caused the case to be decided as it was. Despite the great length of most cases, the *ratio* is often quite simple. For example, the *ratio* of *Partridge* v *Crittenden* might be that 'magazine advertisements, which describe goods and the price for which they will be sold, are not contractual offers but only invitations to treat'. As we shall see when we consider the law of contract, this is a relatively straightforward statement of law.

Ultimately the *ratio* of a case will be decided by future courts when they are considering whether or not to apply the case.

Partridge v *Crittenden* was decided by a Divisional Court of the High Court. It would not therefore be binding on the House of Lords or the Court of Appeal. But other High Courts, as well as County Courts, Crown Courts and Magistrates' Courts, would be compelled to follow it (unless they were confronted with a statute or higher ranking precedent to the contrary).

Statements of law which did not form the basis of the decision are known as **obiter dicta** (other things said). Examples of *obiter dicta* can be found in most cases. For example, in *Partridge* v *Crittenden* all three of the judges were agreed that section 6(1) of the Protection of Birds Act 1954 makes it an offence to offer for sale a wild bird. This statement of law is *obiter* not *ratio* because it was not the reason for deciding that Partridge was not guilty.

Obiter dicta are not binding on judges, no matter what court they were made in. However, if the judges in the House of Lords all express the same *obiter* then a lower court judge would almost certainly follow this in the absence of a precedent which he was compelled to follow.

Courts which hear appeals (appellate courts) usually have more than one judge sitting. Fortunately, it is an odd number of judges rather than an even number. A majority of judges will therefore decide for one of the parties or for the other. If the decision is unanimous, for instance the Court of Appeal decides 3:0 for the defendant, then the *ratio* of the case can be found in the judgments of any of the three judges. If the Court decides for the defendant 2:1, then the *ratio* must be found in the decisions of the two judges in the majority. The decision of the judge in the minority may be persuasive as *obiter*, but it cannot form a *ratio* which will bind future courts.

Disadvantages of the system of precedent

There are currently 95 High Court judges. Every word of every judgment they make might contain a precedent which would be binding on future judges. It is an impossible task for anyone to be aware of all of these potential precedents. In fact, so many High Court judgments are made that most are not even reported in the Law Reports.

Law reporting is not a government task but is carried out by private firms. The law reporters are barristers and they weed out the vast number of judgments which they consider to be unimportant. Even so, as students become aware when they step into a law library, the system of precedent does mean that English law

is very bulky. There are hundreds of thousands of precedents and it can be very hard for a lawyer to find the law he is looking for.

Precedent suffers from another disadvantage, and that is that bad decisions can live on for a very long time. Before 1966 a House of Lords decision was binding on all other courts, including future Houses of Lords. If a bad decision was made then it could only be changed by Parliament, which was generally far too busy to interfere unless grave injustice was being caused.

These disadvantages of the system of precedent are thought to be outweighed by two major advantages.

Advantages of the system of precedent

The first advantage is that the device of **distinguishing** a case means that the system of precedent is not entirely rigid. A judge who is lower down the hierarchy can refuse to follow a precedent if he distinguishes it on its facts. This means that the judge will say that the facts of the case he is considering are materially different from the facts of the case by which he appears to be bound. This device of distinguishing gives a degree of flexibility to the system of precedent. It allows judges to escape precedents which they consider inappropriate to the case in front of them. For example, if a County Court judge strongly wanted to hold that a television advertisement was an offer to sell, it is possible that he might distinguish *Partridge* v *Crittenden* on the ground that a television advertisement is materially different from an advertisement in a magazine.

The second and more important advantage of precedent is that it causes high quality decisions to be applied in all courts. Judges in appellate courts have the time and the experience to make very good decisions, often on difficult or philosophical matters. These decisions can then be applied by much busier and less experienced lower court judges, who do not have to consider whether the decisions are right or wrong.

It must be realised that the House of Lords, the highest English court, is a totally different institution from the parliamentary House of Lords. It is possible for people of no great ability, whether through inheritance or public service, to gain entry to the parliamentary House of Lords. It is impossible for any but the very able to become House of Lords judges.

Until recently judges were chosen only from the ranks of barristers. Now solicitors too can become judges. The Bar is a career, rather like acting, which has extremes of success, and very many talented young people enter it. If a barrister gains promotion and becomes a circuit judge he will sit in the Crown Court or the County Court. This is an honour and an achievement. But even so, he will make no law. He will supervise proceedings, decide who wins civil cases, award damages and sentence criminals. But no matter how brilliant his analysis of the law might be, it will not form a precedent.

High Court judges are a different matter. There are only 95 of them, and they make the law of England from the very first case in which they sit. Every word of their judgements is open to scrutiny by the other judges, by lawyers and by academics. If they were not very able, this would soon be noticed.

About 45 judges are promoted beyond the High Court to the House of Lords or Court of Appeal. These days it seems unthinkable that any but the very able should go this far.

It is not only on the grounds of ability that the House of Lords ought to come to very high quality decisions. Unlike the lower court judges, the House of Lords judges do not decide a case there and then. They hear the facts and the arguments in the case and then reserve their judgment. They talk to each other informally to see whether there is a consensus of opinion. If there is a consensus one of the judges is chosen to write the judgment. If there is no consensus the minority will write their own dissenting judgments. In a particularly difficult case the process of writing the judgment can take a very long time.

In *Airedale Hospital Trust* v *Bland*, for example, the House of Lords had to decide whether Mr Bland, a football fan injured in the Hillsborough tragedy, had the right to die. The 17-year-old Mr Bland was injured on 15 April 1989. He was in a persistent vegetative state, only kept alive by a life support machine. His parents wanted permission for the machine to be switched off. The case was presented to the House of Lords on 14 December 1992, and on 4 February 1993 the Lords ruled that the machine could be switched off. (They decided that the object of medical treatment was to benefit the patient, and that his being kept alive was no benefit to Mr Bland.)

So the five Law Lords took seven weeks to formulate their judgments. Obviously it would be unthinkable for a busy circuit judge, under pressure to get through his cases quickly, to consider such a difficult question at such length.

Alternatives to the system of precedent

As already stated, most other countries do not use a system of precedent. France, which is fairly typical of European countries, has a codified system of law known as a civil law system. All of the criminal law is contained in the Penal Code and all of the civil law is contained in the Civil Code.

French judges, who are civil servants rather than lawyers, do not feel compelled to interpret the Codes according to previous decisions until those decisions have for some time unanimously interpreted the Codes in the same way.

Scotland has a mixed legal system. It is based on the civil law system, but has strong common law influences. In Scotland the system of precedent is used, but a precedent does not have quite the same force as in England.

European Community Law

The United Kingdom joined the European Community, the Common Market, in 1973. In order to be admitted as a member, the UK Parliament passed the European Communities Act 1972. Under this statute the United Kingdom agreed to apply EC law in British courts. It was also agreed that if there was any conflict between EC law and UK domestic law then the EC law would prevail. British statutes would have to be interpreted in a way that was consistent with Community law.

When the European Communities Act was passed several politicians argued that this meant the end of Parliamentary sovereignty. In one sense this is true. By passing the statute, Parliament recognised that it was subject to laws made by the European Community and that it was no longer free to pass whatever statutes it pleased. However, Parliament is still supreme because the European Communities Act is just another statute, and like any other statute it could be repealed by a future Parliament. To repeal it would, however, mean leaving the EC. It is extremely unlikely that a British Government would vote to do this. So while the UK remains a member of the Community, Parliament is no longer truly sovereign.

At the time of our joining the Community, EC law made up a very small percentage of English law. But it is a percentage which is constantly growing, and it is possible that eventually it will come to replace English law. (Whether or not this happens is a matter of politics. It is most unlikely to happen in the near future.)

The Treaty of Rome

The original Treaty of Rome was signed in 1957, long before the United Kingdom joined the Community. On joining, the UK agreed that it would be bound by all the Articles of the Treaty. There are 248 Articles, and these are said to make up the **primary legislation** of the EC.

Some of the Articles are much more important than others. For example, Article 119, which states that there should be no sex discrimination anywhere in the Community, has been the subject of a good deal of litigation. At the time of joining the European Community, the UK Parliament had already passed the Equal Pay Act 1970, and shortly after joining it passed the Sex Discrimination Act 1975. It might be thought that because two UK statutes deal with the subject, cases alleging sex discrimination are purely domestic and have no Community law element. This is not the case. Because sex discrimination is mentioned in an Article of the Treaty of Rome, any case on the matter is regarded as being covered by EC law. The practical importance of this is that in a case where a party alleges sex discrimination the final court to which an appeal can be made is no longer the House of Lords but the European Court. (The English courts which hear the case on the way to the European Court will of course be bound to apply Article 119 as well as the two statutes.)

The **secondary legislation** of the EC is found in three types of rules:

- **Regulations** are directly applicable in all member States without the approval of the Parliaments of those States. Nor can any Parliament pass a statute which conflicts with a regulation. Most regulations are on fairly technical matters, such as what type of additives may be added to the foodstuff of animals.

- **Directives** are not immediately binding, but require member States to pass legislation which bring them into effect within a reasonable time. The United Kingdom Parliament has passed several important statutes, such as the Consumer Protection Act 1987, because EC directives ordered it to do so.

- **Decisions** bring in broad new policies. They are immediately binding, but only on those to whom they are addressed, usually member Governments or corporations.

The European Community institutions

It should be noted that it is not the European Parliament which makes this secondary EC law. The legislation is made by the Council of Ministers or the European Commission.

The Council of Ministers will contain one minister from each member State. With the recent joining of the Scandinavian countries each minister no longer has a veto. Countries are given a certain number of veto points depending upon their population. To secure a veto they must make political alliances with other countries. For example, Britain is thought likely to align itself with two of the smaller Scandinavian countries. In many areas Britain's interests are similar to theirs. In other areas deals can be worked out.

The European Commission is made up of full-time representatives from the member States. Britain and four other large countries get two commissioners each; the smaller countries get one. Leon Brittan is currently an enthusiastic British member of the Commission. Roy Jenkins went one stage higher and became President of the Commission.

The European Court of Human Rights

It should be noted that the European Court of Human Rights has nothing whatsoever to do with the EC. The United Kingdom signed the European Convention on Human Rights in 1952. If UK citizens feel that their human rights have been breached they can, after exhausting other avenues of complaint, present their case to the European Court of Human Rights. This Court can declare that the person's rights have indeed been infringed. It can award the payment of compensation and order the Government to change its future behaviour. However, if a member country refuses to comply with these orders the Court has no real sanction, other than to expel a country from the Convention.

The United Kingdom was found to have breached the Convention in its treatment of IRA prisoners but chose to ignore the ruling. This led to bad publicity, but short of expelling the United Kingdom there was nothing that the Court could do. The European Court, by contrast, is the EC court. If the United Kingdom Government refused to comply with a ruling of the European Court this could, ultimately, lead to the expulsion of the United Kingdom from the EC.

Delegated legislation

Parliament has not got the time to pass all the necessary legislation into statutes. It therefore delegates to ministers the power to make some legislation. This legislation is theoretically concerned with minor, administrative matters such as traffic regulations, rather than with politically contentious matters such as privatising the public utilities.

If the Minister of Transport is asked to make a new road traffic regulation he will first pass the task on to the branch of the Civil Service which he supervises, the Department of Transport. There civil servants will draw up the legislation and the Minister will then present it to Parliament. MPs vote such regulations through 'on the nod,' that is to say without having a debate or a proper vote on them.

Once delegated legislation has been passed it ranks alongside a statute as a source of law superior to any precedent. The courts can interfere only if the legislation was not formed in the proper manner.

The English legal system

The adversarial system of trial

The English system of trial is adversarial. This means that the lawyers on either side are adversaries, who 'fight' each other in trying to win judgment for their client. The judge supervises the battle between the lawyers, but he does not take part. Today the battle is metaphoric, but in the early Middle Ages many disputes were resolved with a Trial by Battle. The parties would fight each other, both armed with a leather shield and a staff, and it was thought that God would grant victory to the righteous litigant. If either of the parties was disabled, or too young or too old, he could hire a champion to fight for him. This was no doubt considerably more entertaining than a modern trial, but eventually it came to be realised that it was not the best way to achieve justice. Lawyers replaced the champions. But the idea of a battle survived, and a trial is still a battle between the lawyers, even if the shields and staffs have given way to witnesses and precedents.

Most other countries have an **inquisitorial** system of trial where the judge is the inquisitor, determined to discover the truth. A French examining magistrate, for example, has enormous powers. He takes over the investigation of the case from the police. He can interrogate whoever he wishes. He can compel witnesses to give evidence and can surprise witnesses with other witnesses, hoping that the confrontation will point the finger of guilt.

When a French case reaches court it is often all but decided. By contrast, no one can ever be certain of the outcome of an English trial. The lawyers will fight each other on the day and either side might win. The judge should be disinterested, merely ensuring that the lawyers fight by the rules.

Students often ask why they must use cases and statutes to back up the statements of law which they make. They argue that if a statement of law is correct then it does not matter which case or which statute created it. Unfortunately this is no more true for students than it is for lawyers. If a lawyer in court makes a perfectly true statement of law, such as the statement that all goods sold in the course of business must be of satisfactory quality, he must provide authority for this statement. This means that he must quote the case, or in this instance the statute, which made the law. If he cannot do this, the judge has no obligation to apply the authority. The judge no doubt knows the relevant statute, but it is not his job to argue the case for the lawyers. Similarly, students must cite authorities. At all levels of study, a statement of law with no authority to back it up is not regarded highly.

Common law and equity

In 1066 William the Conqueror won the Battle of Hastings and became King of England. King William and his successors were warriors and soldiers rather than lawyers. Perfecting a system of law was not their highest priority, and for some time they allowed local law to be applied, much as it had been before the conquest.

A hundred years later Henry II began the process of applying one set of legal rules, the common law, throughout the country. The King's representatives travelled from London to the provinces, checking on the procedures in the local courts. Gradually these representatives became judges rather than administrators. When they arrived they would try the cases which had been waiting for them, a system which survived into the 1970s. The decisions of these first travelling judges began to be recorded and subsequent judges followed them, in order to provide a uniform system of law.

The common law grew to have several defects. First, legal actions could only be commenced through the issuing of a writ. There were various writs, to cover different types of cases, but under political pressure from the barons a statute was passed which prevented the issuing of new types of writs. The development of the common law was very much hindered by this. Sometimes existing writs could be stretched to cover new situations, but sometimes they could not.

A second defect of the common law was that procedure was extremely hidebound. If a writ contained the slightest defect in its wording it was rendered useless. There were also problems with fictitious defences. Originally the truth of these defences had been checked by the King's knights, but later they became, very effective delaying tactics.

Another major defect of the common law was that it had only the one remedy at its disposal. In civil cases it could only order the payment of damages. In some cases, as where a nuisance was being continually committed, the payment of damages was not much of a remedy. What the plaintiff really wanted was that the defendant be ordered to stop committing the nuisance.

In the Middle Ages people who could not gain a remedy under the rigid procedure of the common law could petition the Chancellor, the highest ranking clergyman, to ask him to intercede.

The Church was the one mediaeval institution where men of ability could better themselves. Generally speaking, only clergymen could read and write. They were trained in canon law, which had an element of natural justice, based on God's law and on the laws of conscience. The Chancellor, who had reached the top of this meritocracy, could order litigants to appear before him, without the use of writs. There were no complex rules of evidence or procedure and the Chancellor could order justice to be done in various ways. In particular, he could issue injunctions which ordered a person to behave in a certain way. This justice dispensed by the Chancellor became known as equity.

Equity was not designed to be a rival system to the common law system. Originally it was intended to supplement the common law, to fill in the gaps. But gradually equity developed into a rival system, and gradually it became just as hidebound as the common law.

For several hundred years, until the Judicature Acts in the late nineteenth century, England had two separate systems of courts and laws. The systems did not always deal with separate matters. In the *Earl of Oxford's Case* in 1615 it was decided that if common law and equity conflicted then equity had to prevail.

In 1875 the Judicature Acts merged the two systems of law. These Acts created the modern court structure, designed to apply the common law and equity side by side in the same courts. But even today equity still has an influence on English law. The administration of law and equity was fused, but the separate rules of each branch of the law lived on.

From a student's point of view it is sufficient to say that certain matters are still 'equitable' and that in these areas help will not be given to a party who has behaved 'inequitably' (unfairly), as we shall see when we consider the law of contract.

Lawyers

Unlike other European countries, England has two different types of lawyers. There are about 8,000 practising barristers and it is their main job to argue cases in court. They also give written opinions in which they state what they consider the law to be. Barristers tend to specialise either in criminal law or in a particular branch of civil law.

A barrister can be hired only by a solicitor. Under the 'cab rank' rule a barrister, like a taxi, is supposed to provide his services to whoever requests them. Theoretically, therefore, any barrister is available to any client whose solicitor asks for him. This is not always true as some barristers' fees are beyond the means of many clients and because barristers' clerks, who arrange what cases a barrister can take, are skilled at deflecting unwanted cases.

Barristers cannot appear in court unless they are robed (dressed in wig and gown). If an unrobed barrister tries to speak the judge will not listen to him. This, like many other aspects of the Bar, seems somewhat out of date. (It is still part of a barrister's training that he should eat a certain number of dinners at one of the four Inns of Court in London.)

Solicitors, of whom there are about 50,000, are the first point of contact for a client with a legal problem. Unlike barristers, solicitors can form partnerships and some of the partnerships are very large.

A solicitor in a one-man firm should have a good idea of most legal areas and should know where he can find out more information if he needs it. In the larger firms solicitors would tend to specialise in one particular area of law.

Until recently solicitors were allowed to argue cases only in the Magistrates' Court and the County Court. Now the barrister's monopoly right to appear in the Crown Court and appellate courts has been removed by statute. However, barristers still perform the vast bulk of advocacy work in these courts.

An analogy is sometimes made with the medical profession. Solicitors, it is said, are like family doctors. They are the first people to approach with a problem and they can almost always resolve the problem. Barristers are considered more like surgeons; they perform a specialist task but in far fewer cases.

Criminal procedure

The first stage in a criminal case involves the police. If the crime is a serious one they will charge the accused immediately and keep him under arrest. If the crime is less serious he will be granted police bail and later summonsed to appear in court on a certain date.

Let us assume that the police arrest John Smith for a serious business fraud. John denies guilt but the police charge him. Next John will be taken in front of a bench of magistrates who must make two decisions. First, they must decide whether or not there is enough evidence to commit John for trial. Second, they must decide whether or not to give John bail. If bail is refused John will stay in prison until the time of his trial.

Over the next few months the Crown Prosecution Service gathers the evidence and decides whether or not to go ahead with the prosecution. Its decision is based on the quality of the evidence against John, and whether it would be in the public interest to prosecute. If it decides to go ahead, John will be tried.

As the crime is a serious one the Crown Prosecution Service will insist on a trial in the Crown Court.

At the start of the trial the charge will be read out to John, and he will be asked how he pleads. If he pleads guilty there will be no trial, but the judge will sentence him. If he pleads not guilty the trial will begin.

First, the prosecution barrister will outline his case to the jury. He will tell them what he intends to prove and how he intends to do it. Next he will call witnesses favourable to his case and cross-examine them. The defence barrister also gets a chance to cross-examine any of these witnesses if he so wishes.

After the prosecution barrister has presented his case, the defence barrister sets about trying to disprove it. He calls his own witnesses, and after his own cross-examination the prosecution barrister gets a chance to cross-examine them.

After all the witnesses have been in the witness box, the prosecuting barrister sums up his case. The defence barrister then sums up. Finally, the judge gives his summing up. In this he carefully instructs the jury on the circumstances in which they should either convict John or acquit him. The judge chooses his words very carefully because if he uses inappropriate words a conviction could be over-turned on appeal.

The jury then retire and decide upon a verdict. When they return to court the usher asks them what their verdict is. If they find John not guilty, the judge will tell him that he is free to go. If they find him guilty, John will either be sentenced immediately or the judge will delay sentence until he has received social enquiry reports.

If John spent eight months in prison awaiting trial and is eventually sentenced to three years in prison, the eight months will be taken into account in deciding how much longer he has yet to serve.

Over 90 per cent of criminal cases are tried in the Magistrates' Court rather than the Crown Court. The procedure in the Magistrates' Court is much the same, except that there is no jury and the lawyers involved are likely to be solicitors rather than barristers. The atmosphere in the Magistrates' Court is markedly less formal than in the Crown Court.

Civil procedure

Civil disputes which go to trial are heard either in the County Court or the High Court, depending on the amount of money claimed as damages. Disputes concerning less than £50,000 are usually heard in the County Court: disputes concerning more than £50,000 are usually heard in the High Court.

Procedure in both courts is much the same, and is commenced by the issuing of a writ. This tells the defendant that he must reply with some kind of a defence or he will lose the case. After the defendant has replied there follows a series of pleadings in which each side must explain their legal position in more detail.

If a dispute does actually go to trial then the plaintiff's lawyer begins by outlining his case, calling whatever witnesses he considers relevant. The defendant then replies, calling his own witnesses. Both sets of witnesses can be cross-examined by the other side.

After hearing all the evidence the judge will decide the facts of the case, perhaps commenting on the credibility of the various witnesses. He will then apply the relevant law and, if the plaintiff wins, award a remedy.

Apart from defamation cases, it is most unusual to have juries in civil cases. If there is a jury it will decide the facts of the case and award damages. Juries have tended to award very excessive damages when given the opportunity to do so.

Civil procedure is considered in more detail in Chapter 2.

Summary

From the divided legal profession to the adversarial nature of a trial, English law is full of anomalies and peculiarities. These anomalies have come about because the English legal system has developed gradually over many centuries with no sudden, reforming upheavals. Countries tend to make radical changes to their legal systems after a revolution or a conquest. The new rulers usually throw away the old law and start again from scratch. For over 900 years, England has suffered no lasting revolution from within or conquest from abroad.

Element 15.1

THE EFFECT OF LAW ON BUSINESS OPERATIONS AND ACTIVITIES

PERFORMANCE CRITERIA

A student must:

1 Outline the **types of law** which may affect a business

2 Describe and give examples of the **types of legal duties** arising from business operations and activities

3 Identify and give examples of **legal rights of groups** affected by business operations and activities

4 Explain the **types of legal processes and procedures** which may result from the bringing of legal actions against a business

1 The effect of law on business operations and activities

Every business is regulated by the laws of the country in which it operates. This regulation affects all aspects of business activity. It begins before the business starts trading, making rules about the ways in which the business can be formed. It might continue after the business has ceased to exist, perhaps deciding who owns the assets of the business or whether the owners of the business are personally liable for its debts.

A great deal of English law was created with business in mind. But, surprisingly, English law recognises no separate category of business law. The reasons for this are largely historical. The existing categories of law evolved under the feudal system before business became important. But one reason why a separate category of business law has not developed may be the very size of the subject. Another reason may be that much of the law which affects business, the law of contract for example, applies just as much to people who are not in business.

Whatever the reasons, many different areas of law affect business activities and operations. In order to understand the ways in which they do this, we need to become familiar with the areas of law which might apply.

Areas of law which may affect a business

No lawyer knows all of the law. Some specialists do know one particular area of law in complete detail. The majority have a general knowledge of all areas and know where to find specialist help when it is needed. But when any legal advisor is faced with a problem, his first task is not to consider the specific laws which might apply to the problem but to decide which areas of law the problem concerns.

Most of us have more dealings with doctors than with lawyers, and an analogy can be drawn with the medical profession. When a doctor treats a patient, he must first make a number of preliminary decisions before he can consider prescribing treatment. The doctor will need to decide whether the complaint is physical or psychological, whether it has been caused by an injury or an illness, whether it affects one part of the body or several. These 'areas' of medicine are not mutually exclusive, often they overlap. Very similar questions arise when a legal advisor is faced with a problem. Does the problem concern civil law or criminal? Is the client making a claim or defending one? Does the case concern employment law, or contract law, or maybe both?

This process of sorting problems into their areas becomes instinctive to lawyers, just as it does to doctors and other professionals. But the process is not so automatic when a person first studies the law. So in this opening section of the book we examine the different areas of law which might affect a business, and explain how these areas can be recognised.

Civil law and criminal law

The distinction between civil and criminal liability is fundamental to English law. The courts themselves are divided into civil courts and criminal courts, and the two sets of courts have quite different purposes. The civil courts are designed to **compensate** people who have been injured by others. The criminal courts are designed to **punish** people who have committed a crime.

Table 1.1 shows the essential differences between civil and criminal law.

Despite the differences shown in Table 1.1, it is quite possible that the same wrongful act will give rise to both civil and criminal liability. For example, if a motorist injures a pedestrian by his dangerous driving then both a crime and a tort (a civil wrong) will have been committed.

The State might **prosecute** the driver for the crime of dangerous driving, and

Table 1.1

	Criminal	Civil
Purpose	To punish wrongdoers.	To compensate the injured.
The parties	The State prosecutes a citizen (the defendant). *Regina (Queen)* v *Smith*.	An individual (the plaintiff) sues an individual (the defendant). *Smith* v *Jones*.
Outcome	The defendant is either convicted or acquitted.	The plaintiff wins or loses.
Consequence	If convicted the defendant will be sentenced.	If the plaintiff wins he will be awarded a remedy.
The courts	The case starts in the Magistrates' Court or the Crown Court.	The case starts in the County Court or the High Court.
The costs	Legal aid is usually available to the defendant. If convicted he must pay towards costs.	The loser usually pays all the costs. Legal aid is available to the very needy.
The facts	Decided by magistrate or jury.	Decided by the judge.
The law	Decided and applied by the judge.	Decided and applied by the judge.
Standard of proof	The prosecution must prove all the case beyond reasonable doubt.	The plaintiff must prove his case on a balance of probabilities.
Examples	Murder, theft, driving offences, false trade descriptions, unsafe workplaces.	Negligence, trespass, breach of contract, disputes as to ownership of property.

if the driver is found guilty he will be punished. (He will probably be banned from driving, and might also be fined or imprisoned.) The **injured pedestrian** might **sue** the driver in the civil courts for the tort of negligence. If the driver is found to have committed the tort then he will have to pay damages to compensate for the pedestrian's injuries.

The different functions of the civil and criminal courts can be further demonstrated if we consider what would have happened if the driver's behaviour had been much worse.

Let us now assume that the driver was very drunk, driving very badly, and that he killed the pedestrian. Under the criminal law the driver would be charged with the more serious offences of causing death by reckless driving and of driving with excess alcohol. The purpose of charging him with these more serious offences would be to punish him more severely. He would almost certainly be imprisoned.

However the civil courts would not order the defendant to pay more damages merely on account of his behaviour having been worse. In fact, if the pedestrian was killed, the damages might well be less than if he had been badly injured. It is possible that damages would only be awarded to cover the cost of his funeral expenses. But if the pedestrian was injured in such a way that he would require nursing care for the rest of his life, damages might well exceed a million pounds.

This example demonstrates the different purposes which the two sets of courts are trying to achieve. The criminal courts are designed to punish bad behaviour. The worse the behaviour the greater the punishment. The civil courts are not concerned with the heinousness of the defendant's behaviour, they are concerned with the amount of injury which the victim has suffered.

Crimes which cause injury to a victim will also give rise to a civil action. But 'victimless' crimes will not. Possessing a dangerous drug, for example, is a crime. But the fact of the defendant's possessing the drug does not directly injure anyone else.

Most civil wrongs are not crimes. If a person breaks a contract or trespasses on another's property he might well be sued, but he has committed no crime. Notices on private land which state that 'trespassers will be prosecuted', are misstating the law. Trespassers commit a tort and might be sued for it. However, they do not commit a crime and so they cannot be prosecuted.

ACTIVITY QUESTIONS 1.1

Could the following wrongful acts give rise to criminal liability, civil liability or both?

1 An accountant steals money from a client.

2 In a company newsletter, it is mistakenly stated that an ex-employee has been convicted of fraud.

3 A haulage company's drivers take a short cut across a farmer's field, accidentally damaging crops.

4 A self-employed electrician buys a van with a stolen cheque.

5 Partners in a firm of painters and decorators drive the firm's van without taxing or insuring it.

6 To avoid having to explain his incompetence to the shareholders, a company director burns company documents.

Contract and tort

A tort can be defined as *'a civil wrong which is not a breach of contract'*. This definition makes it plain that civil liability can be broadly classified into two types: liability arising in contract and liability arising in tort.

Most people are familiar with the concept of a contract, and for our purposes here (comparing contract and tort) it is not necessary to expand on this knowledge.

The word 'tort' is not commonly used, but the names of specific torts are well-known. Most people have heard of trespass, libel and negligence, and have some idea of what they are. The exact nature of these torts is considered later in this book.

Liability in contract and tort

When we study contract we will see that liability under a contract is liability **voluntarily undertaken**, and for which something was given in return. For example, if Business A makes a contract to buy a computer system from Business B, then both the decision to buy and the decision to sell will have been freely made. In addition, both sides will have made a bargain. By this we mean that the liabilities which they assumed under the contract will have been given in exchange for the rights which they gained under the contract.

Liability in tort is not undertaken voluntarily. It is **imposed by the courts** who have decided that certain types of behaviour give rise to tortious liability. If a person injures another by such behaviour the injured person may sue. If, for example, a delivery driver injures a pedestrian by driving badly then the injured pedestrian will be able to sue for negligence. The driver has no choice about whether or not to accept such liability, the courts will impose it. Nor will the driver have received any benefit in return for accepting the liability. It will have arisen not as a result of a bargain, but as a consequence of having committed a tort.

Another difference is that **liability in contract is strict**, whereas **liability in tort is based on fault**. As we shall see, a person who fails to perform a contract can be liable for breach of contract even if it is not his fault that he cannot perform. The law takes the attitude that he should have considered such a possibility before he made the contract. But in tort a person will only be liable if his conduct does not match up to an objective, reasonable standard.

For example, once Business B has made a contract to supply the new computer system to Business A, it will have to do so or face the legal consequences. It will be no excuse for Business B to show that it was unable to deliver on time because its workforce went on strike or because vital components became more expensive. But the delivery driver who injured the pedestrian will only be liable if it can be shown that he drove badly and failed to take reasonable care. If it cannot be shown that the driver drove badly then he will not be liable, no matter how severe the pedestrian's injuries.

Contract remedies and tort remedies

Both the breaking of a contract and the commission of a tort give rise to liability in damages. However, the purpose of contract damages is not the same as the purpose of tort damages. Both of course are designed to compensate. But contract damages achieve this by putting the injured party in the position he would have been in **if the contract had been performed.** Tort damages achieve it by putting the injured party in the position he would have been in **if the tort had never been committed**.

For example, if the computer system which Business B agreed to sell to Business A was delivered one month late, then Business A would be entitled to damages. These damages would be calculated by asking how much it cost Business A that the computer system was not delivered on time. Such damages might include an amount for business lost as a result of the computers not being available, or for the cost of employing extra workers who were needed to do the work which the computers were meant to do.

The pedestrian run over by the delivery driver would get tort damages, and the purpose of these would be to put him in the position he would have been in if he had not been run over. He would get an amount for pain and suffering, for lost wages and perhaps for damage to his clothes. These losses would all be recoverable because if he had not been run over, none of the losses would have arisen.

It should however be pointed out that the two methods of assessing damages will often arrive at the same result. If a person loses two months' wages as a result of his contract of employment being broken, he will get damages to cover this loss, on the basis that if the contract had been performed he would have received the wages. If a person loses two months' wages as a result of being run over, he will receive the same compensation in respect of the lost wages, on the basis that if the tort had not been committed he would have earned the wages.

Often a person affected by a tort sues for an injunction rather than for damages. If the injunction is granted, the person committing the tort will be ordered to stop doing so, on pain of a fine or imprisonment. Injunctions can also be ordered to prevent a person from breaking a contract. Such injunctions are, however, very rarely granted.

Consumer law

Later in this book we will see that several important statutes give rights to consumers. There is no universal definition of a consumer. Instead, each statute defines those who are given special protection. The Consumer Credit Act 1974, for example, protects borrowers of less than £15,000 as long as they are not companies. The Consumer Protection Act 1987 protects anyone injured by an unsafe product.

It is in the law of contract that consumer protection is most important. In the past businesses could evade their contractual liability by inserting 'exclusion clauses' into contracts which they made with their customers. The customers had little choice but to agree to these clauses, which in effect took away all of their rights.

The Unfair Contracts Terms Act 1977 provides that consumers cannot lose their rights in this way. The Act says that when a business sells goods or services to a person who buys otherwise than in the course of business, the buyer is to be regarded as a consumer. So a market trader would be a consumer when he bought a pint of beer, but he would not be a consumer when he bought the stock for his stall. A 1995 EC Directive on Unfair Contract Terms in Consumer Contracts has adopted a very similar definition of a consumer, and in a contractual context this definition may well become standard.

As we shall see later, the consumer protection offered by the Act and by the Directive are extremely significant to all businesses which sell goods or services to the public.

Employment law

Although some businesses are run without the help of employees, most employ workers of one sort or another. All employees will have a contract of employment, although such a contract may be very informal. This contract will have been made in exactly the same way as any other contract, and the usual rules of contract law will apply.

But in addition the courts and statutes imply special terms into contracts of employment. The courts, for instance, imply a term that the employer should treat all employees with care and respect. An important statute, the 1978 Employment Protection (Consolidation) Act, gives employees who have worked for at least two years many other rights, such as the right not to be unfairly dismissed.

Every employer will be bound by these special terms, which cannot be excluded by the contract of employment.

Property law

English law classifies property into two different types:

- **Real property** cannot be moved and is limited to land and things attached to the land. Both a factory and the fittings in it would be real property.

- **Personal property** consists of two different types of property. First, it consists of things which can be physically possessed, such as cars and fax machines. Second, it consists of rights which can only be enforced by taking out a legal action, such as copyright, debts or patents.

Most businesses will own both real and personal property. The criminal law will protect such property against theft or destruction. But a dispute about the ownership of property, or the right to possess it, will be a civil matter.

It should be noticed that ownership of property and the right to possess it do not always run together. For example, if a building company hires a mechanical digging machine from a hire firm, then the building company will have the right to possess the machine even though the hire firm has ownership of the machine.

Finance

Few businesses are entirely self-financing. At some time or other most businesses need to borrow money to finance their operations. There can be no borrowers without there also being lenders, and it is the role of many businesses, particularly the banks, to lend money. Naturally, lenders and borrowers will have competing interests.

Lenders are always likely to want security for their loans. A borrower will provide security by agreeing that in the event of the loan not being repaid, the lender will be entitled to sell certain assets belonging to the borrower. When business assets are given as security the lender does not usually take physical possession of them, but he does usually restrict the borrower's right to dispose of the assets or take any action which would reduce their value.

If, for example, a manufacturing company needed money to update its machinery it might borrow the money from a bank. The bank would want security for the loan, and the company might provide this by mortgaging its factory to the bank. The manufacturing company would continue to occupy and use its factory, just as if it had never been given as security. But under the contract which gave the loan, the manufacturing company would be obliged to keep the factory in good condition, and if the loan was not repaid as agreed, the bank would be able to sell the factory and take the amount owed from the proceeds.

ACTIVITY QUESTIONS 1.2

1 A company hires a car from a car-hire firm for one week.
   (a) Who is entitled to possession of the car?
   (b) Who has legal ownership of the car?

2 A customer goes to a large department store to buy a cooker. Would the customer have the right to sue in contract, or in tort, if:
   (a) The cooker did not work properly?
   (b) When entering the shop, he slipped on a pool of oil on the shop floor, injuring his back?

3 Would the customer be a consumer, within the meaning of the Unfair Contracts Terms Act 1977, if:
   (a) He was a postman, buying the cooker for his family?
   (b) He was a cafe owner, buying the cooker for his cafe?

4 A retired teacher wants to start a language school. She needs to borrow money, and mortgages her house to a bank.
   (a) Will the teacher continue to have the right to live in the mortgaged house?
   (b) What rights over the house will the bank have?
   (c) Is the house real property or personal property?

Types of legal duties which arise from business activities and operations

Civil duties and criminal duties

An enormous number of duties are imposed on businesses. Some of these duties are imposed by the criminal law and others by the civil law.

Many of the duties imposed by the criminal law, such as the duty not to steal, are imposed on all citizens. Such duties will, of course, apply just as much to those who run a business as to anyone else. In addition, however, several statutes impose criminal duties which apply only to businesses. The Trade Descriptions Act, for example, makes it a crime to apply a misleading trade description 'in the course of a trade or business'. The Consumer Protection Act 1987 makes it an offence to give misleading indications of prices, but only as regards those who do so in the course of business.

Although these offences which apply only to businesses may seem fairly technical, they are crimes nevertheless. If a business commits one of these offences it will be liable to punishment in the criminal courts.

Again, much of the civil law applies to all citizens, making no distinction between those who are in business and those who are not. However, certain obligations are imposed only on businesses. The Sale of Goods Act, for example, requires that goods sold 'in the course of a business' must be of satisfactory quality. No such obligation is imposed on private sellers.

Common law duties and statutory duties

In the Introduction to this book it was explained that legal rules are made either by the judges or by Parliament. It was also explained that the legal rules made by the judges are known as the common law, whereas Parliament makes law by passing statutes.

The law of contract, the law of tort, and much of the criminal law are essentially judge-made common law. But most of the rules which apply specifically to businesses are statutory. In this section of the book we have already seen that the Trade Descriptions Act and the Sale of Goods Act impose special duties on business. Later on we shall consider other statutes, such as the Companies Act and the Partnership Act which apply only to those in business.

This distinction between common law and statutory rules is important in understanding how the law was created and how it might develop. But once a rule is in existence, it will be applied with equal vigour whether it was made by the common law or by statute. The only restraint on the application of common law rules is that they are not allowed to contradict a statute.

Limited and unlimited liability

A defendant who incurs civil liability will find no artificial limit on the extent of this liability. If a court orders a defendant to pay £1 million damages for breach of a contract, or for having committed a tort, then the defendant must pay in full. If the defendant is unable to do this, then all of his assets will be sold and the proceeds will be paid to the plaintiff. In addition, the defendant will either remain liable for the rest of the debt or will be made bankrupt.

But the owners of corporations may have limited liability for the debts of the corporation. Almost all corporations are registered as limited companies. This means that in the event of the companies owing money, the liability of the shareholders, the owners of the companies, is limited to paying any amount of the purchase price of the shares which has not yet been paid. Beyond this they have no liability for the debts of the company, no matter how much money they might have made from the company in the past.

So, if Company X, with a fully paid up share capital of £100, and assets of £1,000, owes £1 million to a creditor then the creditor will only receive £1,000. Once this has been paid the shareholders will not be obliged to pay any more, even though they own the company. This is true even if the company is a 'one-man' company, with only one shareholder.

It should be noticed that it is not the company itself which has limited liability, it is the shareholders in the company. If the company cannot pay its debts in full it will be liquidated and cease to exist as a company. But as long as there had been no fraud there would be nothing to prevent the shareholders from creating a new company.

This limited liability of shareholders has always seemed very unfair to those who do not receive full payment of their debts. As long ago as 1755, Lord Chancellor Thurlow said: '*Corporations have neither bodies to be punished, nor souls to be condemned, they therefore do as they like.*'

Fault based liability and strict liability

Almost all common law liability in tort is fault based. As we have already seen, this means that a person will not usually be liable in tort unless he was in some way at fault. However, an increasing number of statutes are imposing liability without fault.

The leading case on negligence, *Donoghue* v *Stevenson*, decided that a manufacturer of ginger beer was liable to an eventual customer for allowing the customer to be injured by a snail which had found its way into a bottle of ginger beer. The customer won the case in the House of Lords, but only by three votes to two. She had to prove that the manufacturer had been negligent, and this was not an easy thing to do.

Nowadays, under the Consumer Protection Act 1987, the manufacturer would be strictly liable in the absence of certain narrow defences. This means that the plaintiff would win without having to prove that the manufacturer had been at fault.

Similarly, the Sale of Goods Act 1979 makes shops which sell unsatisfactory goods liable to their customers, even when the shop is quite without fault for the defect in the goods.

It is a general principle that a person cannot be guilty of a crime if he did not know that he was committing the crime. However, the courts occasionally impose criminal liability without fault on the basis that this is in the best interests of justice. In *Hobbs* v *Winchester Corporation*, for example, the Court of Appeal held that a butcher who sold meat which was unfit for human consumption should be convicted even though he did not know, and could not have known, that the meat was unsound. The Court took the view that convicting an innocent butcher was a price worth paying to make sure that all butchers were as careful as they could possibly be.

The liability imposed in *Hobbs* v *Winchester Corporation* was imposed by the common law. But it is much more common for statutes to impose strict criminal liability on business. The Consumer Protection Act Part II, for example makes it a criminal offence to supply a dangerous product. There are defences, but these are very limited.

The different types of legal duties imposed on business can of course overlap, as can be seen from the following case study.

An accident at work

A small bakery is under pressure to meet a deadline to fill a big order for a local supermarket. Recently one or two orders have been delivered slightly late, and the supermarket has made it plain that if this happens again they will buy from elsewhere.

The main problem in the bakery is that the loaves do not feed properly through the slicing and wrapping machine. Having called the fitter to the machine several times, the shift supervisor removes the guard and tells the machine operator to push the loaves through with his hand. This does not appear to be all that dangerous because it is easy to see where the blades of the machine operate. While pushing a loaf through, the machine operator slips and his hand makes contact with the blades of the slicing machine. The operator is badly injured. The shift supervisor stops production and takes the operator to hospital, where it is discovered that he will lose the use of three fingers.

The manager of the bakery rings the supermarket to tell them what has happened and to explain that the delivery of bread will not be made. The supermarket ask the manager to deliver what bread has been made, and the manager delivers half the order.

One of the loaves delivered contained a metal bolt, which had fallen from the slicing machine when the guard was removed. A customer who bought this loaf from the supermarket broke a tooth when he bit the bolt.

This case study raises several different areas of law, involving several different types of legal duties.

First, the bakery are liable to be **prosecuted under the criminal law.** The Health and Safety at Work Act 1974 imposes criminal liability on employers who fail to operate a safe system of work. By using the slicing machine without a guard the bakery would have broken this duty and would be liable to a fine.

Next, the bakery will be sued by the employee who was injured. The bakery will have committed **the tort of negligence** by asking him to use the machine without a guard. The bakery will have to pay damages to compensate the employee for the loss of his fingers and for the consequences, such as lost wages, which flow from this loss.

The bakery have **broken their contract** with the supermarket. The supermarket might be justified in not continuing with the contract and will be entitled to damages to compensate them for the bread not being delivered as agreed. The accident at work will not be a defence to having broken the contractual obligation to deliver the bread on time.

The **supermarket will be strictly liable**, under the Sale of Goods Act, to the customer who broke his tooth. It is no defence that it is not their fault that the loaf they sold was not of satisfactory quality. In turn the supermarket would be able to sue the bakery under the Sale of Goods Act, because the loaf was not of satisfactory quality when the bakery sold it to the supermarket.

Alternatively the customer might sue the bakery under the Consumer Protection Act. The **bakery would be strictly liable** because their product caused personal injury to the customer.

The liability of both the bakery and the supermarket might be **limited** if they are both companies. In the case of the supermarket this is not likely to make much difference, as they are likely to be a large company with sufficient assets to meet any claim. But if the bakery is a small company, with an unhealthy balance sheet, it might be unable to meet the claims of the injured parties. This would mean that the company would go into liquidation and cease to exist. The injured parties would have a claim, alongside others, to any assets of the business. The owners of the company would find that their shares in the company were worthless. But the owners would not incur any personal liability for the company's debts.

If the bakery was run as a partnership, then all of the partners would be **jointly liable**. This would mean that the people injured could claim against any of the partners, and that any partner sued would be liable for the debt in full. A partner who was sued, and who paid damages, could recover a share of the debt from the other partners. This sorting out of liability between the partners themselves would not concern the person who sued.

Legal rights of groups affected by business activities and operations

Generally civil rights attach to individuals rather than to groups. Rights under a contract, for example, are only conferred on the person who made the contract. Similarly, only a person who is injured by a tort can sue for damages in respect of that tort.

But sometimes groups of people are identically affected by the activities of a business. Members of such groups will have rights in common with each other, and they are likely to find that they can more easily enforce these rights as a group than they can as individuals.

Employees

We mentioned earlier that the 1978 Employment Protection (Consolidation) Act gives employees with two year's continuous employment the right not to be unfairly dismissed. But having a right is not the same thing as being able to enforce it. An employee who feels that he has been unfairly dismissed might or might not seek compensation. He is much more likely to do this if he is backed by a group of fellow employees, perhaps a trade union, than if he is not.

Employees of a business can also use their collective strength to increase their bargaining power when negotiating the terms of their contracts. If, for example, only one employee says that he wants a pay rise or an extra day's annual holiday, an employer will not see this demand as too much of a threat. But if the whole workforce make such a demand, and say that they are prepared to go on strike to back it up, then the employer will be under considerably more pressure to respond.

It is not only because of their legal obligations that businesses should consider their relationship with their workforce. It is obvious good sense for a business to remain on good terms with its employees. A disgruntled workforce is likely to be considerably less efficient than a contented one.

Consumers and customers

Earlier in this chapter we saw examples of the type of special rights which can be conferred on consumers. These rights are well established, and individual consumers who are injured are likely to sue to enforce them. If a large number of consumers are injured by the same product, as has happened with several drugs, the consumers might join together to fight a representative action in order to establish the extent of their rights.

Individual consumers have little chance of changing the way a business operates or the products it produces. They could always write to the business, but a letter from one individual consumer is unlikely to force change. However, organised groups of consumers can have an enormous influence on even the largest businesses. CAMRA (The Campaign For Real Ale) has been one of the most successful consumer groups of recent years. It has forced radical change on the whole brewing industry, which contains some of the largest and most powerful companies in the country.

A business must always be thinking of the eventual consumers of its product, not only to avoid legal liability but also to keep itself in business. If the consumers stop buying the product then obviously the business will cease to exist.

Shareholders

A company is owned by its shareholders, but it is managed by its directors. In small companies the shareholders and the directors are often the same people. But the larger the company the more likely it is that the shareholders will appoint a group of professional directors.

As long as the directors are in office they have the right to manage and the shareholders do not have this right. However, the shareholders do have very considerable power. At a company meeting, 50 per cent of the shareholders present and voting can vote to remove a director and appoint a different one. Furthermore, 75 per cent of the total shareholders of a company can vote to change the company's rules. They can also vote to liquidate the company, even if the company is making money.

So the shareholders in a company are a very powerful body, and the managers of any business which operates as a company should ensure that the shareholders are happy with the way things are going.

Creditors

Even when a business is solvent its creditors will have the rights which they demanded as a condition of giving the credit. Creditors tend to be cautious, and these rights might be much more extensive than seems strictly necessary. If the creditors lose confidence in a business they are likely to enforce these rights, causing the very thing they had begun to fear, the downfall of the business. It is therefore important that businesses should have regard to creditors as a group, and try to ensure that they are well-informed and satisfied with the financial health of the business.

If a business becomes insolvent then the creditors as a group assume immediate rights over all the business property. If a company is liquidated because it is unable to pay its debts, the liquidator will take over the director's powers and will have to take note of the decisions of a committee of creditors. The creditors do not need to insist that the company is wound up. They can keep the company going if this seems the best way of recovering their money.

In the context of a company liquidation, creditors are likely to act as a group with similar interests rather than as a collection of competing individuals.

Community

If business activity causes inconvenience to a community as a whole, then it might be possible for that community to take action to prevent further inconvenience.

Later in this book we will see that a business which prevents others from enjoying the use of their land will be liable in the tort of nuisance. Usually a business would commit this tort by making excessive noise or emitting excessive fumes. If only one individual is inconvenienced he might find it hard to take legal action against a large business. But if a whole community is inconvenienced that community might be much more willing to take action. Usually in such cases the plaintiffs do not want damages for inconvenience already suffered, so much as an injunction to prevent the business from continuing to cause the inconvenience.

There are many other reasons why a business should be aware of the rights and preferences of the community in which it operates. For example, if the business wants planning permission to expand its operations, the objections of the local community will be taken very seriously.

The State

As we have seen, it is the State which enforces the criminal law. The police take the initial decision to arrest a wrongdoer and charge him. The charge is then sent to the Crown Prosecution Service who make the decision whether or not to take the case to court. Both the police and the Crown Prosecution Service act in the name of the Crown.

Many of the more technical business offences, such as offences under the Trade Descriptions Act and the Health and Safety at Work Act, are enforced by local authorities and by special inspectors. Again, these people take action on behalf of the State.

But the State plays a far greater role than merely enforcing the criminal law. It provides the framework for settling business disputes, and regulates the affairs of business through a variety of different means. It regulates businesses directly, by requiring them to hold a licence, as well as indirectly, by issuing codes of practice. Nor should it be forgotten that the State owns a big part of British business. The Government is the complete owner of nationalised industries, and is a major shareholder in several private ones.

In addition, the State uses economic means to regulate business. The Chancellor of the Exchequer, for example, uses interest rates as a means of slowing down or speeding up the economy. When rates are raised businesses have to pay more interest on their loans and are therefore less likely to expand.

The Confederation of British Industry, the largest pressure group representing business, is well aware of the influence of the State and exists to put forward the point of view of business.

TASK 1

Carlill's case

In *Carlill* v *Carbolic Smoke Ball Co* (1893, Court of Appeal) the facts of the case were as follows:

The defendants manufactured a medical product called a 'Carbolic Smoke Ball'. On November 13 1891 they placed the following advertisement in the Pall Mall Gazette and other newspapers:

£100 reward will be paid by the Carbolic Smoke Ball Company
to any person who contracts the increasing epidemic influenza . . . after having used the ball three times daily for two weeks according to the printed directions supplied with each ball. £1000 is deposited with the Alliance Bank, Regent Street, to show our sincerity in this matter.

During the last epidemic of influenza many thousand carbolic smoke balls were sold as preventatives against this disease, and in no ascertained case was the disease contracted by those using the carbolic smoke ball.

One carbolic smoke ball will last a family several months, making it the cheapest remedy in the world at the price 10 shillings, post free. The ball can be refilled at a cost of 5 shillings, Address, Carbolic Smoke Ball Company, 27 Princes Street, Hanover Square, London.

The plaintiff, a lady, bought a smoke ball on the strength of this advertisement and used it as directed, three times daily, from 20 November 1891 to 17 January 1892 when she caught influenza. The plaintiff claimed to be entitled to the £100 reward, on the basis that there was a contract between herself and the Smoke Ball Company.

The court held there was a contract, and that under the terms of this contract the plaintiff was entitled to the £100 reward.

Questions

1 Was the case a civil case or a criminal one?

2 The defendants were found liable to Mrs Carlill. Was this liability voluntarily undertaken by the Smoke Ball Company or was it imposed by the courts?

3 Which group within the company would have been responsible for the management of the company?

4 Assuming that the company was prosperous before the advertisement was placed, and that the advertisement caused the company to go into liquidation, explain how this would affect:
   (a) the shareholders in the company,
   (b) the employees of the company.

5 If the company had been a partnership, and if the actions which caused the partnership to lose money had been taken by only one particular partner, would the other partners be liable for the debts of the partnership?

6 Assume that one smoke ball exploded and injured a user.
   (a) On what basis, if any, would a shop which sold the smoke ball to the customer be liable for the customer's injuries?
   (b) On what basis, if any, would the manufacturer be liable to the customer who was injured?

7 Would Mrs Carlill nowadays be regarded as a consumer, as defined by the Unfair Contracts Terms Act 1977?

8 Plainly, the smoke balls did not work as described. If the company were to advertise similarly today, under which statute would it commit a crime? On whose behalf would a prosecution be instigated? What could be the consequences for the company?

9 If the smoke balls had been so successful that there were huge, noisy queues of customers in Princes Street, all waiting to have their smoke balls refilled, what action might the residents take to make the company move?

10 If one batch of smoke balls had been poisonous, and had killed several users, could the manufacturers be criminally liable even though they had no idea that this might happen? If so, on what basis might this liability be imposed?

2 The resolution of business disputes

Throughout this book we shall be examining business rights and obligations. Ultimately these rights and obligations can be enforced only by taking a case to court. For all business organisations this is a last resort. The process is lengthy and expensive, and it is also likely to cause ill will. If a business sues a customer then, win or lose, the customer is unlikely to deal with the business again.

The vast majority of legal disputes do not go to court. They are settled between the parties themselves. This saves time and money, and perhaps keeps a business relationship alive.

Jurisdiction of the civil courts

All civil cases are first heard either in the High Court or in the County Court. Both courts can award the same remedies.

The County Court

The County Court sits in county court districts throughout England and Wales. It hears contract and tort cases where the damages claimed are less than £25,000. It also shares jurisdiction with the High Court in contract and tort cases where the damages claimed are between £25,000 and £50,000. In addition the court deals with bankruptcy, the winding up of small companies and consumer credit cases.

Appeals from the county court go to the Court of Appeal, and possibly from there to the House of Lords, as shown in Fig. 2.1.

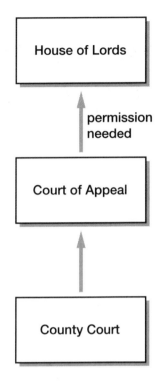

Fig 2.1 Appeals from County Court decisions

The High Court

The High Court sits in London and several provincial towns. It deals with the more serious civil matters.

The High Court is split into three divisions. The largest of these is the Queen's Bench Division, and this is the one which deals with business disputes.

The High Court hears contract and tort cases in which the damages claimed are over £50,000. Disputes in which the damages claimed are between £25,000 and £50,000 can also be heard by the High Court, although this is not usual.

Appeals from the High Court normally lie to the Court of Appeal and from there to the House of Lords. It is however possible to appeal straight to the House of Lords, under the 'leapfrog' procedure. This is possible only if the High Court judge thinks that the case involves a point of law of public importance, and if the House of Lords gives permission for the appeal.

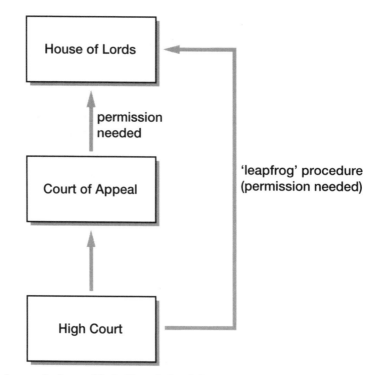

Fig 2.2 Appeals from High Court decisions

Civil procedure

The way in which a case proceeds through the civil courts can be a somewhat dry subject. If we study a particular legal dispute, rather than procedure in general, the process of dispute resolution can be made more interesting and more comprehensible. Throughout this chapter, therefore, I intend to consider the position of Acme Co Ltd, a company involved in two legal disputes, which arose as follows:

Dispute 1   Acme supplied a new boiler to Kwikclean's laundry. The contract price was £10,000, none of which has been paid. Acme has sent several letters demanding payment, but these have been ignored. Kwikclean finally responds by saying that the boiler was defective, and that as a consequence the laundry has lost £4,000 worth of business. Kwikclean offers to pay £6,000, but only on condition that Acme's engineers overhaul the boiler.

Dispute 2   Bob Charles, a factory foreman with 24 years' experience, has been injured at work. He slipped on oil lying on the factory floor, and his hand was crushed in an unguarded machine. Bob's injury is severe. He is likely to be off work for four months and will never be able to perform his old job. Bob was a semi-professional darts player. He had won several local events and once reached the televised stage of the World Darts Championship. His injury means that he can never play darts again. It was Bob's responsibility as foreman to ensure that all the machines in his area of the factory were guarded. He is claiming damages of £75,000.

The two disputes are of a different nature. Acme is suing Kwikclean in debt, and Kwikclean might be counterclaiming for breach of contract. Bob Charles is suing Acme in tort (negligence).

The first case will be heard in the County Court and the second in the High Court. As we have seen, it is the amount of money claimed, rather than the type of dispute involved, which has allocated the two cases to the different courts. We saw earlier in this chapter that tort disputes in which the amount claimed is over £50,000 are heard in the High Court, and that contract cases where the amount claimed is less than £25,000 are heard in the County Court.

Dispute 1 – A County Court case

Acme will be the plaintiff in its dispute with Kwikclean because Acme is the party who is suing. Acme's first move will be to go to the County Court office and fill in a form asking the Court to issue a summons. This form sets out the names and addresses of the parties, the nature of the dispute and the amount claimed as damages. In this case the precise amount would be stated as Acme is suing in debt.

The County Court will send the summons to Kwikclean, the defendant, who has four choices:

(a) Ignore the summons.
(b) Agree to pay the whole amount claimed.
(c) Offer to pay less than the full amount claimed, or offer to pay by instalments.
(d) Defend the action by denying liability, or counterclaiming damages from the plaintiff.

The consequences of Kwikclean's actions will be as follows:

(a) If it ignores the summons, judgment can be entered against it in its absence and it will lose the case.
(b) If it agrees to pay the whole amount claimed, there will be no need for a court case.
(c) If it offers to pay less, or by instalments, then it is up to the plaintiff whether or not to accept this. If the plaintiff does accept it then there will be no need for a court case because the parties will have settled out of court. If the plaintiff does not accept the defendant's offer then the case will proceed.
(d) If Kwikclean says that it intends to defend the action, or to counterclaim, then the case will proceed.

Fig 2.3 Effect of various responses to a County Court summons

Let us assume that Kwikclean offers to pay £6,000 rather than the £10,000 claimed. It is perfectly possible that Acme will simply refuse to accept this and make no more contact with Kwikclean until the date of the trial. However, Acme is quite likely to begin negotiating to try to reach an agreement, particularly if Kwikclean is a regular or an important customer.

Acme might well send around one of its engineers to make a report on the condition of the machine supplied. The engineer would decide whether or not the machine was defective, or whether Kwikclean was merely trying to delay or avoid payment. After the engineer's report Acme's legal department might try to suggest a compromise. A process of bargaining might be conducted. Neither side would be keen on a court case in which it was publicly suggested that one side did not pay its bills and the other supplied defective machinery.

Alternatively, Acme might well have started negotiations before the summons was issued. All the time the threat of the summons would have been there, in case Kwikclean did not produce a satisfactory response.

As part of the negotiations Acme might be prepared to accept that there were defects with the machine supplied and reduce the price accordingly.

When the court case actually begins, both sides are likely to be legally represented by either a solicitor or a barrister. First Acme's lawyer will present the plaintiff's case, calling whatever witnesses seem necessary. The defendant's lawyers will get a chance to cross-examine all the plaintiff's witnesses. Then the defence answer the plaintiff's case, calling their own witnesses. Again, the other side gets a chance to cross-examine these witnesses.

The judge will be the final arbiter of both fact and law. In this case he will decide whether or not the machine supplied to Kwikclean was in fact defective. He will then apply the relevant law and give judgment accordingly.

The losing side may be able to make an appeal to the Court of Appeal.

Dispute 2 – A High Court case

The nature of Bob Charles's dispute with Acme was spelled out on page 43. Bob will begin his quest for damages by going to see a solicitor. This might be a high street solicitor, perhaps the one who acted for him when he bought his house, or it might be a trade union solicitor. The solicitor's first move will be to issue a writ.

The writ

When the writ is served on Acme this amounts to a formal notification that Bob Charles has a claim against the company. The writ sets out brief particulars of what the claim is. The precise amount of damages being claimed is not included.

As soon as the writ is served Acme's insurers will take over all the tactics of the case. (As an employer, Acme must have insurance to cover itself for injury to workers.) It is of course Acme, and not the insurers, which is being sued, but since the insurers are the ones who will end up paying they are likely to call the shots.

Acknowledgement of service

If Acme does not reply to the writ within 14 days it will automatically lose the case. Judgment would then be recorded against it, and the only matter left to be resolved would be the amount of damages.

Acme's insurers will probably insist that the writ is acknowledged. This means that Acme must complete the acknowledgement form and return it to the court within 14 days. Acme fills in its name and ticks boxes to indicate whether or not it is contesting the claim.

If the insurance company think that the injury was caused by Acme's negligence they will tell Acme not to contest the proceedings, and again the only dispute will be as to the amount of damages. (Such a dispute can of course give rise to a High Court action. Many High Court cases are concerned solely with the quantification of damages.)

The negotiations

The issuing of the writ and the acknowledgment of service will certainly not stop the negotiations between Bob Charles's solicitor and the insurance company. Bob's solicitor might have begun negotiating before the writ was issued, or might have waited until after the writ was served. This is a matter of personal preference.

The next stage will be for Bob's solicitor to send Bob for a medical examination. On the basis of the report, the solicitor will arrive at a figure to claim as damages. These damages will comprise **special damages**, such as loss of earnings, which are relatively easy to calculate, and **general damages** which are harder to quantify.

The special damages will cover Bob's pain and suffering and his loss of ability to work and enjoy himself in the future. (A reference book, Kemp and Kemp, *The Quantum of Damages*, keeps an up-to-date record of the amount the courts have awarded for various injuries. Judges follow these awards fairly closely. Currently the loss of an arm is worth about £50,000.)

Acme's insurance company are likely to want Bob to visit their own medical consultant. If his report agrees with the other doctor's report then the case will probably have to be settled in the near future. However, insurance company consultants often tend to take a more optimistic view of a patient's health. The consultant might well feel that Bob's injuries are not as severe as the other doctor thought. He might also feel that a more complete recovery is likely.

The pleadings

Over the next few months the parties to the case will exchange documents. This stage is known as the pleadings and is designed to give both sides a good idea of the other side's case.

The pleadings begin with a **statement of claim** from the plaintiff. This is a detailed description of the plaintiff's case. For instance, Bob's statement of claim would describe how Bob's injuries were caused, in what way this amounted to negligence on Acme's part, and the precise extent of the injuries.

The defence might reply with a **counterclaim**. This would not only deny liability under the plaintiff's claim, but would also allege that the plaintiff is liable to the defendant.

One side may ask for **further and better particulars**, meaning that it is demanding that the other side must supply detailed information to support its statement of claim. If the information is not supplied the statement of claim can be **struck out** and discontinued.

Payment into court

If the amount of damages is disputed then the defendant might pay a sum of money into court. This means that the defendant is offering to settle the case for that amount of money. Acme's insurers, for example, might pay £50,000 into court. If they do this Bob Charles is faced with a difficult decision. He can take the £50,000, or he can proceed with his action in the hope of getting more. If the judge eventually does award him at least £50,000, then Bob will be pleased that he did not accept the payment into court. If, however, the judge awards any less, even one penny less, then Bob will have to pay the legal costs of both sides from the moment when the payment into court was made. As this is a High Court case these costs could be very high. If the case was protracted Bob could even end up out of pocket, his damages being less than the costs.

The judge who tries the case must not be told that a payment into court has been made until he has decided on liability and awarded a sum as damages.

Insurance companies find payment into court a powerful weapon in persuading a client to settle. The amount paid in is often considerably less than the amount being claimed. But the plaintiff's barrister will not be able to give a cast iron assurance that the judge will award more.

Bob is suing in negligence and so his damages will be reduced if the judge decides that he was partly to blame for his own injuries. It was Bob's responsibility as foreman to ensure that machines in the factory were guarded, and Bob's hand was crushed in an unguarded machine. The judge will want to know why the machine was unguarded, and might well decide that this amounted to contributory negligence on Bob's part.

The judge will also have to decide which of the two medical reports most accurately describes Bob's injuries. It is not easy to say how the judge will view Bob's loss of ability to play darts.

If Bob accepts the payment into court that will be the end of the case. If he does not, it is quite possible that a higher payment will be made just before the case is about to begin. It is estimated that such higher payments are offered 'at the doors of the court' in one-third of cases which go to the High Court.

The trial

In the trial the judge will be the sole arbiter of law and fact. Both the plaintiff and the defendant will be legally represented. The lawyers of both sides will almost certainly be barristers, although solicitors are now allowed to present cases in the High Court.

The plaintiff's barrister will begin by summing up the position of both sides. After this the barrister will call witnesses to establish the plaintiff's case. These witnesses may be cross-examined by the defence.

Bob Charles would be the crucial witness in this case. The judge would have to decide how he was injured and how serious the injuries were. Bob's barrister would perhaps also call the doctor who first examined Bob. He might call some of Bob's work mates who saw exactly how the accident happened. The defence barrister will probably cross-examine these witnesses, trying to weaken any good impression they have made.

Then the defence call their witnesses. In this case the only witness is likely to be the insurance company medical consultant. He is cross-examined first by the insurance company's barrister and then by Bob Charles's barrister.

After hearing all the evidence the judge makes his decision. Let us assume that he awards special damages of £26,800 and general damages of £42,000. He also decides that Bob was 10 per cent to blame for the accident. His damages will therefore be £61,920 (£68,800 less 10 per cent). This figure is well above the amount the insurance company paid into court. Bob therefore gets this amount and his costs are paid by the insurance company.

Appeal

An appeal against the amount of damages awarded, or against the law applied by the judge, could be made to the Court of Appeal.

An appeal against the amount of damages is possible only if the amount is totally unreasonable, or if the damages were assessed on the wrong basis.

An appeal on a point of law would allege that the judge misapplied the law in deciding that Acme was negligent.

Arbitration

Commercial disputes are often settled by arbitration. If a dispute is settled in this way then it is resolved by an impartial referee, an arbitrator, who takes over the role of the court.

Advantages of arbitration

The main advantage of arbitration is that the proceedings are conducted **privately**, whereas court proceedings are held in public. Privacy can be a very important factor in commercial disputes. In Acme's dispute with Kwikclean both sides would want to avoid damaging publicity. Acme would not want a public airing of allegations that its boilers are defective; Kwikclean would not want to become known as a business which does not pay its bills.

A second advantage of arbitration is that an arbitrator with **specialist knowledge** can be chosen. Eventually the dispute between Acme and Kwikclean would depend upon whether or not the boiler supplied was defective. If the case went to court the judge would listen to expert witnesses on both sides and then make his decision. It is highly unlikely that the judge would know much about boilers. The side which loses the case would be likely to feel that the judge got it wrong. Both Acme and Kwikclean might have more faith in the decision if it was taken by an expert in the field, perhaps by the chairman of the local Boiler Makers Federation.

Arbitration might also be **cheaper** than going to court. However, this is by no means certain. Arbitrators can demand good money for their skills, and the lawyers arguing the case in front of an arbitrator will charge the client the same rate as they would for going to court.

A dispute sent to arbitration is likely to be resolved relatively **quickly**. It takes a long time for a case to get to court, whereas arbitration can be quickly arranged. Delays in arbitration are usually caused because the parties cannot agree who the arbitrator should be.

A final advantage of arbitration is that the **right to appeal is severely restricted**. The parties know that once the arbitrator has made his award that is the end of the dispute. If a dispute is taken to court, an appeal, or the threat of one, can hang over the winner for some considerable time.

Reference to arbitration

A dispute can be referred to arbitration only if **both sides agree** that it should be. If the dispute is a contractual one then a term of the contract may provide for arbitration. Such terms are common in contracts made in the context of certain industries, including the insurance industry and the building industry. But arbitration clauses are by no means restricted to contracts made in those industries. The contract between Acme and Kwikclean might have contained a clause stating that any dispute arising under the contract should be resolved by arbitration.

Alternatively the parties might agree to arbitration once the dispute has arisen and both sides have made their position clear. Perhaps the arrival of Acme's writ would be enough to convince Kwikclean that the dispute was serious, and lead it to suggest arbitration.

Whether the agreement is made in the contract itself or later, the important thing is that once the parties have agreed to arbitration they will not be able to unilaterally to change their minds. If a party who has agreed to an arbitration clause tries to take the dispute to a court instead of to the arbitrator the court will stay (discontinue) the proceedings.

It is a principle of contract law that no clause in a contract may oust the

jurisdiction of the courts (prevent matters of law from being decided by the ordinary courts of the land). Arbitration is the only exception to this principle.

The Consumer Arbitration Agreements Act 1988 prevents the abuse of arbitration in consumer contracts. Consumers are unlikely to quibble about an arbitration clause when they make a contract. But such clauses could be used unfairly, perhaps to appoint an arbitrator who is sympathetic to the business rather than to the consumer. The Act therefore provides that arbitration clauses in consumer contracts have no effect if the amount of the consumer's claim is less than £1,000. Later in this chapter we will see that if the claim is less than £1,000 the case could be taken to the small claims court. If the amount claimed is over £1,000, the Act states that the arbitration clause can only be effective if the arbitration would not be detrimental to the consumer's interests.

Alternative dispute resolution

Ombudsmen and other dispute resolution schemes

Many public services have been privatised in the past two decades. The courts, like the legislature, seemed to be one of the few services where privatisation was inconceivable. To some extent, though, a privatisation of the courts has occurred.

Arbitration, for example, can be seen as the resolution of disputes by the private sector, whereas litigation is resolution by the public sector.

This privatisation differs from the privatisation of the public utilities in that it has not been imposed by Government but sought by customers. (It also differs in that it has not taken a significant amount of work away from the State-owned service.)

Litigation and arbitration are no longer the only way in which commercial disputes can be settled. Various industries have set up **ombudsmen**, who pursue disputes on behalf of dissatisfied customers without prejudicing the customers' rights. The insurance industry, for example, has created the Insurance Ombudsman, and the major insurance companies have pledged themselves to abide by his decisions. Customers who complain to the ombudsman do not give such a pledge, and their legal rights remain unaffected should they later wish to take the dispute to court.

In addition, experimental dispute resolution schemes have been set up in the United States. These schemes make their own rules about the maximum length of a party's submission, the number of documents which can be presented, and the procedure to be adopted when the dispute is heard. Essentially these schemes are arbitration because they can resolve the dispute only if the parties involved agree that they should. But the schemes differ from traditional arbitration in that under the schemes the arbitrators go out looking for customers. Traditionally it is the customers, those with disputes, who seek out the arbitrators. Whether or not such schemes will catch on in the United Kingdom remains to be seen.

The small claims court

Disputes in which the claim amounts to **less then £1,000** are usually dealt with by 'arbitration' in the small claims court. The disputes can be about any civil matters. Usually they are about unpaid debts or breach of contract, but claims in tort are also covered.

Each side pays its own legal costs, and this discourages the use of solicitors.

Again, the procedure to be followed is perhaps best understood by looking at a particular dispute. Let us assume that Acme has installed a solid fuel boiler in Mr Smith's house, but that Mr Smith has not paid the bill of £868.

Procedure

The claim is commenced by sending in three copies of a completed N1 form (**the summons**). A copy of this form is reproduced on pages 366–7. The other small claims forms follow on pages 368–73.

A fee must be sent along with the forms. Typically this is about £40, but it can be as much as £70. The fee paid by the plaintiff is added to the amount claimed. One copy of the form is retained by the plaintiff, one is sent to the defendant, and one is retained by the court. If the plaintiff pays another £10 fee, the court will send the summons to the defendant, along with a **reply form**.

Acme might complete the summons form by inserting the following information into the relevant boxes:

- its own name and address;
- Mr Smith's name and address;
- details of the claim made; and
- the amount claimed.

The defendant must reply to the summons within 14 days of receiving it. If the defendant does not reply, the plaintiff can ask the court to enter judgment by default. Acme would do this by completing the 'Request for Judgment' form and ticking box A.

If the court does enter judgment by default it will send Mr Smith a form telling him how much to pay and when to pay it.

If the defendant admits the plaintiff's claim he will fill in the 'Admission', which was sent along with the summons. On this form the defendant can ask for time to pay. So Mr Smith might send a completed Admission form, agreeing that he does owe the money, but asking to pay at £20 a week. Acme can accept this or not. If it does accept it it uses the details from this form to fill in a 'Request for Judgment' form, this time ticking box B. The court then issues judgment for Acme. Alternatively Acme might tick box B and the box at the foot of the Request for Judgement form, to indicate that it does not accept payment as proposed by Mr Smith.

If the defendant admits part of the claim only, or if he wishes to make a counterclaim, then he must send a 'Defence and Counterclaim' form along with his form of admission. For example, Mr Smith might say that he is paying only £700 because the boiler supplied was defective.

If Acme accepts this offer to pay £700 it ticks Box B on the 'Request for Judgment' form. Judgment for the £700 offered by Mr Smith will then be entered for Acme.

If the plaintiff does not accept the defendant's defence or counterclaim then the documents are sent to a district judge. The judge will probably fix a date for the arbitration, but he might first invite the parties to a preliminary hearing. Such a hearing is designed not only to clarify each side's position, but also to suggest a way in which the dispute can be settled.

It is also possible that the judge will decide that the case is difficult enough to warrant a full hearing in the County Court. This is unusual. However, it does present a problem to a plaintiff in that if he loses a County Court case he will probably have to pay the other side's legal costs as well as his own.

The hearing itself is informal. The arbitrator will ask questions of both sides and examine statements made by witnesses. The plaintiff does not need to know the exact legal basis of his claim. If, for instance, he was injured by a badly driven car he would not need to know that what he was alleging was the tort of negligence. When he has sufficient information the arbitrator will make his decision, known as an award.

Tribunals

Certain types of disputes go before special courts known as tribunals. The disputes tend to be between the individual and the State. For example, an individual who thought that he was not being given enough unemployment benefit would not be able to take his case to the ordinary courts. He would first appeal to a higher grade civil servant, and if still not satisfied could take his case to the **Social Security Appeals Tribunal**.

The only tribunals which are likely to involve a business are the **Industrial Tribunal** and the **Employment Appeal Tribunal**.

The Industrial Tribunal is the court which hears disputes about employees' rights. An appeal from the Industrial Tribunal lies to the Employment Appeal Tribunal. Such appeals can only be on matters of law.

Tribunals are courts, but the members of the tribunals are not judges. The chairman of an industrial tribunal will be legally qualified and he will sit with two others who will have been chosen because of their knowledge of employment problems.

Both parties can take lawyers to present their case. However, tribunals have the advantages of being much quicker and cheaper than the ordinary courts. The hearings are public. The procedure is informal and each side will pay its own costs.

An appeal from the Employment Appeals Tribunal can be made to the Court of Appeal.

The courts control tribunals through the process of judicial review. This does not mean that they check that the tribunal applied the law correctly (an appeal would achieve that). Rather it means that the courts check that the tribunal followed the laws of natural justice and followed the correct procedures.

ACTIVITY QUESTION 2.1

For many years a wholesaler has supplied a garden centre with flower seeds. The wholesaler and supplier have always enjoyed good relations, but a serious dispute has now arisen over the quality of seeds delivered last year. The garden centre say that many of the seeds did not produce flowers and that customers have been complaining. The wholesaler has not received any similar complaints from other retailers supplied from the same batch of seeds.

(a) List, in order of importance, the reasons why the parties might prefer to resolve this dispute through arbitration rather than through the courts.

(b) If the dispute eventually did lead to a court case, in which court would the case be heard if the damages claimed were:
   (i)   £800?
   (ii) £22,000?
   (iii) £63,000?

(c) To which court could the loser appeal if the case was first heard in:
   (i) the County Court?
   (ii) the High Court?

TASK 2

Mrs Macleod bought some flower seeds from Greenco Garden Centre. Mrs Macleod is claiming that the seeds did not produce flowers and that this entitles her to damages of £300. Greenco Garden Centre are prepared to concede that the seeds did not work, but are prepared to pay Mrs Macleod only £46.50, ten times the cost of the seeds.

(a) As Mrs Macleod, fill in a summons (Form N1) claiming the £300.

(b) As Greenco Garden Centre, fill in a Defence and Counterclaim form, offering to pay £46.50.

(c) As Mrs Macleod, fill in the appropriate form to accept Greenco's offer to pay £46.50.

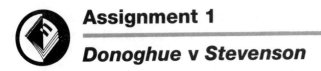

Assignment 1

Donoghue v Stevenson

The facts of *Donoghue* v *Stevenson* (1932, House of Lords) were as follows:

The plaintiff and her friend visited a cafe in Paisley. The plaintiff's friend bought a bottle of ginger beer for the plaintiff. The proprietor of the cafe took the top off the ginger beer bottle and poured a little beer into a glass. The plaintiff drunk some of the beer. Later, when the plaintiff poured out the rest, she discovered that the bottle had contained the remains of a decomposed snail. The sight of this snail made the plaintiff ill. She sued the manufacturer of the ginger beer in negligence.

The court held that the plaintiff won. The manufacturer was liable in negligence because he had broken the duty of care which he owed to the plaintiff.

Tasks

A group of catering students at your college want to know about the areas of law which might affect a business. These students are familiar with the facts of *Donoghue* v *Stevenson*. They would like you to write a report, dealing briefly with the following matters:

1 Explain whether this was a civil case or a criminal one, and give a brief explanation of the different purposes which the civil and criminal law try to achieve.

2 Explain whether the plaintiff was suing the manufacturer in contract or in tort, and briefly outline the distinction between contractual and tortious liability.

3 If the facts of the case had been different, and the plaintiff had herself bought the bottle of ginger beer, describe:
    (a) the basis on which the plaintiff might have sued the cafe, and
    (b) whether she would have been a consumer within the meaning of the Unfair Contracts Terms Act 1977.

4 Explain why the plaintiff would nowadays prefer to sue the manufacturer under the Consumer Protection Act 1987, rather than under the common law.

5 If several ginger beer bottles had contained a deadly virus, the manufacturer might have been criminally liable even though he had no means of knowing that the virus existed in the ginger beer. Explain how the courts can justify the imposition of this type of strict liability.

6 Outline the extent to which shareholders in a company might be personally liable, if their company were to go into liquidation as a result of manufacturing defective products.

7 Explain what the shareholders could do if they thought that the company was being badly managed.

8 Assume that as a result of the plaintiff's case the business which manufactured the ginger beer was likely to go into liquidation. Assume also that a bank had lent the business £30,000. Describe the kind of security which the bank would have been likely to have demanded, and the effect on the business of giving this security.

9 Explain whether the plaintiff would have been entitled to any compensation if she had suffered no harm as a result of consuming the ginger beer. Explain also whether the absence of harm would affect the business's criminal liability for manufacturing a dangerous product.

10 Describe the steps which the local residents could take if the manufacturer of the ginger beer began to use a new powerful chemical to clean their bottles, and if this chemical caused the local streets to be full of choking fumes.

11 Assume that the cafe has not paid the manufacturer for £1,500 of soft drinks supplied. Describe:
    (a) the type of action which the manufacturer might bring to get the money, and the court in which such an action would be brought
    (b) who would be liable for the cafe's debts, if the cafe was run as a partnership by three brothers.

12 If the manufacturer blamed one particular employee for the accident, and dismissed the employee, describe:
    (a) any group which might help the employee seek compensation
    (b) the type of court which would hear such a case.

13 As Mrs Donoghue, fill in a summons form (N1) claiming £650 for gastroenteritis, resulting in two weeks off work.

14 As the manufacturer, Stevenson, fill in a Counterclaim and Defence form, offering to pay £500.

15 As Mrs Donoghue, fill in the appropriate form to accept the payment of £500.

Element 15.2

THE LEGAL STATUS OF BUSINESSES

A student must:

1 Describe the **legal characteristics** of different types of businesses

2 Explain factors that can affect the choice of **legal status** for a **business**

3 Outline the **legal process of formation** of different types of businesses

3 The characteristics of businesses

There are many types of business organisations, and each type has its own characteristics. In order to understand the nature of the different types of organisations it is necessary to classify them. We do this by categorising them according to their characteristics.

It is possible to classify business organisations in many different ways. We could divide them into those which are profit-making and those which are not, or into those which are large and those which are small, or into those which are publicly owned and those which are privately owned. The most useful classification, the one which tells us most, is to divide businesses into those which are incorporated and those which are not. Almost all incorporated businesses are registered companies, and so we begin by considering the characteristics of companies.

Companies

A company is created by registration under the Companies Act 1985. The process of registration is considered in Chapter 5. Here it is enough to say that the promoters of the company must send certain documents to the Registrar of Companies. If the documents are in order the Registrar will issue a certificate of incorporation and the company will then exist as a corporate body.

Incorporation has several important consequences. To some extent these are interconnected, but they are easier to understand if considered separately.

The company is a separate legal entity

The most important consequence of incorporation is that a company is regarded as being a legal person in its own right. This means that it has a legal identity of its own which is quite separate from the legal identity of its owners. If a wrong is done to a company, the company and not its owners must sue. Conversely, if a company injures another person, that person must sue the company and cannot sue the owners. This well-established principle was laid down by the House of Lords in the following case.

Salomon v Salomon and Co Ltd (1897, House of Lords)

For several years Salomon had carried on a business as a boot repairer and manufacturer. He formed a limited company and sold his business to the company for £39,000. The company paid the purchase price by issuing Salomon with 20,000 £1 shares, by regarding him as having loaned the company £10,000, and by making up the balance in cash. Salomon took all of the company's assets as security for the loan. Unsecured creditors lent the company a further £8,000. Shortly after its incorporation the company got into financial difficulty and was wound up. The assets of the company amounted to about £6,000. Creditors who have been given security for their loan are entitled to be repaid before unsecured creditors. As such a secured creditor, Salomon therefore took all of the £6,000. The unsecured creditors claimed that Salomon should repay their loans himself because he was the same person as the company.

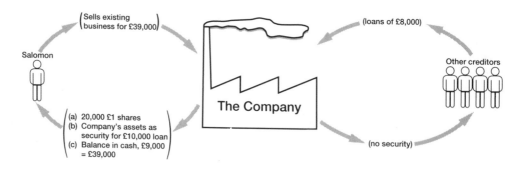

Fig 3.1 *Salomon v Salomon and Co Ltd*

Held The company had been formed properly and without any fraud. Although Salomon owned all but seven of the issued shares he was one person and the company was another. Salomon therefore had no more obligation to pay the company's debts than he had to pay his next-door neighbour's debts.

Salomon's case is regarded as one of the most important in English law, mainly because of the protection which it offers to the owners of companies. However, the decision that a company has a legal identity of its own has many other consequences, as the following two cases show.

Macaura v *Northern Assurance Co Ltd* (1925, House of Lords)

Macaura and his nominees owned all of the shares in a timber company. The company owed money to Macaura but not to anyone else. Macaura insured the company's timber in his own name. Two weeks later the timber was destroyed by fire and Macaura claimed on his insurance.

Held Macaura could not claim on the insurance policy because he did not own the timber. The company owned the timber, and it is a rule of insurance law that goods can only be insured by the person who owns them.

Tunstall v *Steigmann* (1962, Court of Appeal)

Mrs Steigmann ran a pork butcher's shop and leased the shop next door to Mrs Tunstall. Mrs Steigmann wanted to end the lease. Under the Landlord and Tenant Act 1954 she could order Mrs Tunstall to leave only if she intended to occupy the building herself, to carry on a business there. Mrs Steigmann did intend to occupy the shop herself to carry on her butchery business. But before the case came to court she turned her business into a company. Mrs Steigmann claimed that as she owned all but two of the shares in the company it was still herself that wanted to take over the premises.

Held Mrs Steigmann lost. It was not her that wanted to take over the business, but her company.

> Willmer LJ 'There is no escape from the fact that a company is a legal entity entirely separate from its corporators – see Salomon v Salomon and Co. Here the landlord and her company are entirely separate entities. This is no matter of form; it is a matter of substance and reality. Each can sue and be sued in his own right; indeed, there is nothing to prevent the one suing the other. Even the holder of 100% of the shares in a company does not by such holding become so identified with the company that he or she can be said to carry on the business of the company.'

ACTIVITY QUESTIONS 3.1

1 If Salomon had not formed a company, but had carried on his business as a sole trader, would the unsecured creditors have been entitled to the £6,000 which the assets of the business generated?

2 In *Macaura* v *Northern Assurance*, did the shareholders in the company own the timber when it was destroyed?

Further activity questions 3.1

1 It is now possible for a person to own all of the shares in a company. If X owned all of the shares in X Co Ltd, and X Co Ltd owed no money to any creditors:
(a) Could X steal from the company?
(b) Could he sue the company?
(c) Could he be employed by the company?

2 In *Lee* v *Lee's Air Farming Ltd* (1961, Privy Council), Mr Lee owned 2,999 of the 3,000 shares in a crop-spraying company. While at work he crashed his plane and was killed. His widow sued under a statute which required employers to pay compensation if an employee was killed at work. The company's insurers refused to pay, arguing that Lee was employed by himself, and could not therefore be an employee. Did the insurers have to pay up?

3 In *Firsteel Cold Rolled Products Ltd* v *Anaco Precision Pressings Ltd* (1994), Owen J had to decide whether or not a company could sue for 'stress and aggravation,' which it claimed to have suffered as a result of a breach of contract. What do you think the judge decided? Can a company suffer stress?

Limited liability

In *Salomon's* case we saw that Salomon was not personally liable for the debts of the company. When people buy shares in a limited company the only commitment which they make is that they agree to pay the price of the shares. Often they do not pay the full price immediately. When the public utilities were privatised, for example, investors generally paid half of the share price when subscribing for the shares and remained liable for the other half. If one of these privatised companies had gone into liquidation before shareholders had paid this second instalment they would have been liable to pay the amount outstanding. However, beyond this they would not have been liable for the debts of the company.

It must of course be emphasised that it is the shareholders and not the company who have limited liability. If a company has debts it must pay these debts, even if this means selling all of its assets.

Perpetual succession

The members of a company can decide to liquidate it at any time. If they do liquidate then the company will cease to exist. However, companies can continue in existence indefinitely, and therefore it is said that they have perpetual succession.

Shareholders, of course, must die. But even if all the shareholders in a company die, their shares will be inherited by others and the company will continue in existence. The Hudson Bay Company has been in existence for over 300 years. Generations of its shareholders have died, but the company still exists.

As we shall see, the death of a partner ends a partnership (unless the partnership agreement provides otherwise).

Ownership of property

A company can own property, and this property will continue to be owned by the company regardless of who owns the shares in the company. This can be important when a company is trying to borrow money, because the company can give its own property, both present and future assets, as security for a loan.

Contractual capacity

A company has the power to make contracts and can sue and be sued on them. This power must be delegated to human agents, and it is the company directors who actually go through the process of forming the contracts. But the important point is that it is the company itself which assumes the rights and liabilities which the contract creates.

A company can also sue and be sued in tort. (A tort is a civil wrong other than a breach of contract, for example negligence, trespass or defamation.)

Criminal liability

To commit a crime the accused must commit a guilty act (*actus reus*) while having a guilty mind (*mens rea*). At first sight it would seem that companies cannot commit crimes because they have not got minds of their own. However, the courts are sometimes prepared to regard the controllers of the company as the minds of the company.

Tesco Supermarkets Ltd v Nattrass (1972, House of Lords)

Tesco were charged under the Trade Descriptions Act 1968 with selling washing powder for 19½ p when it had been advertised at 14½ p. An assistant had put the full price powder on the shelf without telling the manager of the shop. The manager, who had failed to notice the discrepancy, had not taken all reasonable precautions to see that the offence was not committed. Tesco (the company) were prosecuted.

Held Tesco were not liable because the manager was not sufficiently senior to be regarded as the company. The manager was regarded as the hands of the company rather than as the mind of the company. If a sufficiently senior manager had failed to take all reasonable precautions, the company would have been guilty of the crime.

Lord Reid 'A living person has a mind which can have knowledge or intention or be negligent and he has hands to carry out his intention. A corporation has none of these; it must act through living persons, though not always one or the same person. Then the person who acts is not speaking or acting for the company. He is acting as the company and his mind which directs his acts is the mind of the company. . . . If it is a guilty mind then that guilt is the guilt of the company. It must be a question of law whether, once the facts have been ascertained, a person in doing particular things is to be regarded as the company or merely as the company's servant or agent.'

ACTIVITY QUESTIONS 3.2

1 Does the concept of limited liability mean that companies do not have to pay their debts?

2 Shabana buys shares in a limited company. What is the maximum amount she can be required to contribute towards the company's debts?

3 Companies are said to have perpetual succession. What does this mean?

4 Can a company:
   (a) Own property?
   (b) Make contracts in its own name?
   (c) Be found guilty of a crime?

Further activity questions 3.2

1 The decision in *Salomon*'s case means that investors in a limited company do not have to pay the company's debts. They may lose the value of their shares, but they can lose no more. Why is this regarded as such an important rule in a capitalist society? In what way would society be different if members of companies did not enjoy limited liability?

2 In 1768 Lord Blackstone said: '*A corporation cannot commit treason, or felony, or other crime, in its corporate capacity; though its members may in their distinct individual capacities.*' In the *Tesco* case, and in others, it has been recognised that nowadays, a company can commit a crime. Why do you think that this change in judicial attitudes has taken place? Is it only relatively trivial crimes which a company could commit, or could a company be found guilty of a crime such as murder or manslaughter?

3 The Race Relations Act 1976 makes discrimination on racial grounds unlawful. Can a company commit such discrimination? Could a company be liable under the Sex Discrimination Act 1975?

4 People who refuse to obey court orders can be fined, or imprisoned, or have their assets seized. In *Re Supply of Ready Mixed Concrete (No 2)* (1994) the House of Lords had to decide whether or not a company could be in contempt of court if it's employees deliberately broke a court order. What do you think the House of Lords decided?

Lifting the corporate veil

We have seen that a company has a legal identity of its own. A natural consequence of this is that only the company itself can be liable in respect of a wrong done by the company. The owners of the company will normally be free of any liability. They are said to be protected by the '**veil of incorporation**'. The company's artificial legal personality is regarded as a veil, and the members of the company stand behind it, protected.

As we have already seen, this idea is very well established. But there are circumstances in which the court will lift the corporate veil so that the members of the company are not protected by the company's artificial legal personality.

These circumstances are as follows.

Where the company was formed for a fraudulent purpose

Gilford Motor Co Ltd v Horne (1933, Court of Appeal)

Mr Horne was employed as managing director of GMC Ltd. In his contract of employment Horne agreed that after leaving GMC he would not solicit its customers. When his contract was terminated he did begin to solicit GMC's customers. He knew that GMC would not allow him to get away with this, so he formed a company, the sole purpose of which was to employ him while he continued to solicit the customers. When GMC sued Horne his defence was that his promise in his contract of employment was binding only on himself, not on the new company.

Held An injunction was granted preventing either Horne or the company from soliciting GMC's customers.

> Lord Hanworth MR '*I am quite satisfied that this company was formed as a device, a stratagem, in order to mask the effective carrying on of a business of Mr E.B. Horne. The purpose of it was to try to enable him, under what is a cloak or a sham, to engage in business . . . in respect of which he had a fear that the plaintiffs might intervene and object.*'

If the company can be characterised as an enemy in time of war

When a country is at war with another country it is likely to restrict the activities of citizens of the other country. If a company is owned by enemy aliens then the court may lift the veil and regard the company itself as an enemy alien.

Daimler Ltd v Continental Tyre and Rubber Co Ltd (1916, House of Lords)

The Continental Tyre Co was registered in England. It was owed money by Daimler and sued to recover the debt. Daimler argued that as all but one of the shares in the Continental Tyre Co were owned by German residents the company should not be allowed to sue on the debt when Britain was at war with Germany.

Held The company could not sue on the debt. Because the shareholders were German, the company itself could be regarded as an enemy.

Groups of companies regarded as one

DHN Food Distributors Ltd v London Borough of Tower Hamlets (1976, Court of Appeal)

DHN ran a wholesale cash and carry business through two subsidiary companies, both of which it wholly owned. One of these subsidiaries, Bronze, had only one asset, the premises from which DHN carried on business. The second subsidiary owned the vehicles which DHN used, but like Bronze it carried on no operations of its own. The local authority compulsorily purchased the premises owned by Bronze and as a result DHN had to close down its business. DHN claimed damages from the local authority, who argued that the matter was nothing to do with DHN.

Held The group of companies could be treated as one economic enterprise, and DHN could receive the same damages as if it had owned the premises itself.

Other situations where the court thinks it right to lift the veil

Judges have the power to lift the veil in other situations if they think that this is the best way to do justice in the case.

Goodwin v Birmingham City FC (1980)

Mr Goodwin was appointed manager of Birmingham City Football Club. He formed a company and supplied his services through the company. After three years of a five-year contract Goodwin was sacked. If he had not found another job he would have been able to sue for the remaining two years' salary. Shortly afterwards though Goodwin found another job at a higher salary. This meant that the Football Club's breach of contract had cost Goodwin nothing. If he had sued he would have received only nominal (token) damages. The company sued for full damages, claiming that it had suffered the loss of two years' salary.

Held The company was also entitled only to nominal damages. Its only asset was its contract with the plaintiff and so the plaintiff and the company could be regarded as being the same person.

ACTIVITY QUESTIONS 3.3

1 Was Salomon protected by the corporate veil? If so, how did it protect him?

2 When Salomon was a sole trader was he protected by the corporate veil?

Further activity questions 3.3

1 In *Jones* v *Lipman* the defendant had made a contract to sell land, but later changed his mind and refused to sell. The court ordered him to perform his contract. He tried to evade this court order by forming a company and conveying the land to the company. Do you think that this defeated the court order?

2 In *Tunstall* v *Steigmann*, Mrs Steigmann could not force Mrs Tunstall to quit the shop because it was not Mrs Steigmann but her company which intended to occupy the premises. Could Mrs Steigmann have got around this by winding up her company, and then occupying the premises herself? If so, could she later have formed another company once she was in possession of the premises?

3 The First World War was fought economically as well as militarily. Both sides attempted to bankrupt the economy of the other. Do you think that this was the reason why the court refused to allow a company owned by Germans to sue on a debt? In the *Daimler* case Lord Parker said: '*The acts of a company's organs, its directors, managers, secretary, and so forth . . . are the company's acts and may invest it with enemy character.*' Do you think that this is true or was this a policy decision? (A policy decision is one where the judge is more concerned with creating the correct policy than with doing justice in the case.)

4 Was the decision in *Salomon*'s case a policy decision?

5 In the *DHN* case the three companies were regarded as one economic enterprise, with the result that DHN received damages for a wrong done to one of the other companies. Could this principle also work in reverse? If one of the smaller companies had gone into liquidation with massive debts could DHN have been forced to cover these debts?

Classification of companies

Companies can be classified in several different ways, but from a business perspective only three classifications are useful.

Public companies and private companies

Public companies can offer shares and debentures for sale to the public. The articles of private companies usually restrict the sale of the companies shares. The most common restrictions are either that the shares must first be offered to other members of the company, or that the shares can only be sold to persons of whom the directors approve. It is a criminal offence to advertise the sale of shares in a private company to members of the public.

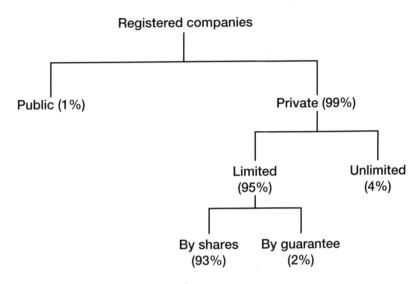

Fig 3.2 Classification of companies

Although public companies, such as Marks and Spencers and ICI, make up only about 1 per cent of all companies they tend to be very much larger than most private companies. The assets of the 1 per cent of companies which are public would far outweigh the assets of the 99 per cent of companies which are private.

Limited and unlimited companies

Unlimited Companies

About 4 per cent of registered companies are unlimited companies. These companies do have a legal personality distinct from that of the company members, but the members have agreed that they will have unlimited liability for the debts of the company.

Unlimited companies enjoy some advantages over limited companies. For example, their accounts need not be published or delivered to the Registrar of Companies. However, these advantages are generally considered to be far outweighed by the unlimited liability of the members.

The names of unlimited companies must not contain the words 'limited' or 'Ltd'.

Public companies may not register as unlimited companies.

Limited Companies

Limited companies can themselves be classified into two types:

Table 3.1 Differences between public and private companies

Public companies	Private companies
Must have at least two members.	Need only one member.
Name must end with the words 'Public Limited Company' or 'PLC'.	Name must end with 'Limited' or 'Ltd' (unless the company is unlimited).
Must have £50,000 allotted share capital, one-quarter of which must be paid up.	No limit on share capital.
Shares can be quoted on stock exchange.	Shares cannot be quoted on stock exchange or advertised for sale.
Must be at least two directors.	Need only one director.
Shares must be paid for in cash (or independent expert must value assets given as payment).	Shares can be given away.

(a) Companies limited by shares

The vast majority of companies are limited by shares. As we have seen, this means that in the event of liquidation a member's liability is limited to paying off any amount unpaid on his shares.

(b) Companies limited by guarantee

The liability of members of these companies is limited to an amount which they have agreed to pay in the event of the company going into liquidation. This amount is usually small, typically £5, and is spelt out in the documents registered with the Registrar of Companies when the company is formed.

Before the Companies Act 1985 a company could be limited by shares and by guarantee, in which case the members were liable to pay both the amount guaranteed and the amount unpaid on their shares. Some such companies, formed before 1985, continue to exist, but since the 1985 Act a company must either be limited by shares or be limited by guarantee.

Most companies limited by guarantee are educational or charitable. Guarantee companies are not a suitable medium for trading companies.

Public limited companies have never been allowed to be limited by guarantee. They must be limited by shares.

Method of creation

Companies can be created by registration under the Companies Act, by statute, or by Royal Charter.

By registration under the Companies Acts

Almost all companies currently in existence were created this way. It is quick and cheap, and it is generally understood that when people speak of a company this is the type of company which they mean.

By statute

Most of the public utilities (such as gas, electricity and water) needed special powers to enable them to purchase land compulsorily, and to prevent competition. These powers could only be granted by Parliament and so the companies were created by statutes.

Many of these utilities have now been privatised. In effect this means that other statutes changed their status so that they became registered public limited companies.

By Royal Charter

A company can be created by Royal Charter. Unless created a very long time ago such companies will not be trading companies. It is far easier to register under the Companies Act than to gain a Royal Charter.

If an institution is granted a Royal Charter this is usually seen as conferring a special prestige. The BBC, Oxford and Cambridge Universities and The Institute of Chartered Accountants were all created by Royal Charter.

ACTIVITY QUESTIONS 3.4

1 A company is registered under the name Acme Trading Ltd. Which one of the following might the company be?
  (a) A Public Limited Company.
  (b) A partnership.
  (c) A private limited company.
  (d) Either a private limited company or a private unlimited company.

2 Arthur owns 100 shares in a private limited company which has gone into liquidation with heavy debts. Arthur has paid half the price of his shares. Which one of the following statements would be true?
(a) As the company is limited it need not pay its debts.
(b) Limited liability will mean that Arthur has to pay nothing towards the company's debts.
(c) Arthur must pay the amount unpaid on his shares. Beyond that he need pay no more.
(d) The amount of the company's debts must be paid by all shareholders in proportion to their shareholding.

3 Which one of the following statements is true?
(a) A public company need only have one director.
(b) A public company cannot be unlimited.
(c) A public company's shares must be quoted on the stock exchange.
(d) A public company's shares must be offered for sale to the public.

Further activity questions 3.4

1 Which one of the following is not a legal person?
(a) A small family company.
(b) A Public Limited Company.
(c) The BBC.
(d) A firm of chartered accountants.

2 Which one of the following statements is not true of a private limited company?
(a) The company will continue in existence indefinitely unless it is liquidated.
(b) The company can sue on contracts made in its name.
(c) The company can employ the person who owns all the shares in the company.
(d) A major shareholder in the company cannot hold shares in a rival company.

Partnerships

Definition

Partnerships, commonly known as firms, are defined by section 1(1) of the Partnership Act 1890, which states: *'Partnership is the relationship which subsists between persons carrying on a business in common with a view to profit.'*

This definition is deceptively complex. It is best understood if broken down into sections:

(a) '**The relationship which subsists between persons**' This opening phrase is revealing. A partnership is not a separate entity with a legal personality of its own. It is merely a relationship between persons. Such a relationship gives rise to legal rights and liabilities, but it does not create a new legal person.

(b) '**Business**' is defined by section 45 of the Partnership Act 1890 as including '*every trade, occupation or profession*'. However, some professionals, such as barristers, have their own rules which prevent partnership between their members. *Mann* v *D'Arcy* (1968) established that even if the business is only to make one deal (in this case to buy and sell 350 tons of potatoes), this can be enough to create a partnership.

(c) '**In common**' means not only that all of the partners carry on the business, but also that the business is carried on for the benefit of all of them. It is quite common for partnerships to employ workers. These employees are not partners. They may help to carry the business on, but it is not carried on for their benefit.

(d) '**View to profit**' does not mean that the business must make a profit, but rather that the partners should intend to make a profit. This intention to make a profit distinguishes partnerships from non profit-making members clubs, such as social clubs.

Despite the statutory definition provided by section 1(1) of the Partnership Act 1890, it is often very difficult to tell whether or not a business is or is not a partnership. Some slight help is provided by section 1(2) of the Act which states that a company cannot be a partnership.

Characteristics of a partnership

Agency

Every partner is an agent of the firm and of his fellow partners. This means that every partner can make contracts which are binding on the partnership. The other partners will not be able to avoid liability under these contracts by saying that the partner who made the contract had no right to do so. Even contracts which a partner has been expressly forbidden to make will still be binding on the firm.

Unlimited liability

Partners are not protected by limited liability. As the partnership is not a corporate body there is no corporate veil to hide behind. Every partner is liable for the firm's debts to the full extent of his personal wealth.

Consequences

These concepts of agency and unlimited liability can have extremely serious consequences, as is demonstrated by the classic quotation from James LJ in *Baird's Case* (1870):

> *'Ordinary partnerships are by the law assumed to be based on the mutual trust and confidence of each partner in the skill, knowledge and integrity of every other partner. As between the partners and the outside world (whatever may be their private arrangements between themselves), each partner is the unlimited agent of every other in every matter connected with the partnership business. . . . A partner who may not have a farthing of capital left may take money or assets of the partnership to the value of millions, may bind the partnership by contracts to any amount . . . and may even – as has been shown in many painful instances in this court – involve his innocent partners in unlimited amounts for frauds which he has carefully concealed from them.'*

ACTIVITY QUESTIONS 3.5

1 If Salomon had carried on his business as a partnership with his family:
   (a) Would he have had to repay the unsecured creditors their £8,000? *No*
   (b) Would his fellow partners (who might have had nothing to do with the loans and known nothing of them) have had any liability to repay the money? *yes*

2 (a) Who makes business contracts on behalf of a partnership? *Any partner*
   (b) When a person goes into partnership with another, what is the maximum liability that person can incur?
   (c) A cleaner is employed by a partnership of doctors. Does this make the cleaner a partner?

Further activity questions 3.5

1 In *Macaura* v *Northern Assurance Co*, Macaura had no insurable interest in the timber because he had sold it to the company. What if Macaura had formed a partnership not a company? Would he have had an insurable interest in the timber?

2 Alma, Billy and Claire go into business together to make a film, imagining that this will make them a lot of money. They do not form a company or give any thought as to what sort of business they might be. Alma and Billy, without Claire's knowledge or permission, make contracts to hire actors, sets and costumes. The project is abandoned when Claire discovers that the other two have no money. None of the money spent is recouped by the business. Which one of the following statements is true?

(a) As a partner, Claire is liable for all of the debts incurred.

(b) Claire has no liability. The business cannot be a partnership because no profits were ever made.

(c) Claire has no liability. She did not know of the contracts and gave no permission for them to be made.

(d) Claire has no liability because she is protected by the corporate veil.

Sole traders

A person can be in business on his own, without being a partnership or a company. Such a person, and there are a good number of them, is called a sole trader. He might well employ other people but is not in business with them.

Sole traders have unlimited personal liability for the debts of their business. If necessary they must sell all of their possessions, and can even be made bankrupt, in order to pay the business debts.

When a sole trader dies the business comes to an end. Somebody else might buy the business as a going concern and take it over, but if this happens the purchaser will be regarded as a new business. The sole trader's estate will not be liable for any debts which the business incurs after it has been taken over.

No formalities are attached to the formation of a business carried on as a sole trader. The trader creates the business as soon as he begins to trade.

Non profit-making organisations

Some of the largest organisations in Britain are non profit-making. The lack of an intention to make a profit debars these organisations from being partnerships. They can however be corporations. Although the organisations do not set out to make a profit their vast spending power makes them important in a business context. The major types of non profit-making organisations are as follows.

Unincorporated associations

Unincorporated associations consist of groups of people who pursue some common purpose other than as companies or partnerships. There are a large number of these associations, such as member's clubs, trade unions and friendly societies.

Unincorporated associations have no legal status distinct from that of their members. That is to say that in the eyes of the law the associations do not exist. This seems an obvious nonsense because anyone can see that the local tennis club does exist. But what is being said is that the tennis club has no legal personality of its own – it cannot sue or be sued.

This gives rise to a number of questions. What, then, if the tennis club has a legal grievance? What if a builder has broken his contract to repair the clubhouse? Can nothing be done? What if the activities of the tennis club injure someone – perhaps a slate falls off the clubhouse roof and injures a passer-by? Has he no one to sue?

It is perhaps easiest to understand the law here if we separate contract from tort. Because unincorporated associations have no legal personality they have no capacity to make contracts. The tennis club itself will not make a contract with a builder. One of the members, or perhaps the committee, will have to make the contract personally. If the builder breaks the contract, he can be sued by the person who made the contract.

If the activities of the unincorporated association injure someone then the injured person will sue in tort. If he can identify the particular member who injured him then he will sue that member.

If all of the members of the association have an identical interest in defending the case then the injured person can sue a **representative sample** of the members and, if he wins, enforce the judgment against any of the members.

This happened in *Campbell* v *Thompson*, where all of the members of an unincorporated association were regarded as the employers of the plaintiff. It was held that the plaintiff had the right to sue two members of the association, rather than having to sue all of them. Similarly, a representative sample of members can sue in tort if all of the members have an identical interest in pursuing the case.

Trade unions are unincorporated associations, but various statutes have given them the right to sue and be sued in their own name.

When a member joins an unincorporated association he makes a contract with it. The rules of the association are part of the contract, and so the member automatically agrees to the rules by joining the association. These rules may well determine a member's liability.

ACTIVITY QUESTIONS 3.6

1 To what extent are sole traders liable for the debts of their businesses?

2 Why are non profit-making organisations, such as member's clubs, not classified as partnerships?

3 Can an unincorporated association make contracts in its own name?

Further activity questions 3.6

O'Connor J in *EETPU* v *Times Newspapers* (1968) said:

'. . . *a voluntary unincorporated association cannot maintain an action for libel on itself. Let me give an example. If one says of the Longbeach Anglers' Association that at the competition last Saturday they cheated, there is a defamatory statement; but the Longbeach Anglers' Association cannot maintain an action in respect of it. It may be that the individuals of the association who were partaking in the competition could successfully sue by saying that, although they were not named, the defamatory statement pointed at them with sufficient clarity and was so understood by those who knew that they were members of the association to enable them to sue for libel; but the association could not do so, and it could not do so, as I see it, on the principle that it has no personality of its own which is capable of being defamed.*'

1 Why could the Longbeach Anglers' Association not sue?

2 If the Longbeach Anglers' Association, like other fishing clubs, had allowed only its champion angler to take part in the competition, could the Longbeach Anglers' Association's champion have sued?

3 One of the Longbeach Anglers, while taking part in the competition, negligently injures a rival angler. Can anyone be sued in respect of the injuries inflicted?

4 O'Connor J went on to say whether or not companies can be defamed. Can they?

Government departments

Some government departments, such as the Department of Education, are incorporated. As corporations they have perpetual succession, can make contracts in their own name and can own property. Other government departments, such as the Civil Service Department, are not incorporated. They therefore cannot own property or make contracts in their own name. For example, the Department of Education employs teachers in State schools. But civil servants are employed by the Government. They cannot be employed by the Civil Service Department.

Local authorities

Local authorities are statutory corporations established to perform a wide variety of local functions. As corporations they too have perpetual succession, can own property and make contracts.

Local authorities act through democratically elected councillors. To some extent they are controlled by central government upon whom they depend for much of their income.

Quangos

Quangos are 'quasi-autonomous, non-governmental organisations'. This definition was invented to make the easily pronounced acronym 'quango'. Essentially they are companies created to take over the running of services previously run by local authorities.

Colleges of further education and opted-out schools are now quangos. In the past they were funded and controlled by local authorities. Central government did not approve of the way local authorities performed these tasks and made colleges quangos. Each college is now a company and therefore now has the powers of a corporation.

Health Authority Trusts, Training and Enterprise Councils, and Local Police Authorities are all quangos.

Ultimately quangos are controlled by their governors or trustees (who are politically appointed) and by central government which supplies their funding.

Charities

There are about a quarter of a million charitable organisations in Britain; 160,000 are registered with the Charities Commission. Charities are given considerable tax advantages but are not allowed to engage in any political activity. They are run by trustees, and it is a strict rule that trustees are not allowed to benefit from their position other than through their contracts of employment.

Charities must be created entirely for one of four purposes:

(a) The relief of poverty.
(b) The advancement of education.
(c) The advancement of religion.
(d) Other purposes beneficial to the community.

Not all charity is given to the poor; Eton College, for example, is a charity school.

Charities can be unincorporated associations or they can register as companies. If they do register they are usually limited by guarantee.

If charities are not registered as companies then the trustees will have unlimited liability. They will make contracts on behalf of the charity in their own name.

On dissolution all the assets of a charity must go to another charity or to charitable purposes.

ACTIVITY QUESTION 3.7

Complete the chart on page 80 by filling in the vacant boxes. Some of the boxes have been completed to help you get started.

Further activity question 3.7

In this chapter we have considered public companies, private limited companies, unlimited companies, partnerships, sole traders, unincorporated associations, local authorities, government departments, quangos and charities. Of these organisations which **could** a golf club be? (Consider **all** of the possibilities.)

	Incorporated? (Yes/No/Maybe)	Profit-Making? (Yes/No)	Government Funded? (Yes/No)
The Body Shop PLC	*Yes*	*Yes*	*No*
Acme Ltd			
Unlimited Company			
Practising barrister			
Firm of accountants			
Oxfam			
Westminster City Council			
Clarendon College Corporation			
Blagdon Darts Club			
Department of Education			
The Civil Service			

TASK 3

A friend of yours has for some time supplied T-shirts to a partnership of market traders. Usually the partnership make an order and pay for the T-shirts some weeks later. The market traders have recently turned their business into a company. Now they have placed a very large order.

Write a report for your friend, indicating the differences between a company and a partnership. In particular, explain the liability of shareholders and partners to unsecured creditors.

4 Choice of legal status

People going into business together must choose what sort of business organisation they wish to form. Often they might have very clear views. They might be quite sure that they want to be either a company or a partnership. In many other cases, however, the choice may not be so clear cut.

When a business is being set up there are often many matters requiring urgent attention. Perhaps staff must be employed, money borrowed or premises leased. It is easy to regard the decision as to whether to form a company or a partnership as less pressing. However, the choice of business status is a very important one. Prospective business people should consider the advantages and disadvantages of both companies and partnerships in some detail.

Limited liability

We saw in *Salomon*'s case that shareholders in a limited company cannot be forced to pay more than the price of their shares. Partners on the other hand are completely liable for the firm's debts to the full extent of their personal fortune. This is, perhaps, the principal advantage of a company over a partnership.

There is another side to limited liability, though, and that is that creditors may be much less willing to extend credit to a small company than they would be to a partnership.

In business it is not usual to pay for goods and services in advance. If suppliers are eager to do business they will probably accept deferred payment. But they will naturally be less keen to extend this credit to businesses of which they know nothing. This can make a company's limited liability something of a disadvantage. Suppliers dealing with a partnership need not have any worries about getting paid as long as they know that some or all of the partners are financially sound. But suppliers dealing with a small company should be very careful. If the company fails, as very many have over the past few years, then suppliers who are owed money will find themselves at the back of the queue as unsecured creditors.

In August 1994, CCN Business Information published a survey of almost a million company directors. This showed that 23.9 per cent had also been directors of companies which had failed in the previous six years. A thousand of the directors had been involved in more than 10 failed companies. The directors involved in the failed companies were not all rogues. (Many of them were!) But each time a company failed, the unsecured creditors did not receive full payment of their debts.

The right to manage

This topic is considered in more depth in Chapters 11 and 12. In essence the position is that all partners have a right to manage the partnership's affairs, and all partners are agents of the firm as regards contracts made in the normal course of the firm's business.

Shareholders, no matter how large their percentage holding, do not have a right to manage a company. This right is vested in the Board of Directors which is elected by a simple majority of the shareholders voting at a general meeting. Therefore a shareholder with over 50 per cent of the shares has the power to change the directors. But it must be emphasised that until the shareholder exercises this power the directors in place have the right to manage the company's affairs.

A shareholder with less than 50 per cent of the votes can be outvoted on a resolution to appoint or change the directors. So minority shareholders are in the unfortunate position of having no right to manage the company's affairs, and no power to change this situation.

A person going into business with one other might therefore be very unwilling to form a company unless he was to own 50 per cent of the shares. Similar problems arise when there are several other shareholders. If the other shareholders have a closer relationship with each other than they have with the minority shareholder then a minority shareholding can again be a very precarious position.

Agency

The directors of a company are agents of the company, and this means that the Board of Directors can make binding contracts on the company's behalf. The shareholders, no matter how large their shareholding, are not the company's agents and cannot make contracts on its behalf.

Every partner is an agent of the firm in respect of contracts made in the ordinary course of the firm's business. It is therefore absolutely vital that partners trust each other implicitly. A dishonest partner can bankrupt his fellow partners and there have been countless cases where this has happened.

As an agent, a partner can order anything which the firm might use. A dishonest partner can order goods in the firm's name and take possession of the goods. If he then steals the goods the other partners are absolutely liable to the suppliers for the price of the goods.

It is possible to have some safeguards over matters such as signing cheques, but liability to outsiders dealing with a partner in good faith cannot be excluded. Of course it is not a good idea to form a company with a rogue, but at least limited liability restricts the amount which can be lost.

Nor is it only a dishonest partner who can bankrupt his fellow partners. An incompetent partner may be just as bad. If he makes disastrous contracts on the firm's behalf the firm will be bound to honour them.

ACTIVITY QUESTIONS 4.1

1 Jane buys 500 £1 shares in a company which she and her friends have formed. What is her maximum potential loss if the company should fail?

2 John goes into partnership with his friends and invests £500 in the business. What is his maximum potential loss?

3 Edward owns 40 per cent of a business. The other 60 per cent is owned by Edwina, his sister. Edward regards Edwina as very autocratic, wanting to make every decision herself. Which type of business organisation would give Edward more power to manage the affairs of the business?

4 Xavier, who is not a director, owns 75 per cent of a company's shares. Can he buy a car on the company's behalf?

5 Helen is very much the junior partner in a market gardening partnership. She has contributed no capital and receives 10 per cent of the profits. Her father has contributed all the capital and receives 90 per cent of the profits. Can Helen buy a new tractor for the firm?

Further activity questions 4.1

1 Your firm has been asked to supply goods on credit to another business. You know that the owners of the business are financially sound. Would you be more willing to supply the goods if the other business was a company, or if it was a partnership?

2 Bearing in mind the definition of a partnership, can a person still be regarded as a partner if the partnership deed states that he has no right to manage the partnership's affairs.

Withdrawal from the business

Partnerships are either entered into for a fixed period of time, or they are partnerships at will, in which case any partner can withdraw from the partnership by giving notice. If a partner does withdraw, the firm will then be dissolved, and each partner will recover his share of the assets. If a partnership is for a fixed term a partner wishing to withdraw must wait until the end of that term. Even so, an end is in sight.

It is possible for a partner to assign his share in the firm before the end of the term. (Unless the partnership deed prevents this.) The assignee will receive the share of the profits to which the partner would have been entitled. But he will have no right to manage the partnership's affairs. This lack of the right to manage might considerably reduce the value of the share which is assigned.

In the case of companies, shareholders may or may not have a right to transfer their shares to whoever they wish. It all depends on the articles, and these might well say that the Board of Directors can refuse a transfer to persons of whom they disapprove. It is even possible for the articles to say that the Board has an absolute veto over any transfer of shares. If this is the case then the shareholders will be locked into the company. No matter how much they dislike the way the company is run they cannot, short of there being a fraud on the minority, sell their shares.

Shareholders who are worried about this happening might do well to insist that they will not buy the shares unless the articles do allow them to be freely transferred. Whether or not the directors would agree to such an article might well depend on how badly they wanted the shareholders' investment.

Business property

Company property belongs to the company and not to the shareholders. An important consequence of this can be that a company is able to give its assets as security on a floating charge, and yet remain free to deal with the assets as it sees fit. (Charges are considered in more detail in Chapter 9.)

Partnership property cannot belong to the partnership because a partnership has no separate legal existence of its own. It therefore belongs to the partners jointly. A partnership is not allowed to offer a floating charge over partnership property. The partners can of course offer a fixed charge but, as we shall see, this restricts the use of the property over which the charge is granted.

Borrowing power

If sole traders want to borrow money then they will need to provide security for the loan. There are several ways in which they might do this, but generally they will either need to find a guarantor (who agrees to repay the loan if the trader defaults) or they will need to mortgage their property. Because of the current high level of business failures banks are demanding very solid security for any money advanced.

Partners are in the same position as sole traders, except that since there are more of them they might well find it easier to find guarantors, or might have more property to mortgage. Creditors who are to be repaid out of partnership profits should make it very clear that they do not intend that this should make them partners.

Members of a company can raise money in the same way as partners or sole traders. But companies also have additional options:

First, companies can sell shares to people who wish to invest in the company but who have no desire to manage it. Shares in a private limited company cannot be offered to the general public but, subject to the articles, they can be offered to individuals.

An investor who is convinced that the company will be a commercial success might be more than willing to pay for shares. Some small companies achieve spectacular success and eventually change into PLCs with enormous assets. If an investor had contributed capital to a company such as The Body Shop when it was first formed for, say, 10 per cent of the shares he would have made an outstandingly good bargain. (In the year to February 1994 the company, now a PLC, reported pre-tax profits of £29 million.) The converse, of course, is that very many small companies go to the wall, in which case the shares become worthless.

Second, companies can raise capital by issuing debentures. We shall examine this in Chapter 9, but essentially it means that the company gives its assets as security for a loan while still maintaining the right to use those assets. As long as the sale of the assets would be guaranteed to raise more than the amount loaned then the creditor has cast-iron security. Many lenders, though, take a particularly jaundiced view of the value of a company's assets. They value them on the basis that everything which could possibly reduce their value will in fact do so. This can make it difficult for companies without substantial assets to raise much money by issuing debentures.

Partnerships are generally limited to 20 partners. But there is no restriction on the number of shareholders in a company. This can give a company an advantage in raising capital in that there may simply be more people willing to contribute to the business than is allowable in the case of a partnership.

Formation

A business which wants to trade immediately will have to do so as a partnership rather than as a company. A partnership can be created without any formalities. As soon as two people carry on a business in common with a view to profit they will be a partnership, whether they realise this or not. It is however quite likely that partners will want to have a deed of partnership drawn up by a lawyer. If so then this too is bound to involve some expense and delay.

A company is formed by registration. As we shall see, this involves sending documents to the Registrar of Companies and waiting for him to register the company. However, it is possible to buy an 'off-the-shelf' company, that is to say a company which has been formed with the sole purpose of selling it to people who wish to own a company but do not want to bother with forming one themselves. If the purchasers of the off-the-shelf company wanted to change the articles or the memorandum they would still have to wait for the Registrar to register the alterations. A shelf company costs about £100.

Formalities

Partners do not need to adhere to any formalities. There is no need for them to hold meetings.

A company will usually have to hold at least one meeting a year (its Annual General Meeting). Notice must be given of meetings and of resolutions to be proposed, and minutes of meetings must be kept.

The current trend is to de-regulate companies. The formalities with which they must comply have been greatly reduced in recent years. As a consequence this particular advantage of a partnership is nowadays less marked.

Publicity

The affairs of a partnership are completely private. Like anyone else, the partners will of course need to declare their earnings to the Inland Revenue. Beyond this there is no need to reveal their accounts to anyone.

Until recently all companies had to publish their accounts. This is no longer true of small companies, and so the advantage of partnerships in respect of publicity has been considerably diminished.

Small companies are defined as having two out of three of the following qualifications:

(a) turnover of less than £2.8 million;
(b) assets of less than £1.4 million;
(c) fewer than 50 employees.

As can be seen, these qualifications are fairly generous. A business which was too large to start trading as a small company would be unlikely to want to trade as a partnership.

Tax

Individuals and companies are not taxed in the same way. Individuals pay income tax and national insurance; companies pay corporation tax.

For tax purposes both partners and sole traders are treated as individuals, and income tax is payable on all of the profits which they make. Even profits which are left in the business are taxed. (The accounts must show whether or not the business assets have increased in value. If they have this is regarded as profit.) However, individuals are given personal allowances for income tax purposes. The single person's allowance is currently £3,525. This means that on the first £3,525 which he earns he pays no income tax. Other allowances, such as the married couple's allowance, might increase this figure.

Once an individual exceeds his allowance he pays tax at varying rates. The single person pays 20 per cent on the first £3,200 in excess of his allowance, 25 per cent on the next £21,100 and then 40 per cent an anything over this.

National insurance contributions must also be paid. The self-employed pay a flat rate of £5.85 a week, regardless of profit. A further 7.3 per cent is payable on profits between £6,640 and £22,880.

It is therefore possible that a self-employed person with substantial other earnings could be paying a tax rate of 47.3 per cent on some of his business profits.

Companies too are taxed on profits made. Profits of under £0.25 million are taxed at 25 per cent. This rate rises by degrees until companies pay the full corporation tax of 33 per cent on profits over £1.25 million.

Money left in the company is taxed at these rates as corporation tax. The owners of the company can withdraw money by paying themselves directors' salaries. Corporation tax would not be paid on such money withdrawn. (Removing the money from the company would reduce the company's profit.) But income tax and national insurance would be payable by the individual receiving the money.

Companies do not receive personal allowances. However, it can be seen that the rates of corporation tax can be considerably lower than the rates of tax paid by individuals.

It would therefore seem advantageous for many business people to form a company. They could pay themselves what they needed to live on as a salary, and leave the rest in the company to grow. However, this is complicated by capital gains tax, which is payable when a person sells assets which have grown in value since he acquired them. If money is left in the company the value of the company, and therefore the value of the shares, will grow. Ultimately the owners must sell their shares in order to take the money.

Capital gains tax, which is payable at 20 per cent, 25 per cent, or 40 per cent (depending on the individual's income tax bracket), could mean that money left in the company is taxed twice (first it is taxed as company profit; when the shares are sold it is taxed as a capital gain). Some relief is provided in that individuals are given an annual capital gains allowance of £6,000 a year.

Capital gains tax liability can be very much reduced by retirement relief available to those over 55. The regulations governing this relief are very complicated, but they can allow an individual selling a private company to take £300,000 free of capital gains tax liability.

For many self-employed people there are definite tax advantages to be gained from forming a company. Some highly paid people who would normally be regarded as employees can reduce their tax liability by arranging to be paid through a company. (See *Goodwin* v *Birmingham City Football Club* on page 67.) However, it must be remembered that the extra administration involved in running a company is bound to involve some cost.

Self-employed people who wish to trade as a company should bear in mind two further pitfalls. First, the Inland Revenue are likely to look to the reality of the situation. They will not accept that the income has been earnt by a company rather than by an individual merely because it is paid into a company bank account. Second, if a person arranges to be paid income by a company then he will be an employee of the company. The company will need to pay the employer's national insurance contribution (10.2%) and the employee will need to pay the employee's national insurance contribution (10%). This combined rate of 20.2% is well in excess of the rate paid by the self-employed.

Perpetual succession

As we saw in Chapter 3, companies continue in existence until they are wound up. The death of a shareholder, or even of all the shareholders, will not end the company.

In contrast, the death of a partner will end the partnership. However, the partnership deed might well provide that the surviving partners should carry on the business. (In which case they must pay an appropriate amount to the estate of the deceased partner.) If the surviving partners do carry the business on then the dissolution of the partnership will only be a technical dissolution.

Numbers

As we shall see, partnerships of 20 or more people are not usually allowed. If 20 or more people want to go into business together they will need to do so as a company.

Sole traders

By definition a sole trader is in business on his own. However, a sole trader should consider the benefits of forming a company. In effect he can trade as a company and still be in business on his own. This is especially true now that it is possible to have private limited companies with only one shareholder.

In this chapter we have considered whether groups of people forming a business should trade as companies or partnerships. Sole traders should consider the same advantages and disadvantages of incorporation.

ACTIVITY QUESTIONS 4.2

1 What methods of raising capital are open to a company but not to a partnership?

2 What type of tax is paid by partners and what type is paid by companies?

3 Which of the following is not an advantage of a partnership?
   (i)   A partnership can begin trading immediately.
   (ii) The affairs of a partnership are completely private.
   (iii) The partners have unlimited liability for the debts of the partnership.
   (iv) Every partner has the right to manage the firm's affairs.

4 Which of the following is not an advantage of a limited company?
   (i)   A shareholder can lose no more than the value of his shares.
   (ii) A company's assets, such as they might be from time to time, can be given as security for a loan.
   (iii) A company can continue in existence indefinitely.
   (iv) A company must comply with certain formalities.

5 Complete the following chart. To get you going some of the sections are already completed.

	Ltd Company	Partnership	Sole Trader
Limited Liability (Yes or No)	*Yes*		
Managed by		*The partners*	
Who are agents of the business?			*The trader*
Who owns the assets of the business?			
Methods of raising capital			*Borrow money*
How is the business formed?			
Liable to which taxes?		*Income Tax National Insurance*	
Perpetual Succession (Yes or No)			
Maximum number in the business			

Further activity questions 4.2

1 Three years ago Sarah finished a college course in health and beauty therapy. After a year working in a salon she spent three months in the United States. On a trip to California Sarah was extremely impressed by some of the alternative beauty treatments available there.

Sarah now wants to market some of the Californian ideas in England, and is worried that if she waits too long others will beat her to it.

Sarah's grandfather, Stanley, has recently retired from the Board of a multinational company. He has a variety of interests but, seeing Sarah as a 'chip off the old block,' he is prepared to invest in her proposed business and help her in the running of it.

Sarah is very fond of her grandfather but thinks that he is too cautious, not realising that in the modern age opportunities must be seized immediately, before it becomes too late. Stanley is very proud of Sarah but feels that, expert though she might be in the field of beauty therapy, she has a great deal to learn as far as business goes.

Stanley has agreed to invest £25,000 in the business and put in three or four hours' work a week. Sarah is putting in her savings of £3,000 and will devote all of her time to the business.

(a) Do you think that Stanley would prefer that the business was a company or a partnership?
(b) Which do you think Sarah would prefer?
(c) As an objective outsider, which type of business organisation do you think they should become?

(It should be pointed out that there are no absolutely right or wrong answers to questions such as these. Both types of business organisation have considerable advantages and disadvantages. However, several of the matters considered in the chapter will have a bearing on the decisions. Try and identify these matters and then decide how important each one is.)

2 Aziz worked as a salesman and his brother, Ahktar, worked as a shop fitter. Four years ago Aziz found Ahktar a one-off job, refitting a friend's office. The job went very well and both Aziz and Ahktar made a good profit.

When Ahktar was made redundant he asked Aziz to look out for any more shop fitting work he could find. To his surprise, Aziz found that he was coming up with quite a few jobs.

Aziz is now ready to leave his full-time job and concentrate on finding shop fitting work for Ahktar and for one or two of Ahktar's friends who were made redundant at the same time as he was. Aziz is also going to sort out the business paperwork and organise materials.

While Aziz was still working full-time he took 15 per cent of the shop fitting profits and Ahktar took the rest. It is proposed that in future they split the profits 50:50. Ahktar's shop fitting friends are to be employed casually, on a daily basis.

List, in order of importance, the factors which should influence their decision as to whether or not to change the existing partnership into a company.

TASK 4

Over the past 40 years Jane has built up a very successful wholesaling business. All three of her children have been employed by the business for the past seven years.

Jane's health is no longer good and she is retiring from the business. Jane has always traded as a sole trader but she realises that if her children are to run the business they will have to trade either as a company or as a partnership.

Jane does not foresee too many problems while she is still alive, but she is concerned that after her death the children may fall out with each other.

Her eldest child, John, has always seen the other two as less hard-working than himself. Mary, the second child, is very easygoing. She is married to a dentist and works only half-time in the business. Anne, the youngest, is engaged to Bill, who seems to dislike John.

John puts a great deal of work into the business. He is the only one of the three who could run it single-handed. However, he has no other qualifications, and if the business were to cease trading he would be poorly placed.

Anne has a Business Studies degree and thinks that with the proceeds from her share of the business she could make a lot more money in some other field.

Jane, who is proud of the business and does not want it to be broken up after her death, wants to explain the choice between company and partnership to each of her three children.

1 Prepare an overhead projector sheet for Jane. On the sheet you should include all the main reasons why one form of business organisation might be preferable to another.

2 Make brief notes for Jane, indicating:
   (a) Which type of business organisation you think John would prefer?
   (b) Which type of business organisation you think Mary would prefer?
   (c) Which type of business organisation you think Anne would prefer?
   (d) Which type of business organisation you think Jane should choose?

5 Formation of businesses

Registered companies

A company is formed by **promoters**, who must register certain documents with the Registrar of Companies. If the Registrar is satisfied with the documents he will issue a **certificate of incorporation**, and the company will then exist as a corporate body.

The documents which must be sent to the Registrar are:

(a) The company's memorandum of association.
(b) The company's articles of association.
(c) A statement giving the names of the company's first directors and of the company secretary (Form 10).
(d) A statement that all the statutory requirements of registration have been complied with (Form 12).

The memorandum of association

A company's constitution is contained in its memorandum and articles of association. The memorandum regulates the company's **external** affairs. It is designed to provide information to outsiders.

Section 2 of the Companies Act 1985 states that the memorandum of a company limited by shares must contain five obligatory clauses:

(a) the company name,
(b) the registered office,
(c) the objects of the company,
(d) the limited liability of the company,
(e) the share capital.

The company name (clause 1)

This clause states the name of the company. If the company is limited then its name must end with the word 'limited'.

The registered office (clause 2)

This clause must state whether the company's registered office is in England, Wales or Scotland. The address does not need to be given here. However, the address will have to be declared in Form 10.

The objects (clause 3)

The objects clause states the purposes for which the company is being formed. Until recently a company could not make valid contracts which were outside its objects clause. For this reason most companies tended to have extremely long objects clauses, often running to several pages. Such clauses are no longer necessary. The liability of companies on contracts made outside their objects clause is considered more fully in Chapter 11.

Limited liability (clause 4)

This clause merely states that the liability of the company is limited.

Share capital (clause 5)

The company must state the amount of share capital with which it is to be registered and the way in which this capital is to be divided into shares. For example, a company might state that it has a share capital of £100, divided into 100 shares of £1 each.

The amount of share capital declared in clause 5 is known as the **authorised share capital**. This is the maximum number of shares, of a stated value, which the company is authorised to issue. Not all of this authorised capital needs to be issued as shares.

Every subscriber to the memorandum must take at least one share in the company. Since a European Directive in 1992 it is now possible to have single member companies. Such a company might have a share capital of £1, made up of a single £1 share.

The articles of association

The articles are the **internal** rules of the company. They bind the members and the company as if signed and sealed by each member.

If a company does not register its own articles a model set of articles will be used. These model articles are contained in Table A of the Companies Regulations 1985. Table A articles are not suitable for all companies, but many do adopt them.

Contents of Table A

Table A runs to 118 lengthy articles, dealing with the following matters:

Article	1	Interpretation of the articles
Articles	2–5	Share capital
Articles	6–7	Share certificates
Articles	8–11	Lien
Articles	12–22	Calls on shares and forfeitures
Articles	23–28	Transfer of shares
Articles	29–31	Transmission of shares
Articles	32–34	Alteration of share capital
Article	35	Purchase of own shares
Articles	36–37	General meetings
Articles	38–39	Notice of general meetings
Articles	40–53	Proceedings at general meetings
Articles	54–63	Votes of members
Article	64	Number of directors
Articles	65–69	Alternate directors
Articles	70–71	Powers of directors

Article	72	Delegation of directors' powers
Articles	73–80	Appointment and retirement of directors
Article	81	Disqualification and removal of directors
Articles	82–83	Remuneration and expenses of directors
Articles	84–86	Directors' appointment and interests
Articles	87–98	Directors' gratuities and pensions
Articles	99	The secretary
Article	100	Minutes
Article	101	The company seal
Article	102–108	Dividends
Article	109	Accounts
Article	110	Capitalisation of profits
Articles	111–116	Notices
Article	117	Winding up
Article	118	Indemnity

There is little point in reproducing all of these articles as many of them deal with technical matters. However, it is important that students have an idea of the complexity and detail of typical company articles. Therefore articles 23–28, which deal with the transfer of shares, are reproduced in full.

TRANSFER OF SHARES

23. The instrument of transfer of a share may be in any usual form or in any other form which the directors may approve and shall be executed by or on behalf of the transferor and, unless the share is fully paid, by or on behalf of the transferee.

24. The directors may refuse to register the transfer of a share which is not fully paid to a person of whom they do not approve and they may refuse to register the transfer of a share on which the company has a lien. They may also refuse to register a transfer unless:

    (a) It is lodged at the office or at such other place as the directors may appoint and is accompanied by the certificate for the shares to which it relates and such other evidence as the directors may reasonably require to show the right of the transferor to make the transfer;

    (b) it is in respect of only one class of shares; and

    (c) it is in favour of not more than four transferees.

25. If the directors refuse to register a transfer of a share, they shall within two months after the date on which the transfer was lodged with the company send to the transferee notice of the refusal.

26. The registration of transfers of shares or of transfers of any class of shares may be suspended at such times and for such periods (not exceeding thirty days in any year) as the directors may determine.

27. No fee shall be charged for the registration of any instrument of transfer or other document relating to or affecting the title to any share.

28. The company shall be entitled to retain any instrument of transfer which is registered, but any instrument of transfer which the directors refuse to register shall be returned to the person lodging it when notice of the refusal is given.

 ## ACTIVITY QUESTION 5.1

Blank copies of Forms 10 and 12 are reproduced at the back of this book. Complete both forms to register a fictitious company. Before starting you will need to decide upon the following information:

(a) The company name.
(b) The address of its registered office.
(c) The name and address of the solicitors or accountants who are to act as agents.
(d) The names of the company secretary and the directors.

Further activity question 5.1

Bulstrodes Ltd is a company which has adopted Table A articles. Bulstrodes has five shareholders, all of whom are directors. One of the shareholders wants to transfer her shares to her sister. None of the others wants this transfer to take place. Can the others prevent the transfer?

Contracts made before the company is formed

A company does not come into existence until the Registrar issues its certificate of incorporation. It follows that until the certificate is issued the company has no capacity to make contracts. However, the promoters might want to make contracts on the company's behalf in advance of incorporation. For example, if a shop intended to begin trading, as a company, on 1 October then the promoters would need to buy stock in advance of that date. It might be thought that the easiest way to do this would be for the promoters to make the contract personally, and for the company to ratify the contract as soon as the company is formed. (A person ratifies a contract if he agrees to be bound by it after it has been made.) Such a ratification would not be effective, as the following case shows.

Kelner v Baxter (1866)

A company was to be formed to run a hotel. Before incorporation the promoters ordered a quantity of wine on the company's behalf. The company came into existence and the directors agreed to ratify the contract on the company's behalf. The wine was delivered and consumed. The company went into liquidation before it had paid for the wine.

Held The company's ratification was ineffective because the company did not exist at the time the contract was made. However, the promoters were personally liable on the contract because they had signed as agents for the company.

If the promoters in *Kelner v Baxter* had not signed as agents or on behalf of the company then they would not have been personally liable on the contract, and the supplier of the wine would never have been paid.

Such a situation is now covered by section 36 (c) of the 1985 Act, which provides:

> *'A contract which purports to be made by or on behalf of a company when the company has not been formed has effect, subject to any agreement to the contrary, as one made with the person purporting to act for the company or as agent for it, and he is personally liable on the contract accordingly.'*

It will be noticed this section applies *'subject to any agreement to the contrary'*. It is therefore possible for the promoter to disclaim personal liability when he makes the contract on the company's behalf. However, it would be inadvisable for others to deal with the promoters on this basis. In effect they would be making contracts which could be enforced against them but which they themselves might not be able to enforce.

Suppliers to the company might do well to insist that the company is actually formed before they make any contract. Another way around the problem would be for the supplier to make two contracts. The first draft contract would be with the company, stating that it will pay as soon as it is formed. The second contract would be a binding one with the promoter, who would agree that he would pay in the event that the company does not.

The company name

Limited or PLC

The name of every public company must end with the words **'Public Limited Company'** or the abbreviation **'PLC'**.

The name of every private limited company must end with the word **'Limited'** or the abbreviation **'Ltd'**.

So the word 'Limited' must appear in the names of both types of companies, although of course it is not the company's liability which is limited, but the liability of its members.

Unlimited companies do not need to include the word 'Limited' in their names.

The word 'company' is not often included in the names of companies. Strangely, the word appears in the names of partnerships more frequently than in the names of companies.

Prohibited names

Section 26 of the 1985 Act lists prohibitions on the use of certain names:

(a) The words 'limited' or 'unlimited' can only be used **at the end** of the name.
(b) The Registrar will refuse to register a name which is **identical** to the name of another company already on the register.
(c) The Registrar will refuse to register a name the use of which would, in the opinion of the Secretary of State, constitute a criminal offence or be offensive.
(d) Regulations made by the Secretary of State prohibit the use of certain words without permission. Currently 79 words are listed, including 'Building Society,' 'Chamber of Commerce,' 'English,' 'Insurance,' 'National,' 'Prince,' 'Queen,' 'Royal,' 'Trade Union,' 'Trust,' and 'Windsor'. The regulations explain the person from whom permission to use the words must be sought. For example, the words which suggest a royal connection can only be used if the Home Office gives permission.

Passing off

If a company registers a name which is too similar to the name of an existing business, a passing off action might prevent the company from trading under its registered name. If such a passing off action is brought the court will grant an injunction to prevent use of that name if it is likely to divert customers away from the existing business or cause confusion between the two businesses. This applies whether the name was deliberately made similar or was done so accidentally. But the fact that it was done deliberately is likely to influence the court's decision against the new name.

Ewing v Buttercup Margarine Co Ltd (1917, Court of Appeal)

The plaintiff carried on an unincorporated business under the name Buttercup Dairy Co. The business dealt in margarine, mainly in Scotland. The defendant company was registered under the name the Buttercup Margarine Co Ltd. It also dealt in margarine, but in the South of England. The plaintiff brought a passing off action.

Held The plaintiff's action was successful. The defendant company was prohibited from continuing to trade under its registered name. The public might have thought that there was a connection between the two businesses.

Section 28 of the 1985 Act gives the Secretary of State the power to order a company to change its name within one year of registration if the name is too similar to one which is already on the register.

Publication of name and address

All companies must publish their names:

(a) Outside all places of business.
(b) On all letters, invoices, notices, cheques and receipts.
(c) On the company seal, if it has a seal.

If the company does not publish its name as required then every one of its officers is liable to be fined. Furthermore, a person who signs company letters or cheques which do not publish the company name will be personally liable to any creditor who relies on the document and loses money. This liability will also be imposed if the company name is incorrectly stated.

For example, in *Penrose* v *Martyr* (1858), a company secretary signed a cheque on the company's behalf and was held personally liable because the word 'Limited' was omitted from the company name.

Change of name

A private limited company may change its name by special resolution.

The same prohibitions will apply to a change of name as applied to the use of a name on formation of a company. The Registrar must register the changed name and has the same powers to refuse.

Business names

Sometimes companies trade under a name other than their registered corporate name. A company which does trade under another name will have to comply with the Business Names Act 1985. The effects of this Act are considered later in this chapter as the Act applies more often to partnerships than to companies.

Even if the company does trade under another name it must continue to print its proper corporate name on all letters and cheques.

ACTIVITY QUESTION 5.2

In which, if any, of the documents sent to the Registrar of Companies will the following information be found?
(a) The company name and the address of its registered office.
(b) The company's capacity to make contracts.
(c) The rules on the transfer of shares.
(d) The name of the company secretary.
(e) A declaration that the necessary formalities have been complied with.
(f) Previous names of the directors.
(g) The authorised share capital.

Further activity questions 5.2

1 Your firm has been approached to refurbish a restaurant on behalf of a company which is soon to be incorporated. The contract is lucrative and you know that the director who approached you is financially sound. Describe the ways in which a contract might safely be entered into.

2 For generations a firm of bakers, Routledge and Ball, has traded in a market town. Now a new firm, Routledge and Ball Ltd, has applied for registration as a company.
(a) Will the Registrar register the company?
(b) Can the established firm prevent the company from trading as bakers in and around the market town?

Would your answer be different if the company intended to make ball-bearings rather than bread?

Partnerships

We saw in Chapter 3 that a partnership is formed merely by the fact of people carrying on a business in common with a view to profit. Such people might or might not enter into a written partnership agreement, usually called a partnership deed.

If a partnership deed is signed by the partners then this will govern their relations. The deed will also state the date at which the partnership commenced. Firms carrying on a professional business, such as firms of accountants or solicitors, would almost certainly regulate their relations with a detailed partnership deed. Other firms, such as firms of window cleaners or market traders, might not have a written agreement. This would not prevent them from being partnerships.

The partnership deed

A very simple partnership deed is reproduced below.

Model Partnership Deed

This partnership agreement is made on (*date*) . . . .

between (*name 1*) . . . . of (*address 1*) . . . .

and (*name 2*) . . . . of (*address 2*) . . . .

and (*name 3*) . . . . of (*address 3*) . . . .

It is agreed as follows:

1) The partners shall carry on business in partnership as (*business*) . . . .

   under the firm name of (*partnership name*) . . . .

   of (*partnership address*) . . . .

2) The partnership will commence on the date of this agreement and shall continue in existence for five years.

3) The partners shall be entitled to the profits arising from the partnership in equal shares.

4) The bankers of the firm shall be (*name*) . . . . .of

   (*address*) . . . .
   Cheques drawn in the name of the firm must be signed by all of the partners.

5) Each partner shall devote his or her whole time to the business of the partnership.

6) Each partner shall be entitled to (*number*) . . . . week's holiday each year.

7) None of the partners shall without the consent of the other: engage in any business other than partnership business; or employ or dismiss any partnership employee.

8) Each partner shall be entitled to draw (*amount*) . . . . as salary from the partnership bank account each month.

Continued overleaf

9) All matters relating to the management of the affairs of the partnership shall be decided by votes taken at a meeting of the partners. At such meetings each partner shall be entitled to one vote and resolutions shall be passed by a simple majority vote.

10) If any disputes should arise as to the meaning of this partnership deed or as to the rights and liabilities of the partners under it, such disputes shall be referred to an arbitrator to be appointed by the President of the Chartered Institute of Arbitrators. The decision of the arbitrator shall be binding on all of the partners.

Signed as a deed by (*name 1*) . . . .

     in the presence of (*witness*) . . . .

Signed as a deed by (*name 2*) . . . .

     in the presence of (*witness*) . . . .

Signed as a deed by (*name 3*) . . . .

     in the presence of (*witness*) . . . .

It should be stressed that such a deed is very brief and is only a model. In its current form it is unlikely to be ideal for many firms. If a firm does use such a model as the basis for its own partnership deed, the partners should ensure that changes are made to suit their particular circumstances.

More complicated partnership deeds can run to several thousand words. They cover the same matters as the simple deed in very much more detail. In addition, they might contain articles dealing with matters such as leasing premises, payment of private debts, negative covenants, banking arrangements, retirement provisions, expulsion of partners, provisions for retiring partners, options to purchase the share of outgoing partners, income tax and retirement annuities.

The partnership deed can be altered by unanimous consent of the partners, unless the articles themselves prevent this. If an article does prevent alteration it should also allow for manifest errors in the deed to be corrected immediately.

Further Activity Question 5.3

A and B are intending to go into partnership as market traders. A is to work full-time in the business, actually standing behind the market stall, and take 75 per cent of the profits. B, who has a full-time job as a sales representative, is to work 10 hours a week and receive 25 per cent of the profits. B is also to act as the firm's buyer and look after the paperwork. A's father, an accountant, is prepared to check the books free of charge on a regular basis.

If B spots a bargain he often has to buy it immediately. A is happy to let B write cheques for up to £100 on the firm's behalf. B has an ambition to work in Australia but would not travel there without a definite job offer. Occasionally he writes to Australian firms, asking for jobs. He realises that he has very little chance of getting a job in this way, but if he was offered one he would want to leave for Australia immediately.

A and B want a partnership deed. They think that the model partnership deed on page 103 is a suitable model but realise that changes would have to be made if the deed was to suit their needs.

(a) List the articles which you think should be changed.
(b) Write alternative articles to replace those which you consider unsuitable.

Absence of written partnership agreement

If there is no written partnership agreement then it may be very difficult to state whether or not there is a partnership. Many people who are partners do not realise that they are. The decision as to whether or not a partnership exists is based on sections 1 and 2 of the Partnership Act 1890.

As we have seen, section 1 provides the classic definition of a partnership as *'the relationship which subsists between persons carrying on a business in common with a view to profit'*. Other matters, such as the joint ownership of property, the sharing of gross returns, or the sharing of profits are likely to be relevant in deciding whether or not a partnership exists. Section 2 of the Act tells us how these matters should be treated.

Joint ownership of property

Joint ownership of property does not on its own indicate that a partnership exists, and this applies whether or not any profits from the jointly owned property are shared.

Davis v Davis (1894)

Two sons inherited a business and three houses in equal shares. They let one of the houses and used the rent to enlarge the workshops attached to the other two houses. They continued to carry on the business, each taking out a weekly sum. No accounts were kept. The rent from the third house was shared between them.

Held There was a partnership as regards the business but not as regards the houses.

The sharing of gross returns does not on its own indicate that a partnership exists

Cox v Coulson (1916, Court of Appeal)

The defendant was the manager of a theatre, and he agreed to put on a play with Mr Mill, the manager of a touring company of actors. The defendant was to pay all of the theatre costs and receive 60 per cent of the gross takings. Mr Mill was to provide the actors and the scenery and receive 40 per cent. During the play an actor shot the plaintiff, a member of the audience. The plaintiff wanted to sue the defendant rather than Mr Mill because the defendant had more money. The plaintiff therefore argued that the defendant and Mr Mill were in partnership.

Held The defendant was not liable because there was no partnership.

> Swinfen Eady LJ '*Although the gross takings were divided between them, there was not any partnership; each had to discharge his own separate liabilities in respect of the venture. The travelling expenses, the remuneration of the actors, the cost of the appliances had to be borne entirely by Mr Mill. The theatre rent and outgoings, the cost of lighting, and the cost of the playbills were wholly to be borne by the defendant. One of them might have made a profit out of the venture, and the other might have made a loss. Neither of them had authority to bind the other in any way; there was no agency between them. The sharing of gross returns does not of itself create a partnership; see the Partnership Act 1890 section 2(2).*'

If a person receives a share of profits then this is prima facie evidence that he is a partner

But as North J explained in *Davis* v *Davis*, even this is not conclusive:

> '*The receipt by a person of a share of the profits of a business is prima facie evidence that he is a partner in it, and if the matter stops there, it is evidence upon which the Court must act. But if there are other circumstances to be considered, they ought to be considered fairly together . . . taking all the circumstances together, not attaching undue weight to any of them but drawing an inference from the whole.*'

Section 2 goes on to say that a receipt of profits is not to indicate partnership if it is received:

(a) As the **payment of a debt**.
(b) To **pay a worker** in the partnership.
(c) As **payment to the widow or child of a deceased partner**.

(d) To **repay a loan** made to the partnership.

(e) To **pay for the goodwill** of a business which has been sold to the partnership.

We see then that although the Partnership Act 1890 appears to give a very neat definition of a partnership it is by no means easy to say whether or not a joint venture amounts to a partnership.

The Partnership Act 1890 was a codifying statute; it meant to put the existing judge-made rules into a comprehensible form. A great deal seems to have been left to the discretion of the judges.

ACTIVITY QUESTIONS 5.4

1 Can people become partners without signing a written partnership agreement?

2 If two or more people own property jointly, does this automatically make them partners?

3 If two or more people share the gross returns of a business venture does this automatically make them partners?

Further activity questions 5.4

1 Using the rules outlined above, do you think that a partnership existed in the following cases? The actual decisions are set out at the end of this chapter.

Pratt v Strick (1932)

A doctor who had sold his practice to another doctor continued to live on the premises for several months so that he could introduce the new doctor to the patients. During this time profits and expenses were shared by the two doctors.

Held

Cox v Hickman (1860)

A trader got into debt and his creditors agreed that instead of making him bankrupt they would allow him to continue in business on condition that he allowed them to supervise the running of the business. The creditors were to receive a share of the business profits until the debt was fully paid. The supervising creditors were sued by another creditor on the ground that they were in partnership with the trader.

Held

Re Jones (1857)

A partnership agreement stipulated that if one of the two partners died then the other partner should continue the business and pay the widow one-quarter of the business profits. A creditor argued that this meant the widow had become a partner.

Held

Keith Spicer Ltd **v** *Mansell* (1970, Court of Appeal)

Mr Mansell and Mr Bishop decided to form a limited company so that they could run a restaurant together. Before the company was formed Mr Bishop ordered goods from the defendant. These goods were to be used by the company, and when the company was formed they were. Mr Bishop went bankrupt and the goods were never paid for. The defendant sued Mr Mansell, arguing that as he was in partnership with Mr Bishop he was liable for goods ordered on the partnership's behalf by Mr Bishop.

Held

2 Two authors jointly write a book. The publisher pays the authors a percentage of the price of each book sold.
   (a) Are the authors in partnership with each other?
   (b) Are they in partnership with the publisher?

3 Mr and Mrs Smith sell their existing house to buy a dilapidated mansion. They intend to live in the mansion for five years during which time they will completely renovate it. At the end of the five years they hope to sell at a much higher price than the one they paid. Are Mr and Mrs Smith in partnership? Would your answer be different if:
   (a) They were not married but were cohabiting?
   (b) They were strangers to each other, each selling their own house in order to buy the mansion?
   (c) They continued to live in their own houses, working on the mansion when-ever they could?
   (d) The mansion was not the only property which they were renovating together?

4 In *Newstead* v *Frost* (1980, House of Lords) an entertainer, David Frost, went into partnership with a company to try and reduce his tax liability. Mr Frost earnt a great deal of money in America, but as he was resident in the UK he had to pay UK tax on foreign earnings. Instead of receiving this money in the UK, Mr Frost formed a company in the Bahamas and went into partnership with it. The company was to receive 5 per cent of Mr Frost's American earn-ings, in return for doing administrative duties. Mr Frost was to receive the other 95 per cent. All of the activity of the partnership was carried on outside the UK and Mr Frost argued that none of its profits were taxable. The Revenue argued that the partnership did not exist.

(a) The whole purpose of this arrangement was to avoid tax. For a partnership to exist Mr Frost and the company must have been *'carrying on a business in common with a view to profit'*. Were they doing this?

(b) Although the Partnership Act 1890 states that a company cannot be a partnership, this case shows us that it is quite possible for companies to enter into partnership with each other or with individuals:

(i) What would be the risks to a company which became a partner with an individual? Would the company be fully liable for the debts of the partnership? Would the company be liable for the debts of the individual? Would the individual be fully liable for the debts of the company?

(ii) What would be the risks to the shareholders in the company? Would they still have limited liability in respect of the debts incurred as a result of the company's partnership?

(iii) As we shall see, the Companies Act 1985 prohibits most partnerships from having more than 20 members. If 100 people formed five companies, each having 20 members, and all of the companies formed a partnership, would this effectively create a partnership of 100 people?

Numbers of partners

Apart from firms of solicitors, accountants and stockbrokers, no firm may have more than 20 members. If more than 20 people want to go into business together they must do so as a company.

Barristers share chambers, but they are not allowed to practise as partners. (The firm might be representing both sides in the same case, or the judge might be hearing a case presented by an ex-partner.)

Illegal partnerships

A partnership formed for an illegal purpose will be void. The purpose will be illegal if either statute or the common law prohibits it. So many statutes prohibit so many types of behaviour that it would be pointless to try to list them all. The common law makes several different types of contract illegal, including contracts to commit a crime, tort or fraud.

Everet v Williams (1725)

Two highwaymen foacted together to rob a coach and share the proceeds. One highwayman sued the other for his share, claiming that they were partners.

Held He could not do this. The 'partnership' business was illegal, and so the partnership did not exist.

If a partnership is declared illegal the courts will refuse to recognise its existence and will not order one partner to pay towards losses suffered by another.

Minors as partners

The law of contract classifies persons under the age of 18 as minors. They do not have full contractual capacity, but can become partners. However, it is not a good idea to go into partnership with a minor as he can avoid the partnership agreement while he is still a minor or within a reasonable time of becoming 18. If a minor does avoid a partnership agreement it will no longer be binding on him.

ACTIVITY QUESTIONS 5.5

1 If 25 small traders wanted to go into business together:
   (a) Could they do so as a partnership?
   (b) How could they go into business together?

2 Can an adult go into partnership with a minor?

3 Two sole traders commit a business fraud together. The object of the fraud was to make money. Would this mean that the sole traders were partners?

Further activity question 5.5

In *Lovell and Christmas* v *Beauchamp* (1894), Lord Herschell said:

> '*I think that it is clear that there is nothing to prevent [a minor] trading, or becoming a partner with a trader, and that until his contract of partnership be disaffirmed he is a member of the trading firm. But it is equally clear that he cannot contract debts by such trading; although goods may be ordered for the firm, he does not become a debtor in respect of them. The adult partner is, however, entitled to insist that the partnership assets shall be applied in payment of the liabilities of the partnership, and until these are provided for no part of them shall be received by the [minor] partner, and, if the proper steps are taken, this right of the adult partner can be made available for the benefit of the creditors.*'

With reference to Lord Herschell's statement, answer the following questions:
(a) Can a minor be partner in a trading firm?
(b) Could a minor validly order goods on behalf of the partnership?
(c) If the firm makes a loss can the minor be sued in respect of this loss?
(d) Sarah, a minor, is in partnership with Sally, an adult. Both contributed assets worth £5,000 towards the partnership. These assets are now worth £11,000. The firm owes £8,000 to a creditor. How will this debt be paid?

The partnership name

Partnerships do not need to register the names under which they trade. Apart from the prohibition as to using the word 'Limited' or 'Ltd,' partners can trade under any name they like, as long as they comply with the Business Names Act 1985, and as long as the name is not designed to confuse the public.

The Business Names Act 1985

This Act applies to partnerships if they carry on business in a name other than the surnames of all the partners.

Section 2 prohibits the use of names which would suggest a connection with Government or local authorities. The Secretary of State can grant permission for such names to be used.

Section 3 prohibits the use of names which would suggest a connection with a Government department, without permission of the department.

Section 4 states that a notice containing the names and addresses of all the partners must be prominently displayed in any business premises to which the customers or suppliers have access. Further, partnerships with fewer than 20 members must include the name of each partner on all business letters, written orders for goods or services, invoices or receipts.

Section 5 states that if section 4 is not complied with then contracts made will be unenforceable by the partners.

Section 6 allows the Secretary of State to make regulations under the Act. Currently these regulations prohibit the use of certain words such as 'Royal' and 'National', as already described on page 100.

Section 7 provides criminal sanctions for use against those who do not comply with the Act.

Confusion with other names

Any person can trade under his own name. So John Lewis may trade under the name John Lewis or John Lewis and Co even though there is an already existing group called the John Lewis partnership.

A person may also trade under a name which is not his own as long as his reason for doing so is not to deceive the public. If the intention is to deceive the public then this can be prevented by a passing-off action.

In *Levy* v *Walker* (1879), James LJ said:

'It should never be forgotten in these cases that the sole right to restrain anybody from using any name that he likes in the course of any business that he chooses to carry on is a right in the nature of a trade mark, that is to say, a man

has a right to say *"you must not use a name whether fictitious or real, you must not use a description, whether true or not, which is intended to represent, or is calculated to represent to the world that your business is my business, and so by a fraudulent misstatement deprive me of the profits of the business which would otherwise come to me."'*

Croft v Day (1843)

A well-known firm of boot polish manufacturers, Day and Martin, carried on business in Holborn. Two people called 'Day' and 'Martin' set up as partners making boot polish with the intention of diverting business from the well-known firm. The established firm applied for an injunction to prevent Day and Martin from trading in boot polish in their real names.

Held The injunction was granted. Although 'Day' and 'Martin' were the real names of the defendants, the intention of the partnership was to deceive the public.

ACTIVITY QUESTIONS 5.6

1 Can a partnership include the word 'limited' in it's name?

2 Do partners have to include their own surnames in their trading name?

3 Are partners **always** entitled to trade under their own surnames?

TASK 5

A group of Albanian students are visiting your college. They want to know how British business organisations are formed.

Using a group of four people who want to start up a car repair business as an example, write a report which indicates:

(a) How a company is formed.

(b) How a partnership is formed.

(c) The main matters which would have to be included in the documents which promoters of companies must send to the Registrar of Companies.

(d) The type of matters usually included in a simple partnership deed.

Case decisions

There follow the actual decisions in the cases set out at page 107.

Pratt v Strick

Held The doctors were not partners. The retiring doctor had sold his business. He did not intend to carry it on with the purchaser.

Cox v Hickman

Held The creditors had not become partners with the trader. They were not carrying on a business in common with him, they were merely trying to ensure that they received payment of their debt.

Re Jones

Held The fact of the widow's receiving a share of the profits did not make her a partner. She was not involved in the running of the business.

Keith Spicer Ltd v Mansell

Held No partnership existed. At the time when the contract was made, Mr Mansell and Mr Bishop were not carrying on a business together. They were preparing to carry on an incorporated business.

Assignment 2(a)

Company or partnership?

Jane has just left college, and is making plans to open a greengrocery shop with two friends. Jane's friends have asked her to find out about the different types of business organisations. Knowing that you are on a Business Studies course, Jane asks for your help in preparing a report which outlines the differences between trading as a company and trading as a partnership.

When Jane and her friends were students, they all worked part-time for a greengrocers called Greens. They acquired some knowledge of Greens, and of one of the companies which supplied it. Feeling that this knowledge might serve as a basis for exploration, Jane supplies you with the following information:

'Greens' is a fruit and vegetable shop which is run as a partnership by Merium and George. The partners own the premises and let two flats above the shop. Merium gets up early to buy from the wholesale fruit and vegetable market, and she also has responsibility for the accounts. George manages the shop and arranges deliveries of vegetables. In addition, the partnership employs an under-manager and several part-time shop assistants.

At the wholesale vegetable market, Merium buys mainly from Bulk Vegetables Ltd. This is a family run company with three directors, Robert, Susan and Trevor. The shares in the company are owned by the three directors and by Robert's mother. Each shareholder owns 25 per cent of the shares. Like Greens, the company employs several staff.

Jane now wants you to prepare a document which will enable her to explain the different types of business organisations to her friends. She would like the document to deal with the following matters:

1 An investigation of the different legal characteristics of a partnership and a limited company.

2 A description of the extent to which Merium and George could be liable for Green's debts, and the extent to which the shareholders in Bulk Vegetables Ltd could be liable for the company's debts.

3 An outline of the way in which a limited company is formed, and of the documents in which the company's rules could be found.

4 A description of the way in which a partnership is formed, and the more important matters which Merium and George might have inserted into a partnership deed.

5 A recommendation as to which type of business organisation would be more suitable for the proposed business venture, bearing in mind the advantages and disadvantages of companies and partnerships.

Using the information which Jane has given you as a basis, draft a suitable report giving Jane the information which she requires.

Assignment 2(b)

Clients and legal advisors

This assignment takes the form of a role play exercise, in which half the students play the role of clients and the other half play the role of legal advisors.

Stage 1
The students should split into two equally sized groups of clients and legal advisors. These groups should then sub-divide into groups of three or four students.

Each group of clients should decide upon a business venture which they wish to set up. They will need to make brief notes, giving details of the venture.

Each group of legal advisors should decide upon the types of questions which they will need to ask, in order to advise the clients of the most appropriate type of business organisation for their particular venture.

Stage 2
Each client should choose a legal advisor. The clients should present their information to the legal advisors. The legal advisors should elicit additional information so that they can advise on the most appropriate type of business organisation, and then advise the clients accordingly.

Stage 3
The clients should return to their original groups, accompanied by their legal advisors, and a consensus should be reached.

Element 15.3

LEGAL RELATIONSHIPS ARISING FROM BUSINESS OPERATIONS AND ACTIVITIES

PERFORMANCE CRITERIA

A student must:

1 Identify the specific **legal responsibilities** of businesses towards **key external parties** to the organisation

2 Summarise the **specific legal responsibilities** of **businesses** towards **key internal parties**

3 Describe the ways in which a business's **legal liability** for civil and criminal wrongs committed can be reduced

6 Legal responsibility to suppliers and customers

Every business wants to remain on good terms with its suppliers and customers. Various disputes are bound to arise but, as we saw in Chapter 2, it is far better to sort these out amicably than to go to court. However, there are two main reasons why a business will want to know its legal position. First, the dispute may end up going to court and the business will want to know its chance of success. Second, if the business knows that its legal position is strong this will strengthen its hand when it is bargaining to reach a settlement.

Businesses make contracts with their suppliers and with their customers. The legal responsibilities which the businesses assume will be governed by the *terms* of the contracts which they make.

Contractual terms

A contract is made up of terms. All the promises which the contract contains, whether they were made expressly or impliedly, will be terms. If any of these terms are broken, then the injured party will always have a remedy.

How do terms arise?

Terms can find their way into contracts in one of two ways: they can be expressed or they can be implied. Express terms are actually agreed upon by the parties; implied terms are implied either by the court (on the ground of the presumed intention of the parties) or by statute.

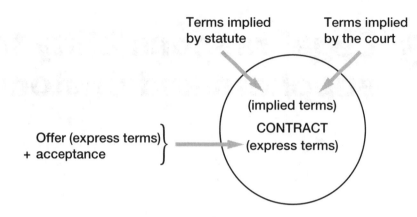

Fig 6.1 Nature of the terms of a contract

Express terms

A contract is formed when an offer is accepted. The express terms of the contract will be contained in the offer. The offeror proposes a set of terms and the offeree accepts them.

Oral contracts usually contain very few express terms. Written contracts, especially business contracts, usually contain far more.

If we look at the specimen contract at the end of this chapter we will see that it contains 26 express terms. People who agree to this contract agree to all of these terms. There is little point in trying to speculate about typical business terms. The doctrine of freedom of contract gives individuals and businesses the right to agree any terms they want. Although similar types of businesses often use similar terms, the terms of business contracts are as various as the operations which the businesses conduct.

Implied terms

Terms implied by statute

As we shall see in Chapter 7, the Sale of Goods Act 1979 implies terms into every contract under which goods are sold. These terms include premises that the seller owns the goods he is selling, that the goods are as he has described them, and that the quality of goods sold in the course of business is as high as can reasonably be expected.

Because a statute implies these terms the parties do not need to mention them when they make the contract. The terms are automatically put into the contract by the statute.

As we shall see, other statutes also imply terms into contracts. These matters are examined in detail in Chapter 7.

Terms implied by the courts

The courts also have the power to imply terms into contracts. Despite having this power, the judges have always made it plain that they are not prepared to make a contract for the parties. But they will imply a term on the basis that it was so obviously intended to be a part of the contract that the parties felt no need to mention it.

As Mackinnon LJ said, in *Shirlaw* v *Southern Foundries* (1939, Court of Appeal), '*that which in any contract is left to be implied and need not be expressed is something so obvious that it goes without saying*'.

Mackinnon LJ went on to formulate his **officious bystander test**. Under this test the courts decide whether or not to imply a term by asking how the parties to the contract would have reacted if an officious bystander had suggested to them that they had better include the term in the contract which they were making. If the parties would irritably have told the officious bystander that the term was so obviously included that it did not need to be mentioned, then the term would be implied by the courts. If the parties would not have reacted in this way, then the term would not be implied.

The test can be demonstrated by looking at the following case:

The Moorcock (1889, Court of Appeal)

A jetty owner made a contract allowing a ship owner to moor his ship at the jetty. Both parties knew that the ship would be grounded at low tide. When the ship did touch the ground it was damaged because there was a ridge of rock beneath the mud. The ship owner asked for an implied term that the jetty owner had taken reasonable care to ensure that the jetty was a safe place to unload a ship.

Held The ship owner won. It was necessary to imply such a term to make the contract commercially effective.

This case arose half a century before Mackinnon LJ formulated his test. Even so, we can see that the officious bystander test would have achieved the same outcome. (If the officious bystander had said to the parties, 'Hadn't you better include a term that the jetty is a safe place to moor a ship?' they would both have told him that such a term was so obvious that it did not need to be stated.)

Customary terms

Terms will be implied by the courts on the ground that they are customary in a particular trade, customary in a particular locality or customary between the parties.

Many trades have customs, and these customs will be implied into contracts made within the context of those trades. In the bakery trade, for example, 'a dozen' used to mean 13, and a baker who sold 20 dozen loaves would be deemed to have sold 260, not 240.

Similarly, customs of a particular locality will be implied into contracts made in that locality.

Hutton v Warren (1836)

A Lincolnshire tenant farmer was given notice to quit the farm. He asked for an implied term that he should be paid an allowance for seeds and labour.

Held The term was implied because it was an agricultural custom in that area.

A term can become customary between the parties if they regularly make contracts which include such a term. In *Kendall* v *Lillico* (1969, House of Lords) a 'sold note' containing a large number of terms was always sent the day after the contract. When a dispute arose as to whether this sold note applied to a particular contract it was held that it did. It may have been too late to be part of the offer and acceptance, but it was implied by the court on the basis of the parties' previous dealings.

Limits of implied terms

Care must be taken when looking for implied terms as the courts do not imply them freely.

Lord Pearson said, in *Trollope* v *NWRHB* (1973, House of Lords):

'The court does not make a contract for the parties. The court will not even improve the contract which the parties have made for themselves, however desirable the improvement might be. . . . An unexpressed term can be implied if and only if the court finds the parties must have intended that term to form part of their contract . . . it is not enough for the court to find that such a term would have been adopted by the parties as reasonable men if it had been suggested to them . . . it must have been a term which went without saying, a term necessary to give business efficacy to the contract.'

The current attitude of the courts was made plain by the following case:

Liverpool City Council v *Irwin* (1977, House of Lords)

Liverpool City Council were the landlords of a multi-storey block of flats. The tenants' leases imposed many obligations on the tenants but none on the landlords. A tenant of the flats refused to pay his rent on the ground that the flats were not being adequately maintained. Liverpool City Council wanted to evict him. It fell to the House of Lords to decide whether any implied terms imposed liability on the council. (Any terms imposing liability on the council had to be implied, as no express terms imposed liability upon them.)

Held The court would only imply terms which were necessary to make the contract work. So a term that the stairways should be kept usable and free from rubbish would be implied, but a term that the stairway should be well-decorated would not.

Exclusion of implied terms

Usually the terms implied by statute cannot be excluded, as we shall see in Chapter 15. But terms implied by the court, being imposed on the basis that they are obviously what the parties intended, can always be excluded by an express term.

If, for instance, the lease in *Hutton* v *Warren* had expressly stated that the tenant farmer would not get an allowance for seeds and labour then he would not have received such an allowance.

ACTIVITY QUESTIONS 6.1

1 In *Liverpool City Council* v *Irwin* the lease contained express terms, such as that the tenant should pay the rent, and implied terms, such as that the stairways should be kept in a usable condition. Who put the express terms into the contract, and who put in the implied terms?

2 If the 'officious bystander' test had been applied in *Liverpool CC* v *Irwin*, would the court have implied a term that the lifts should work? What would the bystander have said, and what would the parties have replied?

Further activity questions 6.1

1 Do you know of any trades or professions which have customs? If not, perhaps your friends or relatives work in such areas. Try and get examples of at least four such customs.

2 If a business hired a cement mixer for a week at a price of £70, would it be

implied that the cement mixer should work? Would it be implied that the business would pay British pounds rather than Irish pounds (which are worth slightly less)? Can you think of other terms which would be implied?

Types of terms

If any term is broken the injured party will always have a remedy for breach of contract. The nature of that remedy will depend upon what type of term was broken.

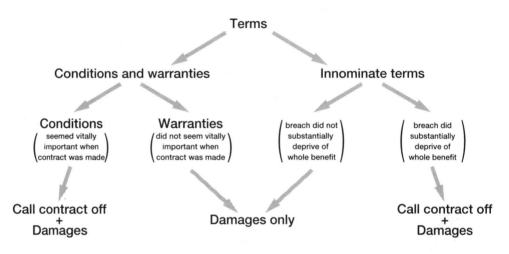

Fig 6.2 Result of breaching different types of terms

Conditions and warranties

Traditionally all terms could be classified as being either **conditions or warranties**.

A condition was a term which seemed very important when the contract was made (a term which went 'to the root of the contract'). If a condition was broken then the injured party could call the contract off and claim damages.

A warranty was a term which did not seem vitally important when the contract was made (a term which did not go 'to the root of the contract'). If a warranty was broken the injured party could only claim damages. He could not call the contract off.

Two cases decided in 1876, both involving opera singers who had broken their contracts, have always been used to demonstrate the difference between conditions and warranties.

Bettini v *Gye* (1876)

Bettini was an opera singer who made a contract to give a series of performances over a three-month period. He fell ill and missed half of the six days rehearsals which the contract demanded. His employer found a substitute and sacked Bettini. It was a term of Bettini's contract that he should attend all six days of the rehearsals, and there was no doubt that he had broken this term. His employers argued that this term was a condition and that they could therefore call the contract off. Bettini argued that the term was a warranty, and that while this made him liable in damages it did not give the employer the right to call the contract off.

Held The term was a warranty. Bettini's breach of the term did not '*go to the root of the contract*'. (So the employer had to pay damages to Bettini for breaking a term by sacking him unjustifiably.)

Poussard v *Spiers* (1876)

The facts of this case were substantially the same as those of *Bettini* v *Gye*, except that Madame Poussard became seriously ill five days before the first performance. She was unavailable for the first four performances of her three-month contract. The employers found it necessary to sack Madame Poussard because they could find a replacement only if they offered her the whole three months' work.

Held The employers were entitled to dismiss Madame Poussard because she had broken a condition. Her breach '*went to the root of the contract*'.

Strangely, these two cases about the opera singers became the definitive cases on conditions and warranties. The cases were applied to commercial contracts in which the right to call the contract off could be worth very substantial amounts of money.

It might be thought that the right to terminate a contract is of little importance if damages are always available. This is not necessarily the case, as the following example shows:

Example   Let us assume that in 1989 Firm A ordered £1,000,000 worth of shipping services a year, for 10 years.

The price of shipping, like the price of many other things, fluctuates considerably. Broadly speaking, shipping is cheaper in times of recession when there are fewer cargoes to be carried, and more expensive in prosperous times.

In retrospect Firm A seem to have made a very bad contract. Due to the world recession the same shipping services could now be obtained at 80 per cent of the price. The contract is therefore costing Firm A £200,000 a year. Still, they have made a contract and they must continue with it or they will be sued.

But let us now assume that the shipper breaks the contract by repeated late arrival. The shipper has broken a term and Firm A see a glimmer of hope. If Firm A can prove that the shipper has broken a condition then not only can they get damages, they can also tear up the contract.

The shipper of course will insist that he has only broken a warranty. He will be glad to pay damages to compensate for any loss suffered by Firm A, but he will insist that the contract remains in place.

There is no dispute about whether or not a term has been broken. Both sides agree that it has. The dispute is about what type of term has been broken, and many such cases go to court because the sums of money involved are so large that it is worth risking a little more to get out of the contract.

Let us finally assume that Firm A have been advised that they have only a 20 per cent chance of proving that the broken term was a condition. Would they risk a court case over the matter? They probably would. If the estimated court costs would be £100,000, and the contract (with four years left to run) represented a liability of £800,000, going to court with a 20 per cent chance of success would offer very good odds. (In gambling terms Firm A is getting 8:1 about a 4:1 chance.)

It is because escaping from a contract can be worth so much money that so many cases revolve around whether a broken term was a condition or a warranty. It has always seemed very odd that in such cases the judges are guided by the opera singer cases of 1876.

Innominate terms

In 1962, Diplock LJ tried to put matters on a more sensible footing by inventing a new type of term, the innominate term, the term with no name.

Hong Kong Fir Shipping Co Ltd v Kawasaki Kisen Kaisha Ltd (1962, Court of Appeal)

A ship was chartered to the defendants for a 24-month period. The engines of the ship were in poor condition and the crew was inefficient. As a result five weeks were immediately lost and a further 15 would be lost while repairs were carried out. However, after the repairs were completed the contract would still have 20 months left to run. One of the terms of the contract said that the ship should be '*in every way fitted for ordinary cargo service*'. Both sides agreed that this term had been broken. The defendants, the hirers of the ship, walked out of the contract, arguing that the broken term was a condition. The plaintiffs sued, claiming that the defendants were not entitled to walk out because the term was only a warranty. (So far the case seemed like a typical condition/warranty shipping case.)

Held The term that the ship should be '*in every way fitted for ordinary cargo service*' could not be classified in advance as either a condition or a warranty. The term covered very minor breaches (such as a rivet being missing) as well as very major breaches (such as the ship sinking). If the term was held to be a condition this would lead to the absurd result that the whole contract could be called off because one rivet was missing. If the term was held to be a warranty this would lead to the even more absurd result that the contract could not be called off even if the ship sunk to the bottom of the ocean. The term was therefore an innominate term, and the contract could not be called off because the defendants had not been deprived of '*substantially the whole benefit which it was the intention of the parties they should obtain*'.

Difference between conditions, warranties and innominate terms

The test applicable to an innominate term is to wait and see what effect the breach of contract has. If the injured party is deprived of '*substantially the whole benefit*' of the contract, he can call the contract off and claim damages. If he is not deprived of substantially the whole benefit , he can only claim damages.

Under the old conditions and warranties approach the courts did not wait and see what effect the breach had. They looked back to the time when the contract was made, and decided how important the parties would have considered the term when they made the contract.

Relationship between conditions and warranties and innominate terms

Innominate terms have not replaced conditions and warranties. Some terms can now be classed as conditions or warranties; others are innominate terms.

Recent statutes, such as the Sale of Goods Act 1979, and the Sale and Supply of Goods Act 1994, still classify certain terms as either conditions or warranties. If a term labelled a condition is broken the injured party can call the contract off; if a term labelled a warranty is broken, he cannot.

The parties themselves can also agree that certain terms will be conditions. If they expressly or impliedly provide that breach of a particular term will give a right to call the contract off then such a term will still be a condition. The court is always trying to give effect to what the parties intended.

In the sample contract at the end of this chapter, for example, term number 15 makes it plain that the customer's obligations are to be regarded as conditions. If the customer breaks any of these conditions then the hire company will be able to call the contract off.

If no term of the contract or rule of law stipulates that a particular term is to be a condition, the courts will regard the term as an innominate term. If a breach of such a term does deprive the injured party of substantially the whole intended benefit of the contract he can call the contract off; if it does not, he cannot.

It should also be remembered that damages will always be available for any breach of contract, whether the injured party has the right to call the contract off or not. The subject of damages is considered in Chapter 15.

ACTIVITY QUESTIONS 6.2

1 In the *Cehave* case (*The Hansa Nord*) the contract was to sell 12,000 tons of pulp pellets which were to be used as cattle food. The goods were to be delivered in consignments. The buyers rejected one consignment of 3,000 tons because about a third of the consignment was damaged. Even the damaged goods could still be used to make cattle food. A term in the contract said that the goods should be '*in good condition*'. The buyer wanted to reject the pulp pellets, but the seller was only prepared to pay damages.
  (a) What type of term would the buyers have argued that the term was?
  (b) What type of term would the sellers have argued that the term was?
  (c) What do you think the court decided?

2 In the *Hong Kong Fir* case, the term in dispute stated that the ship should be 'in every way fitted for ordinary cargo service'. Why did Lord Diplock decide that a broad term such as this could not be classified in advance as either a condition or a warranty?

Further activity question 6.2

(a) If the court had decided that the terms in the opera singer cases were innominate terms, would the results of the cases have been the same?

(b) In the opera singer cases, did the court in fact look back to the term's seeming importance when the contract was made, or did it apply the innominate term test and consider the effect of the breach?

Misrepresentation

We have seen that a business will always be liable if it breaks a term of a contract. In addition, it may incur liability for misrepresentation. Such liability may arise if a representation made by the business causes loss to a supplier or customer. In order to understand this we need to understand the difference between terms and representations.

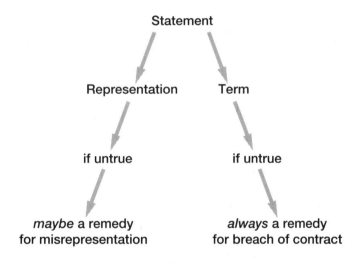

Fig 6.3 Untrue statements – remedies

The difference between terms and representations

We have seen that the terms of a contract are what the parties agree to. One of the parties proposes the terms in his offer and the other party agrees to those terms when he accepts. We also saw that if one of the terms is broken then the injured party will always have a remedy.

Frequently, however, a person is persuaded to make a contract by a statement which is not a part of the contract. Such a statement cannot be a term, it can only be a representation. If this statement turns out to be untrue, the injured party might or might not have a remedy for misrepresentation. But to sue for misrepresentation is not the same as to sue for breach of contract. Not only are the remedies different, but the whole basis of the action is different. It is therefore necessary to distinguish terms and representations.

Written contracts

In written contracts the express terms will be contained in the written document. Statements which are not contained in the document can only be representations.

Let us consider an example: If a person buys a car from a dealer, the terms of sale are usually spelt out in a standard form contract. When both parties sign this form they agree to all of these terms. If any of the terms are broken then the injured party will always have a remedy for breach of contract. But if a customer was persuaded to sign the standard form because the dealer made an untrue statement (perhaps he said that all the cars would be going up in price the following week, when this was not true) then the dealer has not broken a term, he has only made an untrue representation. As no term has been broken the customer will not be able to sue for breach of contract. He might, however, have a remedy for misrepresentation.

Similarly, it might have been the customer who made an untrue statement which caused the dealer to make the contract. If the customer paid with a cheque he would be impliedly making the statement that the cheque was his own and would be honoured. If this implied statement was untrue, because the cheque was stolen and would be dishonoured, the customer would not be breaking a term of the contract. He would, however, be making an untrue representation, and the dealer might have a remedy for misrepresentation. (It is only possible to say that a victim of a misrepresentation **might** have a remedy because he might well not have one. A broken term always leads to a remedy, but as we shall see misrepresentation gives much less potent remedies, which can easily be lost.)

So when both parties have signed a written contract, there is not too much difficulty in telling a term from a representation. Statements included in the written contract will be terms; statements not included can only be representations.

Oral contracts

If the contract is made orally it is much harder to tell a term from a representation. It is still the case that a term is a part of the contract and a representation is not. But it can be much harder to tell exactly which statements were included in the contract.

What if I offered to sell you my car for £1,000, and you accepted because shortly beforehand I had told you that the car had a new engine? Is this statement a part of the contract or not?

The courts decide questions such as this by looking at the opinion of the reasonable man. Did he think that the parties intended the statement to be a term or a representation?

This **objective test** is necessary because there is little point in looking for the opinions of the parties themselves. If the court asks me whether I thought that the statement about the new engine was a term or a representation, I will say that it was just a representation. If the court asks you, it is likely to get the reply that you thought it was a term.

Over the years the courts have devised various tests to decide what the reasonable man would have thought.

Strong statements are likely to be terms

The stronger the statement made the more likely it is to be a term.

Schawel v Reade (1913, House of Lords)

The plaintiff was considering buying a horse to be used for stud purposes. The defendant said, '*You need not look for anything; the horse is perfectly sound. If there was anything the matter with the horse I would tell you*'. Three weeks later the plaintiff bought the horse, which turned out to be utterly useless for stud purposes.

Held The defendant's statement was a term. It was so strong that it was the basis on which the offer and acceptance were made.

The weaker the statement the more likely it is to be a representation.

Ecay v Godfrey (1947)

The plaintiff bought a motor cruiser, the 'Tio Pepe', for £750. The defendant said that the boat was sound and capable of going overseas, but advised the plaintiff to have it surveyed before making the purchase. The plaintiff bought the boat, without having it surveyed, and soon discovered that it was not sound.

Held The statement that the boat was sound was only a representation. It was not a part of the contract because it was a very guarded statement.

The reliance placed upon the statement

If the plaintiff **demonstrated** that he considered the statement to be vitally important then the statement will be a term of the contract.

Bannerman v White (1861)

The plaintiff, a merchant who traded in hops, sent around a circular to all his hop farmers. The circular said that the plaintiff would no longer buys hops which had been treated with sulphur, because the Burton brewers would not use them. When later buying a consignment of hops, the plaintiff asked if they had been treated with sulphur, adding that if they had he would not buy them at any price. The defendant said that they had not been treated with sulphur, but they had.

Held The defendant's statement was a term. The plaintiff had demonstrated that he considered the statement to be vitally important.

Note that since it is the reasonable man's opinion the court is after, the plaintiff must **demonstrate** that he considers the statement to be vital. The reasonable man, although credited with the same degree of expertise as the parties to the contract, is not a mind reader. (Anybody could of course later say that he was **thinking** that the term was vital. The reasonable man would have no means of knowing whether or not this was true.)

The knowledge of the parties

If one party has more knowledge about the subject matter in general then he is likely to make terms. A party with less knowledge is likely to make representations.

Chess (Oscar) v Williams (1957, Court of Appeal)

The plaintiffs, who were motor dealers, took the defendant's car in part exchange. The defendant, a private motorist, told the plaintiffs that the car was a 1948 model. The defendant believed that this was true because the forged registration documents indicated that it was a 1948 model. In fact the car was a 1939 model, and was therefore worth much less than the price the plaintiffs had allowed on it.

Held The defendant's statement was only a representation. The plaintiffs, who had far more knowledge about cars, were at least as well placed as the defendant to know the true age of the car.

Dick Bentley (Productions) Ltd v Harold Smith (Motors) Ltd (1965, Court of Appeal)

A motor dealer sold a car to the plaintiff, saying that the car had only done 20,000 miles since having a new engine fitted. In fact the car had done 100,000 miles.

Held The dealer's statement was a term. The dealer, with his greater knowledge of cars, had much more chance of knowing that the statement was untrue than the plaintiff had.

Statements of opinion

Mere opinions cannot be terms or misrepresentations. But if a party who has vastly superior knowledge states an opinion which the other party relies on, then there may well be an implied term that this opinion was reached with reasonable care and skill.

Esso Petroleum Co Ltd v *Mardon* (1976, Court of Appeal)

Esso's representative persuaded Mardon to take on a filling station by telling Mardon that the station would sell 200,000 gallons of petrol a year within three years. It soon became apparent that no matter how well the station was managed it would never achieve anything like this figure.

Held The statement about the 200,000 gallons was just an opinion, and could not therefore be either a term or a misrepresentation. But a term was implied that the opinion had been made using reasonable care and skill. As this term had been broken, Mardon was entitled to damages.

The contract to take on the petrol station would of course have been in writing, and nowhere in the written contract was there an estimate about the throughput of petrol. If there had been such a statement it would have been a term. So there were two reasons why the statement about throughput was not a term: first, it was not a part of the contract; second, it was just an opinion.

The term that the court did imply was not about throughput of petrol. The term implied was that the statement about throughput of petrol had been made using reasonable care and skill. The court felt obliged to imply this term because a person taking on a new petrol station does so from a very vulnerable position. How can such a person know how many gallons the station will sell? Esso, on the other hand, ought to have known this as it is their business to know such matters.

It should also be noted that it can be very difficult to tell the difference between terms and representations. For this reason the injured party will frequently **argue both** terms and representations. He will start off by trying to prove that the statement was a term (because this gives him the stronger remedy). But he will go on to tell the court that if they do not agree with him, and find that the statement was not a term, then he will prove that it was misrepresentation (which will give him a lesser remedy.

ACTIVITY QUESTIONS 6.3

1 If a written contract is signed by both parties:
   (a) Will the statements contained in the contract be terms or representations?
   (b) Will verbal statements which persuade a party to sign the contract be terms or representations?

2 In oral contracts:
  (a) Are very strong statements likely to be terms or representations?
  (b) Is the party with the greater knowledge about the subject matter in general likely to make terms or representations?

Further activity questions 6.3

1 A customer makes an oral contract to trade his car in to a dealer. Which of the following are likely to be terms, and which representations?
  (a) The customer describes his car as seven years old.
  (b) The dealer describes his car as six months old.
  (c) The customer says that his car has never been involved in an accident. (Unknown to him it had been in an accident before he bought it.)
  (d) The dealer says that he thinks that a motoring magazine said that the car does 50 miles to the gallon about town, but that the customer should check the magazine himself before buying the car.
  (e) The dealer says that his car will do 110 miles an hour, using the words, 'You can take that from me as absolute fact, because I tried this actual car at Donnington and proved it.'

2 The three tests explained above (the strength of the statement, the importance shown to be attached to it and the relative degrees of knowledge) are not exhaustive. The courts have used two other tests to tell the difference between terms and representations. These tests are:
  (a) The lapse of time between the statement and the making of the contract.
  (b) Whether or not the statement was included when the agreement was later put in writing.

How do you think these tests affect the court's decision? For example:
  (a) If the untrue statement was made a month before the contract was made, does this lengthy interval make the statement more or less likely to be a term than if the statement had been made immediately before the contract was made?
  (b) If a statement made orally was not included when the parties subsequently wrote down what they thought the contract was, does the fact that the statement was not included make it more or less likely to be a term?

How a representation becomes a misrepresentation

A broken term always gives the injured party the right to a remedy. An untrue representation will lead to a remedy if it amounts to a misrepresentation. If, however, the representation does not fit within the definition of a misrepresentation then it will be a mere representation and no remedy will be available.

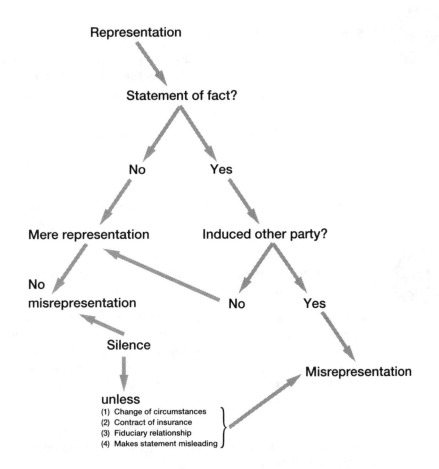

Fig 6.4 How a representation becomes a misrepresentation

Definition of a misrepresentation

A misrepresentation is **an untrue statement of fact which induced the other party to make the contract.**

This definition makes it plain that to become a misrepresentation an untrue representation must meet two requirements:

(a) it must have been a statement of fact; and
(b) it must have induced the other party to enter into the contract.

The statement must be one of fact

Statements of mere opinion are not capable of being misrepresentations.

Bisset v *Wilkinson* (1927, Privy Council)

The plaintiff bought a farm because the defendant told him that the farm would support 2,000 sheep. The plaintiff knew that the farm had never before been used for sheep farming. In fact the farm, no matter how well managed, could not support anything like 2,000 sheep.

Held The statement was just an opinion and could not therefore amount to a misrepresentation.

However, some statements of opinion imply statements of fact, as the following case shows:

Smith v *Land and House Property Corporation* (1884, Court of Appeal)

The plaintiffs offered their hotel for sale, stating that it was occupied by '*Mr Frederick Fleck (a most desirable tenant)*'. Before the sale went through Mr Fleck went bankrupt. The defendants discovered that for some time Mr Fleck had been badly in arrears with his rent. They refused to go ahead with the purchase of the hotel, claiming that the statement that Mr Fleck was a most desirable tenant amounted to a misrepresentation.

Held The statement was a misrepresentation. It sounded like a mere statement of opinion, but it implied facts (such as the fact that the tenant paid the rent) which justified the opinion.

> Bowen LJ '. . . *if the facts are not equally known to both sides, then a statement of opinion by the one who knows the facts best involves very often a statement of a material fact, for he impliedly states that he knows facts which justify his opinion.*'

The statement must induce the other party to make the contract

People do not usually make contracts for just one particular reason. There may be many reasons why they went ahead. However, a statement can only amount to a misrepresentation if it was at least one of the reasons why the plaintiff made the contract.

If a person makes a contract without checking the truth of a statement made to him, this suggests that the statement did induce him to make the contract.

Redgrave v Hurd (1881, Court of Appeal)

A solicitor advertised for a partner who would also buy the solicitor's house. The defendant answered the advertisement and was told that the practice made about £300 p.a. The solicitor produced papers which he said would prove that his statement about the value of the practice was true, but the defendant did not read the papers. If he had done so he would have discovered that the business was worthless. When the defendant did discover this he refused to go ahead with the purchase.

Held The plaintiff's statement about the value of the practice was a misrepresentation. The fact that the defendant did not check the papers showed that the solicitor's statement did induce the defendant to make the contract.

If a person checks the truth of a statement made to him then he cannot later say that the statement induced him to make a contract.

Attwood v Small (1838, House of Lords)

The plaintiff bought a mine because the defendants greatly exaggerated the capacity of the mine. Before buying the mine the plaintiff got his own experts to check the defendants' statement. The experts mistakenly agreed that the defendants' statement was true.

Held The statement about the mine's capacity was not a misrepresentation because the plaintiff did not rely on it. By appointing his own experts to check the statement, the plaintiff proved that he did not rely on it.

Silence as a misrepresentation

Generally silence cannot be a misrepresentation. The old rule *caveat emptor* (let the buyer beware) applies. It follows that a person should not make a contract without making sure that he has asked all the questions to which he needs answers.

Fletcher v Krell (1873)

A woman applied for a job as a governess without revealing that she was divorced. She would have been well aware that she stood no chance of getting the job if her secret had been discovered. The employer did not ask her whether she was divorced, so she did not say. She was given a three-year fixed-term contract to work in Buenos Aires.

Held Her silence did not amount to a misrepresentation.

There are, however, four exceptions to this rule. Silence will amount to a misrepresentation:

(a) If there was a change of circumstances.
(b) In contracts of insurance.
(c) If there was a fiduciary relationship between the parties.
(d) If the silence made another statement misleading.

These exceptions need to be examined individually.

A change of circumstances

If a person makes a statement which is true, but due to a change of circumstances the statement becomes untrue before the contract is made, then it may be a misrepresentation not to reveal that the circumstances have changed.

With v O'Flanagan (1936, Court of Appeal)

A doctor who was selling his practice said that it was worth £2,000 p.a. This was true, but when the sale went ahead three months later the practice was virtually worthless because the doctor had been ill.

Held The doctor's failure to reveal the change was a misrepresentation.

Contracts of insurance

Contracts of insurance are contracts *uberrimae fidei* (of the utmost good faith). In such contracts everything which could affect the price of the premium is a **material fact**. A person taking out insurance must reveal all material facts, whether he is asked about the matter in question or not.

Lambert v Co-op Insurance Society Ltd (1975, Court of Appeal)

The plaintiff insured her own and her husband's jewellery. She did not mention that her husband had been convicted of a small theft some years earlier. When the plaintiff renewed the policy she did not reveal that her husband had recently been sent to prison for 15 months for theft. The insurance company did not ask about convictions so the plaintiff felt no need to mention them. Over £300 worth of the insured jewellery was stolen, and the plaintiff claimed on her insurance.

Held The insurance company did not need to pay on the policy. The convictions were a material fact and the plaintiff should have revealed them.

Where there is a fiduciary relationship between the parties

A fiduciary relationship is a relationship of great trust. In such relationships one of the parties can expect to trust the other implicitly. Examples of such relationships would include doctor and patient, solicitor and client, parent and child. The person of whom the trust is expected (the doctor, the solicitor, the parent) must reveal everything when he makes a contract with the other person. If he does not do so, this silence will amount to a misrepresentation.

Silence makes a statement misleading

Even a statement which is literally true can amount to a misrepresentation if the statement conveys a misleading impression.

Nottingham Patent Brick and Tile Co v *Butler* (1886, Court of Appeal)

A solicitor who was selling a house for a client was asked whether there were any restrictive covenants attached to the land. (The buyer would generally not want restrictive covenants. If there were any, they would be included in documents which the solicitor should have read.) The solicitor replied that he was not aware of any restrictive covenants. This was true, but the reason he was not aware of any was that he had not read the documents. The buyer agreed to buy the land but pulled out of the contract when he discovered that there were restrictive covenants.

Held The solicitor's statement, although literally true, was a misrepresentation.

ACTIVITY QUESTIONS 6.4

1 Can a statement of opinion be a misrepresentation?

2 Will an untrue statement of fact be a misrepresentation if it did not induce the other party to make the contract?

3 X goes for a job as a security guard and does not reveal that he has several previous convictions for armed robbery. The security firm do not ask about previous convictions, and so X, scarcely able to believe his luck, does not reveal his convictions. X gets the job. Has he made a misrepresentation?

Further activity question 6.4

Read the facts of the following cases and decide whether a misrepresentation was made. The actual decisions are available at the end of this chapter.

Hands v Simpson, Fawcett & Co Ltd (1928)

The plaintiff was employed as a commercial traveller and had to use a car in his work. He was convicted of dangerous driving and banned from driving for three months. His employers dismissed him. The fact that the plaintiff had been banned was not enough to justify a dismissal. (A substitute could have been used for three months.) The employer claimed that the plaintiff's not having revealed previous convictions when he took the job amounted to a misrepresentation and therefore justified the dismissal. The plaintiff argued that the employer had never asked about previous convictions.

Held

Dimmock v Hallett (1866)

A landlord sold property which he described as fully let. When the landlord made the statement he was aware that the tenant had given notice to quit. The purchaser argued that the landlord's failure to reveal that the tenant had given notice amounted to a misrepresentation.

Held

London Assurance v Mansell (1878)

The plaintiff bought life assurance from the defendants, whose proposal form asked: 'Has a proposal ever been made on your life at any other office or offices? If so, where? Was it accepted at the ordinary premium, or at an increased premium, or declined?' The plaintiff answered, 'Insured now in two offices for £16,000 at ordinary rates'. The proposal was accepted, but the defendants subsequently discovered that the plaintiff had been declined at several other offices. The defendants claimed that the plaintiff's failure to declare this amounted to misrepresentation.

Held

Brown v Raphael (1958, Court of Appeal)

A trust fund was sold, the seller stating that he did not believe that the fund was subject to estate duty. After buying the fund, the buyer discovered that it was subject to estate duty. The buyer could not easily have discovered this before the sale was made, but the seller should have known it all along. The buyer claimed that the seller's statement, although only an opinion, implied facts which justified the opinion. In particular he claimed that one of these facts (that the seller had reasonable grounds for believing his opinion to be true) amounted to a misrepresentation.

Held

Remedies for misrepresentation

There are three types of misrepresentation. Each type gives rise to different remedies.

	Type of misrepresentation		
	Fraudulent	**Negligent**	**Wholly innocent**
Definition	Made (1) knowing it was false, or (2) without belief, or (3) recklessly carelessly	Made honestly but *unreasonably*	Made honestly *and* reasonably
Remedies	Rescind + tort damages (time does not run until misrep discovered)	Rescind + tort damages (time runs from date of contract)	Rescind usually no damages (time runs from date of contract)

R   E   S   C   I   S   S   I   O   N

Contract is affirmed ◄── lost if ──► Subject matter no longer exists

third party has rights

Fig 6.5 Types of misrepresentation and their remedies

Fraudulent misrepresentation

This was defined in *Derry* v *Peek* (1889, House of Lords), as a misrepresentation made either:

(a) knowing that it was untrue; or
(b) not believing that it was true; or
(c) recklessly, not caring whether it was true or false.

A fraudulent misrepresentation allows the injured party to **rescind the contract** (call it off) **and sue for tort damages**.

Negligent misrepresentation

The Misrepresentation Act 1967 defines a negligent misrepresentation as one made honestly believing that it was true, but without reasonable grounds for such a belief.

A negligent misrepresentation allows the injured party to **rescind and to sue for tort damages**.

Wholly innocent misrepresentation

A wholly innocent misrepresentation is one made honestly believing that it was true, with reasonable grounds for such a belief. The injured party can **rescind** but he has no right to claim damages.

However, section 2(2) of the Misrepresentation Act 1967 allows the court to award damages instead of rescission where the court considers it 'equitable to do so'. It is rare for the courts to use this section to award damages for an innocent misrepresentation, but they sometimes do so when the misrepresentation was so trivial that rescission would be too drastic a remedy.

Example A buys a car from B because B says that the car is five years old. In fact the car is six years old, but B believes that it is only five years old because he was incorrectly told the age of the car when he bought it. B has made an innocent misrepresentation, and a court might well think that a minor, innocent misrepresentation such as this did not warrant rescission. So as not to leave A without any remedy, the court could order B to pay damages to compensate A for the loss he has suffered as a result of the misrepresentation.

Losing the right to rescind

All three types of misrepresentation give the injured party the right to rescind. To some extent rescission is a self-help remedy. A party can rescind merely by letting the other party know that he no longer regards himself as bound by the contract. (However, if the other party then refuses to return what he gained under the contract it may be necessary to go to court to enforce the rescission.)

One of the reasons that a representation is regarded as less potent than a term is that the major remedy for misrepresentation, rescission, can easily be lost.

The right to rescind can be lost in three ways:

(a) If the contract is affirmed.
(b) If a third party acquires rights.
(c) If the subject matter of the contract no longer exists.

If the contract is affirmed

The contract will be affirmed if the plaintiff decides to carry on with the contract after he has discovered the misrepresentation. The plaintiff might make such agreement expressly by saying, 'All right, I've found out you made a misrepresentation, but I'm not going to call the contract off anyway'. If he does say this he will not later be able to change his mind.

The plaintiff might also affirm impliedly, particularly by doing nothing for a long enough time for the court to take the view that the contract has been impliedly accepted.

Leaf v *International Galleries* (1950, Court of Appeal)

The plaintiff bought a painting from International Galleries because of an innocent misrepresentation that the painting was by Constable. Five years later the plaintiff discovered that the painting was not by Constable and he immediately applied to the court for rescission of the contract.

Held The plaintiff was too late to rescind. He had affirmed the contract by doing nothing for five years. (But if the misrepresentation by the gallery had been **fraudulent,** time would have started to run against the plaintiff only from the moment when the misrepresentation was discovered.)

If a third party has acquired rights

Although a misrepresentation gives the injured party the right to rescind, it does not prevent ownership of goods sold under the contract from passing to the misrepresentor. As we have seen, the misrepresentor does own the goods unless and until the innocent party rescinds the contract. The innocent party has no obligation to rescind. We have seen that he may affirm the contract, despite the misrepresentation, and keep what he gained under the contract.

It follows that if the misrepresentor sells the goods on to an innocent third party **before** the contract is rescinded, then the third party can keep the goods forever. This is because when the misrepresentor sold the goods he still owned them, and therefore still had ownership to pass on. Furthermore, section 23 of the Sale of Goods Act 1979 says that although the misrepresentor's ownership was not perfect, because it could be rescinded, the third party who buys from the misrepresentor nevertheless gets complete ownership.

If, however, the goods are sold to the innocent third party **after** the contract has been rescinded, then the innocent third party will get no ownership of the goods. This is because when the misrepresentor sold the goods to the third party he no longer had any ownership to pass on, the contract having been rescinded.

Cases on this matter amount to a dispute about who did what first.

Car and Universal Finance Co Ltd v *Caldwell* (1965, Court of Appeal)

A rogue bought a car with a bad cheque. (This of course was a fraudulent misrepresentation.) The rogue sold the car to a third party who bought it in good faith. Before this second sale the original seller found out about the rogue's misrepresentation. He could not find the rogue to tell him that he was calling the contract off, so he told the police and the AA.

Held Telling the police and the AA was enough to rescind the contract. The original seller therefore got the car back from the third party. If the original seller had not told the police and the AA until *after* the rogue had resold the car he would never have got the car back.

In all of these cases where a rogue buys goods with a stolen cheque one of two innocent parties is bound to suffer a loss. Either the original owner will get the goods back, in which case the innocent third party will have paid money to the rogue in return for nothing at all, or the original owner will not get the goods back, and will therefore have been deprived of his goods in return for a worthless cheque.

Whichever of the two parties suffers the loss will be left with the right to sue the rogue for damages. However, it should be pointed out that this right is likely to be worth very little. First, the rogue must be identified before he can be sued, and not all rogues are caught. Second, rogues who buy goods with bad cheques rarely have enough money to pay damages.

If the subject matter of the contract no longer exists

If it is not possible to give back what was gained under the contract then rescission will not be possible. If, for example, a rogue pays for a holiday with a bad cheque it will not be possible for the holiday company to rescind once the rogue has taken the holiday. The holiday, having been taken, has ceased to exist.

ACTIVITY QUESTIONS 6.5

1 In the following three cases no misrepresentation was made. If the decision had been different, and there had been a misrepresentation in each case, what type of misrepresentation would it have been, and what remedies would have been available to the injured party? If it is possible that the misrepresentation might have been more than one type, consider all the possible types.
   (a) *Bisset* v *Wilkinson* (The 2,000 sheep. Assume that the vendor had used the land for sheep farming for many years.)
   (b) *Attwood* v *Small* (Buying the mine.)
   (c) *Fletcher* v *Krell* (The governess. Assume that the governess was asked if she was divorced.)

2 In the following cases a misrepresentation was made. Decide what type of misrepresentation it was, and what the remedies would have been.

   (a) *Redgrave v Hurd* (the solicitor exaggerating the value of his practice).

   (b) *Smith v LHPC* (the most desirable tenant).

   (c) *Oscar Chess v Williamson* (the motorist who thought that his car was a 1948 model).

   (d) *Nottingham Patent Brick and Tile Co v Butler* (the solicitor who was unaware of the restrictive covenants).

Further activity question 6.5

Martha bought a cafe because the previous owner said that it had a turnover of £120,000 a year. After the first month Martha's turnover is only £5,000. The written contract made no mention of turnover.

(a) Is the statement about turnover a term of the contract?

(b) Has a misrepresentation been made? If so, what remedies would be available to Martha? In practical terms what would you advise her to do?

(c) Could any term relating to the statement about turnover exist?

TASK 6

The Student Union at your college has hired a computer system and software for a two-year period. The contract under which the computer system was bought said that the hiring company would provide technicians to deal with any faults and to train three people how to operate the system. Despite repeated requests for training, none has been provided and no one is able to use the computer. Before buying the software, the purchasing officer of the Student Union asked whether or not it could deal with complex accounts. The salesman assured him that it could. The contract under which the software was sold did not say that it could deal with complex accounts.

Write a report for the Student Union, indicating:

(a) the difference between breach of contract and misrepresentation;

(b) whether or not the Student Union might be able to reject the computer system and get its money back;

(c) what action the Union should take as regards the salesman's promise that the software could handle complex accounts.

HIRE ASSOCIATION EUROPE
A standard format contract designed specially for the hire industry

GENERAL CONDITIONS FOR THE HIRING OF EQUIPMENT

1. DEFINITIONS AND LAW
The Contract is the document or documents that set out these Conditions and all other details about your agreement with us.

"We" and "Us" mean the supplier of the hired equipment.

"You" means the person, firm, company, corporation or public authority or body to whom we supply Equipment on hire.

"Equipment" means the hired items referred to in the Contract.

These Conditions exclude any terms and conditions you may have put forward, except where we have agreed to any amendments or other conditions in writing.

These conditions do not affect the statutory rights of a person dealing as a consumer as defined by the Unfair Contract Terms Act 1977 or any statutory modification of that Act.

The Contract will be governed by and interpreted in accordance with English Law.

2. BASIS OF CHARGING
You will pay the hire charges stated in the Contract. Hire charges will begin at the time stated in the Contract and will continue during the period of hire until we have given you a collection or off-hire number, or until you have restored the Equipment to us in a clean and serviceable condition and we have given you a receipt for it. All time is chargeable including Saturdays, Sundays and Bank Holidays. All charges are payable on demand. If payment is not made when due, we will be entitled to interest on the amount that is overdue at four percent above the prevailing base rate of National Westminster Bank PLC calculated on a daily basis. This will be without prejudice to any other rights or remedies we may have. You will also pay to us any charges we reasonably incur in the recovery from you of money or Equipment.

3. DELIVERY AND CARRIAGE CHARGES
Hire charges do not include carriage. You will pay to us any agreed charges for delivery or collecting Equipment. Where we quote carriage charges, these include only for the time required to load or unload alongside our vehicle at the address you have specified. You will pay extra for any further time or attendance including any attempt by us to carry out your pre-arranged instructions for delivery or collection which is unsuccessful due to your acts or omissions.

4. MAXIMUM PERIOD OF AGREEMENT (If you are not incorporated)
If you are an individual or a partnership, or an unincorporated body of persons, the Contract will terminate not later than three months from the beginning of the period of hire. In such circumstances you must restore the Equipment to us before close of business on the day before the end of the three month period. If you fail to do this we will be entitled to charge you for any financial loss this causes us.

5. WHEN THE CONTRACT COMES INTO BEING
The Contract comes into being when you have placed an order giving details of your requirements and have agreed to be bound by these Conditions and we have accepted your order.

6. SAFETY AND INSTRUCTIONS
It is your responsibility to make sure that all people who use the Equipment are properly instructed in its safe and correct use and that they are in possession of all instructions supplied by us. You must ensure that the Equipment is not misused.

7. WHEN YOUR SIGNATURE FOR RECEIPT OF EQUIPMENT BECOMES EFFECTIVE
Where for administrative convenience, you or your agent are requested by us to sign a receipt for the Equipment before it is handed over, you or your agent will be given the opportunity to examine the Equipment when it is physically handed over to you or to your agent. The receipt will not be effective until immediately after the physical handover.

Fig 6.6 Specimen contract

8. RESPONSIBILITY OF HIRER (YOUR RESPONSIBILITY)

(i) You will be responsible for the loading and unloading of the Equipment at the address specified by you. You will also be responsible for the loading and unloading of the Equipment at our premises when the Equipment is transported by you or your agent. If we supply any person to assist you, he will be under your control at such times.

(ii) Your responsibility for the Equipment begins when you or your agent receive the Equipment. If it is delivered to you your responsibility begins on delivery. Your responsibilities include safekeeping of the Equipment, and protection against the elements, theft, vandalism or improper use. You are responsible for the return of the Equipment or making clear arrangements with us for the collection of the Equipment at the end of hire. Your responsibility ends only when the equipment has been returned or collected and you have our unqualified receipt for all of the Equipment. You must not sell or otherwise part with control of the Equipment.

(iii) You will indemnify us against any and every expense, liability, financial loss, claim of proceedings whatsoever, and in respect of any death or person injury whatsoever or damage to or loss of property whatsoever (other than the Equipment itself, which is governed by Conditions 13 and 14) arising out of the delivery, use, non-use, repossession, collection or return of the Equipment or any part of it. This indemnity will be reduced in proportion to the extent that such expense, liability, financial loss, claim or proceedings or death or personal injury or damage to or loss of property is due to our proven negligence.

9. ELECTRICAL EQUIPMENT

Where any part of the Equipment is electrical it should normally be used with plugs and/or sockets as fitted but if temporarily fitted with other suitable plugs or sockets, this must be carried out by a competent person who must also return it to its original condition. It will be your responsibility at all times to arrange a suitable supply of electricity for use with the Equipment. Under no circumstances should electrical Equipment be used without it being correctly earthed unless it is of double insulated specification. You will be responsible for complying with the requirements of the Electricity at Work Regulations 1989 during the period of your responsibility for the Equipment as defined in Condition 8 (ii) of these Conditions.

10. MAINTENANCE OF EQUIPMENT, BREAKDOWN PROCEDURES AND ACCIDENT REPORTING

You must keep yourself acquainted with the state and condition of the Equipment and ensure that it remains safe, serviceable and clean. Any breakdown or any unsatisfactory working of Equipment must be immediately notified to us. Under no circumstances must you repair or attempt to repair the Equipment unless authorised by us. The Equipment must be returned to our premises for examination except where examination elsewhere has been mutually agreed upon. You must notify us immediately if the Equipment is involved in any accident resulting in damage to the Equipment or to other property, or injury to any person.

11. LOCATION OF EQUIPMENT

Equipment must not be removed without our authority from any site originally specified by you or from any site we subsequently authorise.

12. LIMITS OF OUR LIABILITY

(i) All times which we state or quote for delivery or collection are approximate.

(ii) We will not be liable for any delays caused by any circumstances beyond our reasonable control.

(iii) We will not be liable for any indirect loss, loss of business, profits, savings you expected to make, wasted money, wages, fees or expenses, due to take delivery, non-delivery, unsuitability, breakdown or stoppage of the Equipment or any part of it.

13. INSURANCE AND YOUR RESPONSIBILITY FOR LOST, STOLEN OR DAMAGED EQUIPMENT

You will pay to us the replacement cost of any Equipment which is lost or stolen or damaged beyond economic repair. You are advised to insure the Equipment on this basis. You will hold in trust for us and pay to us on demand all money you receive from an insurance company or from any other source in settlement of any claim relating to the loss, theft or damage of any of the Equipment. You must not compromise any claim without our express consent.

14. NON-RETURNED, LOST, STOLEN, DAMAGED OR UNCLEAN EQUIPMENT

(i) You have full responsibility for the care and safekeeping and return in good order of the Equipment.

(ii) You will pay to us all costs we incur in rectifying any Equipment returned damaged or unclean. Additionally you will pay for our financial loss until such rectification is complete.

(iii) Where Equipment is lost or stolen or damaged beyond economic repair, you will pay for all financial loss to us until you have paid to us the replacement cost. This is without prejudice to our other rights.

15. TERMINATION OF HIRE

We will be entitled at any time if you break this Contract or if any proceedings are commenced in which solvency is called into question to terminate this Contract with immediate effect and to repossess any or all of the Equipment. Such termination will not affect our right to recover from you any money due to us under this Contract or damages for breach of contract.

16. OUR RIGHTS OF ACCESS

You authorise us to enter any land or premises where we reasonably believe any Equipment to be, in order to inspect, test, repair, replace or repossess it.

17. RIGHTS RESERVED

Any failure by us to enforce any or all of these Conditions shall not amount to, or be interpreted as, a waiver of any of our rights.

18. SEPARATE TERM VALIDITY AND HEADINGS

If any term in this Contract is held invalid this shall not affect the validity of the remaining terms. The headings in these Conditions are for reference purposes only and shall not affect the interpretation of these Conditions.

GENERAL CONDITIONS OF SALE

1. DEFINITIONS AND LAW

The Contract is the document or documents that set out these Conditions and all other details about your agreement with us.

"We" and "Us" mean the seller of the Goods.

"You" means the buyer of the Goods.

The "Goods" means all goods to be sold by us to you.

The "Recipient" means the person, firm, company, corporation or public authority to whom the Goods are delivered, when it is not you. These Conditions exclude any terms and conditions you may have put forward, except where we have agreed to any amendments or other conditions in writing.

These Conditions do not affect the statutory rights of a person dealing as a consumer as defined by the Unfair Contract Terms Act 1977 or any statutory modification of that Act.

The Contract will be governed by and interpreted in accordance with English Law.

2. WHEN THE CONTRACT COMES INTO BEING

The Contract comes into being when you have placed an order giving details of your requirements and have agreed to be bound by these Conditions and we have accepted your order.

3. PAYMENT

Where we have granted monthly account facilities to you in writing, all invoices must be paid by the last day of the month following the month of delivery. Where no such facilities have been granted, payment will be with your order, or where previously agreed, on delivery. If payment is not made when due, we will be entitled to interest on the amount that is overdue at four percent above the prevailing base rate of National Westminster Bank PLC calculated on a daily basis. This will be without prejudice to any rights or remedies we may have.

4. RECEIPT

You, or the Recipient on your behalf, will receive and unload the Goods and should check them for quantity and condition in the presence of the carrier. If there is a shortage or if any of the Goods are in an unsatisfactory condition, you or the Recipient must so endorse the carrier's delivery document and must give a separate written notice of this to us within three days of delivery. If this Condition is not observed, no claim in respect of shortage or of unsatisfactory condition of the Goods will be entertained.

5. RISK AND TITLE TO GOODS

(i) The risk in the Goods will pass to you immediately on delivery of the Goods to you or to the Recipient.

(ii) The ownership of the Goods will remain with us and we reserve the right to dispose of the Goods until you have paid in full for all Goods which we have supplied at any time to you. Until such payment has been made in full you will hold the Goods on our behalf and will be under an obligation to return them to us on demand. You will permit us to enter any land or premises of yours to recover our Goods.

6. LIMIT OF OUR LIABILITY

(i) All times which we state or quote for delivery are approximate.

(ii) We will not be liable for any delays caused by any circumstances beyond our reasonable control.

(iii) We will not be liable for any indirect loss, loss of business, profits, savings you expected to make, wasted money, wages, fees or expenses, due to late delivery, non-delivery, unsuitability, breakdown or stoppage of the Goods or any part of them.

7. RIGHTS RESERVED

Any failure by us to enforce any or all of these Conditions shall not amount to or be interpreted as a waiver of any of our rights.

8. SEPARATE TERMS VALIDITY AND HEADINGS

If any term in this Contract is held invalid, this shall not affect the validity of the remaining terms. The headings in these Conditions are for reference purposes only and shall not affect the interpretation of these Conditions.

You and Your Contracts

'Printers Pulls' are available for the HAE General Conditions for the Hiring of Equipment and the HAE Conditions of Sale.

Use of the 'Printers Pull' is strongly recommended. Firstly because they have been checked and are known to be free of error and secondly because they will save you typesetting costs. They are available free of charge in the following formats:
  a. Hire Conditions
  b. Sales Conditions
  c. Hire & Sales Conditions

The HAE Legal Adviser recommends that:

1. The HAE General Conditions for the Hiring of Equipment be printed on the reverse of the document recording the transaction and that a copy be prominently displayed in your hire outlet. Account customers should signify acceptance of the conditions prior to the opening of the account and subsequently whenever the conditions are revised.

2. Although not absolutely essential, the contract will be strengthened if it has provision for two signatures – the first confirming "acceptance of the conditions contained above and on the reverse of this contract" and the second acknowledging receipt of the items hired and that the person receiving the equipment has been instructed in its safe and proper use. When one signature only is required by the Hire Company it must be made clear that this refers not only to the receipt of the equipment, but also to the acceptance of the terms and conditions which include the passing on of instructions to the end user.

Whenever signatures are obtained the name of the individual signing should appear in block capitals.

3. It is important when accepting orders to inform customers that "the acceptance of the order is subject to the HAE General Conditions for the Hiring and/or Sale of Equipment."

Message pads for both hire and sales should have a reminder to this effect and provision should be made for the person taking the order to initial the reminder when it has been given. This applies equally to orders taken by telephone or over the counter.

4. When rehiring from another hire company where ever possible ensure that the transaction is governed by the HAE General Conditions for the Hiring of Equipment. When a supplier to you uses other conditions please ensure that they do not place onerous duties and risks on you compared with the HAE Conditions which you will place on your customers.

Case decisions

There follow the actual decisions in the cases set out at page 142.

Hands v Simpson, Fawcett & Co Ltd

Held The plaintiff won. He had no duty to reveal his conviction. The defendant did not ask, so he did not need to say.

Dimmock v Hallet

Held The seller's statement was a misrepresentation. It might have been literally true but it conveyed a misleading impression.

London Assurance v Mansell

Held The plaintiff had made a misrepresentation. He had plainly failed to reveal a material fact.

Brown v Raphael

Held Following *Smith* v *Land House and Property Corporation*, there was a misrepresentation. The seller had far more knowledge than the buyer and it was implied that he had reasonable grounds for his belief.

7 Legal responsibility to consumers

A business can become liable to consumers either directly or indirectly. When a business makes a contract to sell goods or services to a customer it assumes direct liability under that contract. Indirect liability can also be imposed, even where the business does not deal directly with the eventual consumer. This indirect liability is considered in Chapters 13 and 14. The statutes considered in this chapter confer protection on consumers by directly implying terms into the contracts which the consumers make with businesses.

The Sale of Goods Act 1979

Background

The first Sale of Goods Act was passed in 1893, and for 80 years it was the only statute conferring consumer protection. It is considered first not only because it is the oldest and most important of the statutes, but also because the other statutes based themselves on the Sale of Goods Act. The more recent statutes are certainly the work of Parliament, but the original Sale of Goods Act was merely a codifying statute which put all of the judge-made law into one comprehensible piece of legislation. As we shall see, this has caused difficulty with some of the words used.

Scope of the Act

The Sale of Goods Act 1979 applies only to **contracts** for the **sale** of **goods**. Such contracts are defined by section 2(1):

> *'A contract of sale of goods is a contract by which the seller transfers or agrees to transfer the property in goods to the buyer for a money consideration, called the price.'*

Meaning of 'sale'

Reading section 2(1), we can see that a sale occurs when a buyer pays **money** in return for **ownership** of goods. It does not matter whether the buyer pays cash, by cheque or by credit card. But a free gift, where the buyer pays no money, cannot be a sale. Nor is it a sale where goods are bartered (exchanged) for other goods.

Note also that the seller must transfer the property in goods (ownership of the goods) to the buyer. This requirement rules out contracts to hire or lease, where possession of the goods is transferred but ownership is not.

Meaning of 'goods'

Section 61(1) defines goods as *'all personal chattels other than things in action'*. A **personal chattel** is a physical thing which can be **touched and moved**, for example a car, a cup or a computer. A **thing in action** is a right which can be enforced only by suing (taking out an action). A guarantee, for example, is a thing in action. A guarantee may be written on a piece of paper but the paper is not the property. The property is the right which the guarantee gives and, ultimately, that right can be enforced only by suing the person who gave it.

ACTIVITY QUESTION 7.1

Which of the following contracts would be contracts for the sale of goods?
(a) £5 for a haircut.
(b) A patent on a new invention for £12,000.
(c) A cheque which pays £3,000 for a car.
(d) A trolley of groceries, purchased with a credit card.
(e) A 'free chicken' to customers who spend £20 in a supermarket.
(f) A house for £40,000.
(g) The whole of a farmer's crop of potatoes, next June, for £9,000.
(h) The copyright in a song for a percentage of the royalties.
(i) A pen for £7.

(j) A bicycle in exchange for a personal stereo.

(k) A landscape painting, commissioned for £200.

(l) A ticket to the cinema for £4.

(m) A television, hire-purchased over three years, at £20 a month.

(n) A share in a company.

The terms implied by the Act

Sections 12 to 15 of the Sale of Goods Act 1979 contain five implied terms. These terms do not need to be mentioned by the buyer or the seller, the Act will automatically imply them into all contracts for the sale of goods:

- **Section 12** implies a term that the **seller has the right to sell the goods**.
- **Section 13** implies a term that the goods will **match any description applied to them**.
- **Section 14(2)** implies a term that the goods are of **satisfactory quality**.
- **Section 14(3)** implies a term that the goods are **fit for the buyer's purpose.**
- **Section 15** implies a term that if the goods are sold by sample then **the bulk matches the sample**.

Both sections 14(2) and 14(3) are implied only into sales made **in the course of business**. The other sections are implied into all contracts for the sale of goods.

These implied terms are vitally important, and each one must be examined closely.

Title (ownership)

Section 12(1) says that unless the circumstances show a different intention:

> *'There is an implied condition on the part of the seller that in the case of a sale he has a right to sell the goods, and in the case of an agreement to sell he will have such a right at the time when the property is to pass.'*

This term, like the others, is a **condition**. We have already seen that if a condition is broken the injured party can rescind the contract and, perhaps, claim damages. If a buyer rescinds a contract he will get back the money he paid.

Rowland v Divall (1923, Court of Appeal)

A thief stole a car from its owner and sold the car to the defendant. The plaintiff, a motor dealer, bought the car from the defendant for £334. The plaintiff did the car up and sold it to a customer for £400. On discovering that the car was stolen, the police took it from the customer and returned it to its original owner. The customer went back to the plaintiff who returned his £400. The plaintiff asked the defendant

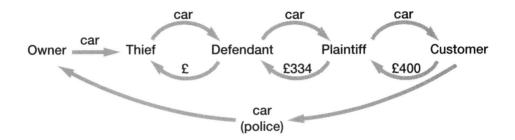

Fig 7.1 Transactions in *Rowland v Divall*

for the return of the £334 he had paid. The defendant refused to pay, saying that he had no idea that the car was stolen.

Held The plaintiff got all of his money back. Section 12(1) says that the seller must have the right to sell, and when the defendant sold the car to the plaintiff he did not have this right because he did not own the car. The thief never owned the car. He therefore could not pass ownership to the defendant, who could not pass ownership to the plaintiff, etc. None of the parties except the original owner ever had the right to sell the car.

> Atkin LJ '*It seems to me that in this case there has been a total failure of consideration, that is to say that the buyer has not got any part of that for which he paid the purchase price. He paid the money in order that he might get the property, and he has not got it. It is true that the seller delivered to him the de facto [actual] possession, but the seller had not got the right to possession and consequently could not give it to the buyer. Therefore the buyer, during the time that he had the car in his actual possession had no right to it, and was at all times liable to the true owner for its conversion.*'

When there is a chain of innocent sellers the loser will generally be the person who bought from the thief, as in *Rowland v Divall*. Of course this person could successfully sue the thief, but in practical terms this would be a waste of money as it is most unlikely that the thief could be found and would have the money to pay. However, if any of the sellers in the chain has become insolvent then the person who bought from him will be the one with no practical remedy.

Example A thief has stolen a car from its owner and then sold the car to A, who sells it to B, who sells it to C, who sells it to D. As can be seen from Fig 7.2, A will be the loser.

But now let us assume that B has become insolvent. D can recover from C, but C cannot recover from B. Nor can C leapfrog B and sue A – there is no contract between the two of them.

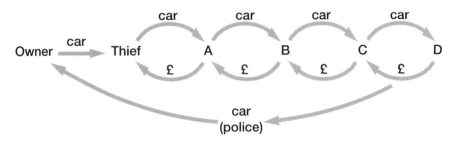

Fig 7.2 Who is the loser?

The goods will always be returned to the owner because he has owned them all along. Others might have had possession of the goods, and believed that they owned them, but ownership never moved from the owner.

ACTIVITY QUESTIONS 7.2

1 Read section 12(1) on page 154. Does it provide that the seller must **have** the right to sell the goods, or does it say that the seller must **think** that he has the right to sell the goods?

2 A grain merchant agrees to sell 1,000 tons of grain to a buyer, delivery to be made next November. The merchant intends to buy the grain from a Canadian exporter, but as yet this contract has not been made and so he does not yet own the grain. Does this mean that the merchant breaks section 12(1)?

3 In *Rowland* v *Divall* Lord Atkin stated that the seller did deliver *de facto* (actual) possession of the car. Why, then, was the buyer entitled to all of his money back?

1 A thief steals a consignment of batteries and, after the batteries have passed through a succession of buyers, a shopkeeper buys them in good faith. The shopkeeper sells the batteries to a customer who uses them until their power is exhausted.

(a) Did the customer ever have ownership of the batteries?

(b) Did he ever have *de facto* (actual) possession of them?

(c) Did he ever have legal possession?

(d) Ought he be able to claim all of his money back from the shop?

2 In *Niblett* v *Confectioners Materials* (1921, Court of Appeal), 3,000 tins of condensed milk were sold. The milk was labelled 'Nissly Brand'. Nestlé warned the buyers of the milk that the word 'Nissly' was too similar to the Nestlé trademark, and that if they attempted to sell the milk they would be prevented from doing so by an injunction. The buyers accepted that this was the legal position, and rejected the milk under section 12(1). The court held that the buyers won. Read section 12(1) and find out why the seller broke it even though he did own the milk when he sold it.

Description

Under **section 13**, *'Where there is a contract for the sale of goods by description there is an implied condition that the goods will correspond with the description'*.

A seller has no obligation to describe his goods, but if he does describe them then the goods must match the description. However, the common law maxim *de minimis non curat lex* (the law is not concerned with trifles) applies. The maxim means that if the failure to match the description was very trivial the seller would not break section 13.

Many cases, such as the one which follows, have hinged around whether or not a failure to match a description was a trifle.

Arcos Ltd v *Ronaasen & Son* (1933, House of Lords)

The seller contracted to sell a quantity of wooden staves to be used for making cement barrels. The seller described the staves as 'half an inch thick'. Ninety per cent of the staves were between half an inch and five-eighths of an inch, but 10 per cent were over five-eighths of an inch. The buyer rejected all of the staves, even though they were perfectly fit for making barrels.

Held The buyer could reject the staves as they did not match the description.

Descriptions can be made in many ways, and a seller may make a description without knowing that he is doing so.

Beale v Taylor (1967, Court of Appeal)

The defendant advertised a car as a Triumph Herald 1200, believing that this description was correct. The plaintiff examined the car and bought it. The rear of the car was indeed a Triumph Herald 1200, but it had been welded to the front of a Triumph Herald 948. The plaintiff had seen a '1200' badge on the rear of the car when he inspected it.

Held The plaintiff got his money back under section 13. A buyer who had noticed the badge could take it as a description, and could assume that the whole car was a 1200.

Note that the parties must intend that the description can be relied upon by the buyer. Whether or not an advertisement such as the one in *Beale v Taylor* will amount to a description will depend upon the thoroughness of the buyer's examination of the car. The more thoroughly the buyer examines the car the less likely it becomes that he relied upon the description in the advertisement.

If a description is made in a commercial contract then the courts are very likely to regard the description as important.

Re Moore and Co and Landauer and Co (1921, Court of Appeal)

A consignment of 3,100 tins of peaches was to be shipped from Australia to a buyer in London. The shipment arrived late. The buyer rejected the consignment on the ground that whereas the peaches had been described as packed 30 tins to a case, about half of the tins were packed 24 to a case instead of 30. The correct number of tins were delivered.

Held The buyer could reject all of the tins. The goods were not as described.

> Scrutton LJ *'The arbitrator finds that 24 tins to the case are as valuable commercially as 30 tins to the case. That may be so. Yet a man, who has bought under contract 30 tins to the case, may have sold under the same description, and may be put into considerable difficulty by having goods tendered to him which do not comply with the description under which he bought.'*

ACTIVITY QUESTIONS 7.3

1 Are the following goods, displayed in supermarkets, likely to be sold by description. If you decide that any are sold by description, in what manner is the description likely to have been made?

(a) A tin of beans.
(b) A jar of coffee.
(c) Cheese ordered from an assistant behind the cheese counter.
(d) Pre-packed potatoes.
(e) Loose potatoes.
(f) Bread which is baked in the supermarket.

2 If a customer orders goods over the phone is the sale always going to be by description? What if he ordered them from a mail-order catalogue?

3 Are vegetables bought from a market stall always sold by description?

Further activity question 7.3

In *Arcos v Ronaasen* Lord Atkin said:

> 'It was contended that in all commercial contracts . . . there must always be some margin . . . I cannot agree. If the written contract specifies conditions of weight, measurement and the like, these conditions must be complied with. A ton does not mean about a ton, or a yard about a yard. Still less when you descend to minute measurements does ½ inch mean about ½ inch. If the seller wants a margin he must and in my experience does stipulate for it. Of course by recognised trade usage particular figures may be given a different meaning, as in a baker's dozen. . . . If a condition is not performed the buyer has a right to reject. . . . No doubt, in business, men often find it unnecessary or inexpedient to insist on their strict legal rights. In a normal market if they get something substantially like the specified goods they may take them with or without grumbling and claim for an allowance. But in a falling market I find that buyers are often as eager to insist on their legal rights as courts of law are ready to maintain them.'

(a) If Lord Atkin had taken the view that a margin of 1 per cent was acceptable, so that a metric tonne of coal could be 10 kilos light, what problems would arise? Would a line still have to be drawn somewhere? What if a coalman delivered 11 kilos light?

(b) Do you think the price of the staves had increased or decreased between the time of the making of the contract and the buyer finding that they did not match the description? How do you think the buyer would have acted if the price of staves had increased dramatically and it would now cost him double to buy similar staves elsewhere?

(c) If the goods do alter in price between the time of making the contract and the time of delivery, would this have any bearing on the court's decision as to whether section 13 had been broken?

(d) When *Arcos* v *Ronaasen* was decided Britain still had an empire and the case would have been a precedent in Commonwealth countries. Would it have been reasonable for an Australian businessman to buy half-inch nuts from a British supplier and half-inch bolts from an Australian supplier, and expect the nuts and bolts to fit together? How would this have been different if Lord Atkin's approach had not been adopted?

Section 14: Quality and fitness in business sales

Section 14(2) implies a term that goods sold in the course of a business must be of **satisfactory quality**.

Section 14(3) implies a term that goods sold in the course of a business must be **fit for the purpose supplied**.

Business sales

These two sections apply only if goods are sold in the course of business. Neither section will apply if the goods are sold by a private seller.

Goods are sold in the course of business if:

(a) the sale is made as an integral part of the business; or
(b) the sale of such goods is fairly regular.

ACTIVITY QUESTION 7.4

Would sections 14(2) and 14(3) apply to the following sales?
(a) An estate agent sells his car to a friend.
(b) A car dealer sells a car to a customer.
(c) A motor manufacturer sells 40 cars to a dealer.
(d) Every two years, a large company sells all of its salesmen's cars to a dealer.
(e) A shopkeeper sells his old till when he buys a new one.

Section 14(2): Satisfactory quality

Until the Sale and Supply of Goods Act 1994, section 14(2) of the Sale of Goods Act 1979 required that goods sold in the course of business had to be of merchantable quality, which was defined by section 14(6) as meaning *'fit for the purpose or purposes for which goods of that kind are commonly bought as it is reasonable to expect having regard to any description applied to them, the price (if relevant) and all the other relevant circumstances'*.

In recent years the exact meaning of this section caused considerable difficulty.

The courts adopted two tests, the acceptability test and the usability test, to decide whether or not goods sold were merchantable. Unfortunately, it was never clear which test a court might use.

The **acceptability test** held that the goods were merchantable if the buyer would still have bought the goods at the same price if he had known of the defects when he made the purchase. The **usability test** held that the goods were merchantable if a reasonable buyer could use the goods for any of the purposes for which goods of that contract description are commonly used.

Section 1 of the Sale and Supply of Goods Act 1994 has changed the requirement that the goods be of merchantable quality to a requirement that they must be of satisfactory quality. Section 2A defines the meaning of 'satisfactory quality':

> 'For the purposes of this Act, goods are of satisfactory quality if they meet the standard that a reasonable person would regard as satisfactory, taking account of any description of the goods, the price (if relevant) and all the other relevant circumstances.'

This definition of satisfactory quality is very similar to the definition of merchantable quality given by section 14(6) of the Sale of Goods Act 1979. However, section 2B of the Sale and Supply of Goods Act 1994 goes on to say:

> 'For the purposes of this Act, the quality of goods includes their state and condition and the following (among others) are in appropriate cases aspects of the quality of the goods –
> (a) fitness for all the purposes for which goods of the kind in question are commonly supplied,
> (b) appearance and finish,
> (c) freedom from minor defects,
> (d) safety, and
> (e) durability.'

This detailed description of the meaning of satisfactory quality reveals that it does not mean the same as merchantable quality. In particular, the usability test seems to have been made redundant. That test required that the goods had to be satisfactory for **any** of their normal purposes. Section 2B requires that the goods be satisfactory for **all** of their usual purposes.

Further activity question 7.5

Read the following cases and:
(a) Decide whether the court used the acceptability test or the usability test.
(b) Decide how the cases would now be decided in the light of the Sale and Supply of Goods Act 1994.

Kendall v Lillico (1969, House of Lords)

The owner of a game farm bought groundnut extract which he used to make food for his birds. Groundnut extract is normally used as cattle food, and the buyer did not tell the seller that he intended to feed it to birds. The extract contained a mould which made it poisonous to birds. It would not have been harmful to cattle. The buyers' birds died and he sued for damages under section 14(2).

Held The groundnut extract was of merchantable quality because it could safely have been used as cattle food, its normal purpose.

Sumner Permain v Webb & Co (1922, Court of Appeal)

A dealer bought a large quantity of tonic water, intending to export it to Argentina. The Argentinian authorities refused to let the tonic water into the country as it contained salicylic acid. Other countries would not have been concerned about this acid, but Argentinian law did not allow it to be present in drinks. The dealer rejected the tonic water on the grounds that it was not of merchantable quality.

Held The tonic water was of merchantable quality because it could have been used for just about any purpose other than the one for which the buyer intended to use it.

Shine v General Guarantee Corporation Ltd (1988, Court of Appeal)

A motorist bought a second-hand specialist sports car which gave him few problems. However, when he discovered that the car had been involved in a crash and totally submerged in water he sought to reject it under section 14(2).

Held The car was not of merchantable quality. Bush J said that no member of the public who was aware of the car's history *'would touch it with a barge pole unless they could get it at a substantially reduced price to reflect the risk they were taking'*.

Rogers v Parish Ltd (1987, Court of Appeal)

A motorist bought a new Range Rover for £16,000. The car had several minor defects (scratches on the paint work, leaking oil seals, and excessive engine noise). But the car was drivable and the defects could have been put right. The motorist rejected the car under section 14(2).

Held The car was not of merchantable quality. The court said that the way in which such cars were marketed conjured up very high expectations, and the car had failed to live up to them.

The seller's liability under section 14(2) is **strict**. He does not need to be at fault in any way. However, section 14(2) itself says that it is not to apply to:

(a) defects **specifically pointed out** to the buyer before the contract is made; and
(b) defects which the buyer ought to have spotted **if he examined the goods**.

Bartlett v *Sidney Marcus Ltd* (1965, Court of Appeal)

A dealer sold a second-hand car and pointed out to the buyer that the car had a defective clutch. The buyer negotiated a reduced price to take account of the defect. Repairing the clutch cost far more than the buyer had anticipated, and he claimed to reject the car under section 14(2).

Held The car was of merchantable quality because the defect had been pointed out to the buyer.

However, it must be remembered that the buyer has no obligation to examine the goods.

Section 14 (3): Fitness for purpose

Section 14(3) states that if the buyer makes known to the seller the particular purpose for which he intends to use the goods then the goods must be fit for that particular purpose. This applies whether or not the purpose made known by the buyer is the purpose for which the goods are commonly supplied. However, section 14(3) will not apply if:

(a) the buyer does not rely on the skill and judgement of the seller; or
(b) it was unreasonable for him to rely on this.

If the purpose for which the goods are to be used is perfectly obvious, then the buyer does not need to state the purpose.

Grant v *Australian Knitting Mills Ltd* (1936, Privy Council)

A customer who bought a pair of underpants from a shop contracted dermatitis because a chemical used in the manufacture of the underpants had not been rinsed out properly. The customer sued under section 14(3), as well as under section 14(2), because the purpose for which he bought the underpants was perfectly obvious.

Held The buyer won under both sections.

Griffiths v *Peter Conway Ltd* (1939)

A customer with abnormally sensitive skin contracted dermatitis from a tweed coat which she bought from a shop. The coat would not have affected most people.

Held The shop were not liable under sections 14(2) or 14(3).

When defective goods are bought for their usual purpose it is common for the buyer to sue under both section 14(2) and section 14(3).

ACTIVITY QUESTIONS 7.6

1 How would *Sumner Permain* v *Webb* (tonic water to Argentina) and *Kendall* v *Lillico* (groundnut extract for bird food) have been decided if the buyers had told the sellers the purpose for which they intended to use the goods?

2 Generally second-hand cars are more expensive to buy from a garage than they are to buy privately. Why might a customer who knows little about cars be better to buy from a garage?

3 David, who knows little about cars, feels that he will get a better price from the garage if he appears to have some mechanical expertise. Before buying a car he therefore kicks the tyres, looks underneath the chassis, and examines the engine. Why might these be unwise moves?

Further activity questions 7.6

1 When section 14(3) was originally passed shop assistants were very different. Often they would be retired tradesmen with a lifetime's experience of the goods they sold. Also, the goods sold were much less technical than many of today's goods. Is it reasonable to impose the same standards on modern shop assistants, who might know very little about the properties of what they sell?

2 In *Manchester Liners Ltd* v *Rea Ltd* (1922, House of Lords), the plaintiffs ordered 500 tons of coal from the defendant, a Liverpool coal merchant. The coal was said to be for 'The Manchester Importer', a steamship which was on the Manchester canal. The defendant supplied a type of coal which was unsuitable for use on this type of steamship. As a consequence the ship had to return to port after it had set off. The coal merchant was held liable under the forerunner to section 14(3) of the Sale of Goods Act because he should have known that the coal was not suitable.

Applying this case, do you think a modern coal merchant would be liable if he supplied ordinary coal to a customer who lived in a smokeless zone? (Assume that the customer merely rung up and asked for a ton of coal to be delivered at his address.)

Sample

Section 15 of the 1979 Act provides that if goods are sold by sample three conditions are implied:

(a) The bulk must correspond with the sample.
(b) The buyer must have a reasonable opportunity of comparing the bulk with the sample.
(c) The bulk must be free from hidden defects, which would render the goods unmerchantable, if these defects would not be discovered on a reasonable examination of the sample.

Godley v Perry (1960)

A six-year-old boy bought a catapult which snapped in use and caused the boy to lose an eye. The boy sued the shopkeeper and won. The shopkeeper sued the wholesaler under the forerunner to section 15 because, before buying the catapults, he had tested a sample by pulling back the elastic, and this sample had not snapped.

Held The shopkeeper won under the forerunner to section 15.

ACTIVITY QUESTIONS 7.7

1 Which of the following sales are likely to be by sample?
  (a) A farmer sells 100 tons of potatoes to a supermarket chain.
  (b) A shopper orders a fitted carpet in a style he saw in the shop.
  (c) After test driving a demonstration model, a motorist buys a new car.
  (d) A shop agrees to stock a new range of pens.
  (e) A householder orders a three-piece suite which he saw pictured in a magazine.

2 In *Godley* v *Perry* the boy sued the shopkeeper and won. Under which section(s) would the boy have sued?

3 In *Godley* v *Perry* there was a chain of buyers.

  Manufacturer .... supplier 1 .... supplier 2. .... shopkeeper ..... boy

  (a) Who was the eventual loser likely to be?
  (b) How would the bankruptcy of supplier 2 have affected the position?

The Supply of Goods (Implied Terms) Act 1973

As we have seen, the terms implied by the Sale of Goods Acts have given excellent protection to buyers of goods since 1893. However, the Acts did not stretch beyond these strictly defined contracts for 'sale' of 'goods', and in other contracts consumers had to rely on case law for protection.

In the 1970s Parliament passed several statutes which extended the Sale of Goods Act implied terms into other types of contract.

The first of these Acts was the Supply of Goods (Implied Terms) Act 1973, which extended the implied terms into contracts of **hire purchase**. The terms, which are almost identical to the terms implied by sections 12 to 15 of the Sale of Goods Act 1979, are contained in the following sections:

- **Section 8**   **Title**
- **Section 9**   **Description**
- **Section 10**   **Satisfactory quality and fitness** (business contracts only)
- **Section 11**   **Sample**

A contract of hire purchase is one whereby a hirer of goods agrees to hire them for a certain period, and is given an option to purchase the goods for a nominal sum at the end of that period.

Example   Mr Smith takes a fridge on hire purchase from a shop. The fridge would have cost £350 to buy, but Mr Smith takes it on hire purchase for three years at £17 a month.

Until the final payment is made Mr Smith is merely hiring the fridge. The last payment he makes will include a nominal purchase price, and when Mr Smith makes the final payment he then buys the fridge. When he eventually does buy the fridge the Sale of Goods Act provisions would apply, but by then it would almost certainly be far too late for any of the implied terms to be of any use to Mr Smith. The Supply Of Goods (Implied Terms) Act 1973 therefore implies terms as to title, description, quality and sample as soon as the hire-purchase agreement begins.

The statute became necessary because customers using hire purchase often did not understand the arrangements they were making, and usually paid an exorbitant price for the hire of the goods. The salesman would dangle the carrot of immediate possession of items such as television sets in front of the customers and tell them that the small print was just a technicality. An anonymous judge described hire-purchasers as '*People who are persuaded by persons they do not know to enter into contracts they do not understand to purchase goods that they do not want with money that they have not got*'.

When we consider the Consumer Credit Act 1974, we shall see that it gives many other rights to hire-purchasers. But in the context of the terms as to title, description, quality and sample it is sections 8 to 11 of the Supply of Goods (Implied Terms) Act 1973 which apply.

Section 10, which implies the term as to satisfactory quality and fitness for purpose, applies only if the hirer makes the hire-purchase agreement in the course of business. The other sections apply to all contracts of hire purchase. In almost all hire-purchase agreements the hirer will make the agreement in the course of business.

The Supply of Goods and Services Act 1982

Part I of the Act

Part I of the Supply of Goods and Services Act 1982 implies terms as to title, description, quality and sample into contracts for the **supply of work and materials**, and into contracts of **barter, hire, rent or leasing**. The terms are contained in the following sections:

(a) *Contracts for work and materials, barter, rent and leasing* –
- **Section 2**   **Title**
- **Section 3**   **Description**
- **Section 4**   **Satisfactory quality and fitness** (business contracts only)
- **Section 5**   **Sample**

(b) *Contracts of hire* –
- **Section 7**   **Hire**
- **Section 8**   **Description**
- **Section 9**   **Satisfactory quality and fitness** (business contracts only)
- **Section 10**   **Sample**

Part II of the Act

Part II of the Supply of Goods and Services Act 1982 implies different terms into contracts for **services**. These terms are as follows:

- **Section 13**   **Reasonable care and skill** (business services only)
- **Section 14**   **Reasonable time** (business services only)
- **Section 15**   **Reasonable price**

Section 13 provides that: *'In a contract for the supply of a service where the supplier is acting in the course of business, there is an implied term that the supplier will carry out the service with reasonable care and skill.'* Note that, like section 14 of the Sale of Goods Act 1979, the term will be imposed only on those who supply **in the course of business**.

The test of whether the service provided was carried out with reasonable care and skill is **objective not subjective.** If a person professes to have a certain level of skill then he must show the level of skill which the reasonable man would expect, and it is no defence that he did his incompetent best. Professionals, such as solicitors and accountants, and tradesmen, such as plumbers and roofers, would automatically be expected to show the skill normal in that profession or trade.

Section 14 applies only to services provided in the course of business. It provides that if no **time** for completion of the task was either expressed or implied then the service should be performed within a reasonable time.

Section 15 provides that if no **price** for the service was fixed then the customer should pay a reasonable price. This section applies to all services, whether provided in the course of business or not.

ACTIVITY QUESTIONS 7.8

1 A motorist buys a new car from a garage but the car has a serious defect in the steering system. Which section of which statute gives the motorist a remedy?

2 How would your answer to question 1 be different if:
  (a) The motorist had hired the car?
  (b) The motorist had bought the car from his friend, an accountant?

Further activity questions 7.8

1 Complete the table opposite to show which sections of which statutes would apply. Put an asterisk next to the sections which would apply only to business deals. To get you started, some of the table has already been completed.

2 Is it normal, when dealing with a professional or a tradesman, to fix the exact price in advance? Is it still necessary to do so? Is it wise to do so?

Type of transaction / Implied term as to:	Sale of goods	Hire purchase	Barter, work and materials	Hire
Title	SGA s.12			
Description		SGITA, s.9		
Quality and fitness			SGSA, s.4*	
Sample				SGSA, s.10

The Sale and Supply of Goods Act 1994

In this chapter we have already seen that the Sale and Supply of Goods Act 1994 changed the requirement of merchantable quality to a requirement of satisfactory quality. In addition, the Act has changed the status of some of the implied terms. Prior to the Act, all of the terms implied by all of the statutes were conditions. This meant that if the seller broke any of the terms the buyer could always rescind and get his money back as well as claim damages. Sometimes rescission seemed a somewhat drastic remedy if the breach of the implied terms was very minor. The courts were faced with an unenviable choice: declare the implied term broken and let the buyer rescind for a very minor defect; or declare the implied term unbroken and give the buyer no remedy at all.

In consumer contracts the law is unchanged – the implied terms are still conditions – but section 4 of the new Act has changed the law in non-consumer cases.

Section 4: Remedies in non-consumer cases

Section 4 states that in non-consumer deals all the implied terms as to description, quality, fitness and sample should be warranties if:

(a) the breach is so slight that it would be unreasonable for the buyer to reject; and

(b) the contact does not show a contrary intention, that the terms are to be conditions.

So now, in non-consumer cases, the courts will have the option of awarding damages for minor breaches.

Exclusion of the implied terms

We shall see later, in Chapter 15, that an exclusion clause is a term in a contract which tries to limit or exclude liability for breach of the contract.

In the same chapter we will also consider the Unfair Contract Terms Act 1977 in some detail. This Act specifically mentions the terms implied by sections 12 to 15 of the Sale of Goods Act 1979, and subsequent legislation has extended it to cover all three of the statutes which we have considered in this chapter.

In this context the Unfair Contract Terms Act 1977 makes a distinction between **consumer** contracts and **non-consumer** contracts. This distinction is vitally important here because:

(a) In **consumer** contracts none of the implied terms as to description, quality, fitness for purpose or sample can be excluded.
(b) In **non-consumer** contracts these terms can be excluded if it is **reasonable** to do so.

The Unfair Contract Terms Act 1977 defines a consumer as:

(a) a person who makes a contract not in the course of business, and not holding himself out to be in the course of business,
(b) with a person who does make the contract in the course of business.

For example, when a customer buys a pint of beer in a pub he is a consumer. The customer is not in the business of buying beer; the pub is in the business of selling beer. When the landlord of the pub orders its weekly supply of beer he is not a consumer. The landlord is in the business of buying beer.

However, not everything the landlord sells to customers will be sold under a consumer contract. If the landlord sells his car to a customer this will not be a consumer contract because the landlord does not sell the car in the course of a business, he sells it privately.

In **non-consumer contracts** the terms implied by statute are excludable if this is **reasonable**, and schedule 2 of the Unfair Contract Terms Act 1977 describes the factors which a court will consider in assessing whether or not the exclusion clause was reasonable. These factors are:

(a) The relative **strength of the parties' bargaining position**, which will include whether or not the customer **could find another supplier**.
(b) Whether the customer was given **any inducement** to agree to the term.
(c) Whether the customer **knew** or ought to have known that **the term existed**.

THE CUSTOMER IS NOT IN THE BUSINESS OF BUYING BEER ...

(d) If the term excludes liability unless some condition is complied with, whether or not it was **reasonably practicable to comply** with that condition.
(e) Whether the goods were manufactured, altered or adapted **at the customer's request**.

These factors were examined by Lord Denning MR in the following case:

Mitchell (George) Ltd v *Finney Lock Seeds Ltd* (1983, Court of Appeal)

A farmer bought his yearly supply of cabbage seeds for £192. Because of a defect in the seed the cabbages did not grow properly and were not saleable by the farmer. The loss of the year's crop cost the farmer £61,000, but an exclusion clause in the back of the seller's catalogue and on the back of the invoice limited the seed seller's liability to the cost of the seed, in this case £192. The farmer sued for his total loss of £61,000.

Held This was not a consumer contract, and the exclusion clause was a term of the contract. The sole question to be considered therefore was whether or not the exclusion clause was reasonable. Lord Denning MR gave the leading judgment and decided that, although a borderline case, the clause was not reasonable. Applying the definition of 'reasonable' contained in the Unfair Contract Terms Act, Lord Denning MR made the following points:

(a) The farmer had little bargaining power – he either agreed to the terms or could not make the contract.
(b) The seed merchants could have known that there was something wrong with the seed; the farmer could not.
(c) The seed merchants could have insured against the risk of the seed being defective; the farmer could not.
(d) The term was usual in the trade.
(e) The seed merchants, or the person from whom they bought the seed, must have been negligent to some extent. The farmer was not negligent at all.

Unlike the other terms, terms as to **title** cannot be excluded by any contract term. If the supplier does not have title to what he supplies under the contract then there has been a total failure of consideration, and no term can protect against this.

ACTIVITY QUESTION 7.9

Which of the following would be classed as consumer contracts?

(a) A motor dealer orders a dozen new cars from Ford.

(b) A customer goes to a salon for a haircut.

(c) A manufacturing company buys a new car for one of its salesmen.

(d) A motorist fills his car with petrol at a filling station.

(e) A lady who has inherited an extremely valuable painting sells it to a gallery.

(f) A postman sells his old television to his neighbour.

(g) A businessman books an extremely expensive meal for a party of foreign customers.

Further activity question 7.9

Which of the guidelines as to reasonableness contained in schedule 2 of the Unfair Contract Terms Act 1977 (the strength of the parties' bargaining position, etc.) would be likely to influence the court's decision on whether or not exclusion clauses in the following contracts are reasonable? How would they be likely to affect the court's decision?

(a) A businessman was to buy an industrial machine for £12,000, but he was given a 10 per cent reduction in the price for signing an exclusion clause.

(b) A businessman designed a new type of machine. A manufacturer built the machine but insisted on the businessman signing a clause that the machine might not work if the design was flawed.

(c) A pottery business needs gas to fire its kilns. The owner of the business objects to one of British Gas's exclusion terms and is told that the contract cannot be altered. There are no other suppliers, and if the business owner wants gas his only option is to sign the contract.

TASK 7

Work out the answers to the following multiple choice questions.

1 Anne hires a television from a shop. The shop assistant says that the television has previously been hired, but works as if new. Anne finds the television most unsatisfactory. It will not receive Channel 4 and the picture is often poor. Under which of the following can she return the television to the shop and demand her money back?

(a) Section 13 of the Supply of Goods and Services Act 1982.
(b) Sections 8 and 9 of the Supply of Goods and Services Act 1982.
(c) Only section 9 of the Supply of Goods and Services Act 1982.
(d) Sections 9 and 10 of the Supply of Goods (Implied Terms) Act 1973.

2 A county cricket club buy three dozen cricket bats from a wholesaler. The bats are sold for a third of their usual price because they have a manufacturing fault in the splice. The wholesaler points this fault out to the cricket club's buyer who signs a note saying that he buys the bats 'aware of defective splice'. The club thought that the bats would be suitable for their junior teams, but most of the bats split as soon as they are used. Which of the following is true?

(a) The club can return the bats under the Sale of Goods Act 1979, sections 14(2) and 14(3), despite the note.
(b) The club can return the bats under the Sale of Goods Act 1979, sections 14(2) and 14(3) unless the note was reasonable.
(c) The club can return the bats under the Sale of Goods Act 1979, section 13 unless the note was reasonable.
(d) The Sale of Goods Act 1979 offers no help to the cricket club.

3 David, a carpenter, buys a new saw from a shop, telling the shop assistant that he intends to use the saw to cut very hard plastic. The shop assistant, a 16-year-old who works only on Saturdays, takes David's money.

David subsequently discovers that the saw will not cut the very hard plastic – a hacksaw will be needed. Which of the following is true?

(a) David has no remedy.
(b) David can return the saw under section 13 of the Sale of Goods Act 1979.
(c) David can return the saw under section 14(2) of the Sale of Goods Act 1979.
(d) David can return the saw under section 14(3) of the Sale of Goods Act 1979.

4 Buildo Ltd, a firm of builders, hire a JCB digging machine from Hire Co Ltd. Buildo's manager signs a contract, without reading it, which contains a clause, 'All terms expressed or implied by statute or otherwise are hereby expressly excluded'. The JCB will not excavate due to a mechanical fault. Hire Co refuse to repair it, to exchange it for another machine or to return Buildo's money. Which of the following is true?

(a) Buildo will win under sections 14(2) and 14(3) of the Sale of Goods Act 1979, unless the exclusion clause was reasonable.

(b) Buildo will win under section 9 of the Supply of Goods and Services Act 1982, unless the exclusion clause was reasonable.

(c) The exclusion clause will be completely ineffective, and Buildo will win under sections 14(2) and 14(3) of the Sale of Goods Act 1979.

(d) The exclusion clause will be completely ineffective, and Buildo will win under section 9 of the Supply of Goods and Services Act 1982.

5 Elaine hires a portrait artist to paint her portrait. The finished work is in a post-modernist style and is unrecognisable as Elaine. Elaine can refuse to accept the picture under:

(a) Section 14(2) of the Sale of Goods Act 1979

(b) Section 9 of the Supply of Goods and Services Act 1982

(c) Section 13 of the Supply of Goods and Services Act 1982

(d) Section 10 of the Supply of Goods (Implied Terms) Act 1973.

6 Geraldine bought a pair of shoes at half price in the January sale. Above the till was a sign 'No refunds on sale goods'. The shop assistant pointed this out to Geraldine when the sale was made. Within a week the heel fell off one of the shoes. Which of the following is true?

(a) Geraldine has no remedy.

(b) Geraldine can get her money back because the sign was unreasonable.

(c) Geraldine can get her money back because the sign was ineffective.

(d) Geraldine cannot get her money back but is entitled to exchange the shoes for another pair.

7 As Harold was about to leave for work he noticed that his bathroom tap was dripping continuously when turned off. He phoned a plumber who said that he could come around immediately and fix the tap. No price was mentioned. When Harold returned home he found that although the tap no longer leaked it could not be turned on fully. Worse still, there was a bill for £250 on the sink. Which of the following is true?

(a) Harold must pay a reasonable price for the job even though it was unsatisfactory.

(b) Harold need not pay anything, he has been deprived of substantially the whole benefit he was meant to receive.

(c) The plumber must come back and put the job right, after which Harold must pay a reasonable price.

(d) Harold need not pay, as in (b) above, and could claim the cost of getting the tap put right.

8 Arthur bought a bicycle from Bill's shop. The bicycle frame was defective and snapped in half, injuring Arthur. At Arthur's request Bill had ordered the bicycle from Charles's wholesale company, which in turn had bought it from the manufacturer. Which of the following is true?

(a) Section 14(2) of the Sale of Goods Act 1979 will protect only Arthur.

(b) Section 14(2) will impose liability on Bill, Charles and the manufacturer.

(c) Bill will not be able to sue Charles under the Sale of Goods Act 1979. It was his business to know about bicycles and he should have spotted the fault.

(d) Bill will be liable under section 13 of the Supply of Goods and Services Act 1982 because he should have serviced the bicycle before selling it.

8 Legal responsibility to the community and to the State

Every business owes duties to the State and to the community in which it operates. Traditionally these duties have been imposed by the common law, but in recent years there has been increasing statutory regulation.

Common law regulation

If a business causes injury, the law of tort will usually provide the injured person with a remedy. Each tort is designed to protect against a different type of behaviour, and it is necessary to examine each tort separately. In this context some torts are far more significant than others, and these torts are therefore considered in greater detail. In this chapter we shall consider the effect of negligence, private and public nuisance, occupiers' liability, strict liability, trespass to land, to the person and to goods and, lastly, defamation.

Negligence

Negligence is the most important tort. It is examined in detail in Chapter 13, as a means of illustrating the distinction between contract and tort. When we consider negligence we shall see that it is very broadly based, flowing from Lord Atkin's 'neighbour speech,' and that it covers an enormous number of situations. In effect, negligence plugs the gaps left by the more strictly defined torts. The judges impose liability in negligence whenever they consider this necessary on the grounds of public policy.

Businesses can be liable for negligence in the same way that individuals can, and this liability can extend to cover environmental damage to the community in which the business operates. Important recent cases have found a farmer negligent for using an inappropriate pesticide (thereby killing a neighbour's bees), and a water authority negligent for not warning of excessive chlorine in a river. However, the courts have been reluctant to use the tort of negligence to control environmental damage. The major reason for this is that the English judges are unwilling, as a matter of policy, to extend negligence as far as it has been extended in the United States.

In England, liability for negligence, and the resulting damages, are decided by a judge. In the United States these matters are decided by a jury, and American juries have extended negligence to absurd lengths and awarded enormous damages for seemingly trivial breaches of duty. For example, an American court recently awarded $2.7 million against a fast food chain for serving coffee that was too hot. Imposing such liability inevitably places an enormous burden on business. The Japanese seem well aware of this – there are more lawyers in the American city of Washington than in the whole of Japan!

Another reason why negligence does not impose a great number of environmental duties on businesses is that other, well-established torts do.

Private nuisance

A private nuisance is an indirect unlawful interference with another person's use or enjoyment of his land. For example, if a manufacturing company makes persistent unreasonable noise in a residential area this would be a private nuisance. There is nothing unlawful in the company manufacturing goods. What makes it unlawful, and therefore a private nuisance, is that it prevents others from enjoying the use of their property.

As private nuisance is an interference with the use and enjoyment of land, only the owner or occupier of land can sue.

Types of interference

A **direct interference** with a person's land, such as dumping rubbish onto it, would be trespass. **Indirect interferences**, such as noise, are nuisance. However nuisance is by no means limited to noise. Vibrations, noxious fumes, encroaching roots from trees, and even the use of premises as a sex shop, have all been held to amount to a private nuisance.

Damage must be suffered

The plaintiff can sue only if he suffers some damage. This need not necessarily involve physical injury or damage to property; it can also include the damage suffered by not being able to enjoy using the land.

Leeman v Montagu (1936)

The defendant bought a house in a residential area which bordered on open countryside. He kept a flock of 750 cockerels in an orchard about 100 yards from the house. These cockerels crowed from 2 am to 7 am, making it impossible for the plaintiff to sleep. The plaintiff asked the court for an injunction to prevent the defendant from keeping the cockerels on his land.

Held The defendant had committed a nuisance and so the injunction was granted.

The interference must be unreasonable

The law attempts to strike a balance between the different people trying to enjoy the use of their land. All users of land must make a certain amount of noise etc. The question is whether this unreasonably prevents neighbours from enjoying the use of their land.

What is reasonable will depend upon the area in which the alleged nuisance was committed. In *Sturges* v *Bridgman* (1879) Thesiger LJ said: '*What would be a nuisance in Belgrave Square would not necessarily be so in Bermondsey.*'

Noisy manufacturing operations have to be carried on somewhere. If they are carried on in an industrial estate the noise (as well as the smell, vibrations etc.) is unlikely to constitute a nuisance. Similarly, if the defendant in *Leeman* v *Montagu* had kept his cockerels in a completely rural area the noise they made would not have constituted a nuisance.

The frequency with which the interference is caused is also relevant. If a manufacturer conducted a noisy cleaning process once a year this would be more likely to be reasonable than if he conducted it every day.

Abnormally sensitive plaintiffs are not protected. The interference must be such that it would prevent an ordinary person from using and enjoying his land.

Robinson v Kilvert (1889, Court of Appeal)

The plaintiff stored brown paper on the ground floor of the defendant's premises. Heat from the defendant's boiler in the basement of the premises damaged the brown paper. The heat generated would not have damaged ordinary paper, but brown paper is especially sensitive to heat. The plaintiff wanted an injunction to prevent the defendant from using the boiler.

Held The defendant was not committing a nuisance and so an injunction was not granted.

> Lopes LJ '. . . *a man who carries on an exceptionally delicate trade cannot complain because it is injured by his neighbour doing something lawful on his property, if it is something which would not injure anything but an exceptionally delicate trade.*'

If a person causes the interference maliciously then this is much more likely to be a nuisance.

Christie v Davey (1893)

Much to the defendant's annoyance, his next-door neighbour, the plaintiff, gave music lessons and held musical parties. The defendant retaliated by blowing whistles, shrieking, shouting, banging trays and hammering. The plaintiff asked the court to grant an injunction to prevent the defendant from continuing to make the malicious noises.

Held The defendant's actions amounted to a nuisance because they were done maliciously. Therefore an injunction was granted.

Remedies

Damages

Damage to property and injury to the person will be calculated in the usual way. Damages can also be awarded for inconvenience suffered, although these damages are more difficult for the judge to assess.

Injunction

An injunction is a court order requiring a person to behave in a certain way. (In nuisance cases the injunction will order the defendant to stop committing the nuisance.) If the defendant disobeys the court order he will be liable to punishment for contempt of court. The issuing of an injunction could be lethal to many businesses. For example, if a business needs to make excessive noise in order to manufacture its products, and an injunction is issued forbidding the business to make the noise in the area where it currently operates, the business will be compelled either to move or to stop manufacturing the product.

An injunction is generally the most sought after remedy for private nuisance. Usually all the plaintiff wants is that the defendant stops committing the nuisance.

Abatement

This is a self-help remedy whereby the victim removes the nuisance himself. It is generally allowed only in an emergency, or if it does not involve entering onto the defendant's land.

 Smith v Giddy (1904)

Large ash and elm trees on the defendant's land overhung the plaintiff's land. The branches of these trees interfered with the plaintiff's fruit trees. The plaintiff cut the branches back so that they no longer hung over his land.

Held The plaintiff was entitled to do this, as well as receive damages for nuisance.

Defences

Statutory authority

A defendant will not be liable for a nuisance which was necessarily committed in order to comply with a statute.

Allen v Gulf Oil Refining Ltd (1981, House of Lords)

An Act of Parliament gave Gulf Oil the right compulsorily to purchase land and build an oil refinery on it. Once the refinery was running a nearby resident said that its noise, smell and vibrations amounted to a nuisance.

Held It was Parliament's intention that the oil refinery be built and operate on the site. As the noise, smells and vibrations were an inevitable consequence of the operation of a refinery, the defendant had a complete defence.

Prescription

If a person has committed a nuisance **continuously for 20 years**, prescription will give him a right to continue committing the nuisance without redress. It is not enough that the defendant has been committing the act complained of continuously for 20 years. It must also have amounted to a nuisance for 20 years.

Sturges v Bridgman (1879, Court of Appeal)

A confectionery manufacturer occupied premises next door to a doctor. For more than 20 years the confectioner had operated heavy pestles and mortars which were noisy and caused vibrations. This did not bother the doctor until he built a consulting room which adjoined the room where the pestles and mortars were used. The doctor applied for an injunction to stop the use of the pestles and mortars.

Held The noise and vibration were a nuisance and the injunction was granted. Prescription was not available as a defence because although the noise had been committed for 20 years, the nuisance had not.

Prescription can apply only if the activity has been carried on openly, without using force and without permission.

Act of God

An Act of God is an event, such as an earthquake, which no human foresight can provide against. If an Act of God causes a nuisance to be committed then the defendant will not be liable.

Consent of the plaintiff

If the plaintiff consents to the commission of the nuisance then this will give the defendant a complete defence. However, the plaintiff does not consent merely by occupying or buying land with the knowledge that a nuisance is being committed.

Public nuisance

A public nuisance is committed by an act or omission which materially affects the comfort and convenience of the public at large. Blocking the highway is perhaps the most common example.

Public nuisance is a **crime**, but a person who has suffered damage over and above that suffered by the public at large can sue.

Occupiers' liability

Occupiers of premises owe a duty of care to all lawful visitors, and a separate duty of care to trespassers. Almost all businesses must occupy some premises, and so almost all are potentially liable.

Lawful visitors

Any person who comes on to premises with either express or implied permission will be a lawful visitor. So delivery drivers or service mechanics would be as much lawful visitors as would invited visitors such as important customers.

The Occupiers' Liability Act 1957, section 2 requires occupiers of premises to take *'such care as in all the circumstances of the case is reasonable to see that the visitor will be reasonably safe in using the premises for the purposes for which he is invited or permitted by the occupier to be there'*.

This standard of care is very similar to the standard required in the tort of negligence. Compare section 2 of the Act, quoted above, with Lord Atkin's 'neighbour' speech on page 287. In some ways the statute has just extended negligence to cover injuries to lawful visitors on premises.

The standard is not an absolute one. It varies with all the circumstances. Some people, such as children, can be expected to be less careful than others, and a higher duty is therefore owed to them. Others, such as contractors, can be expected to look out for themselves rather better than most people, especially if they have been warned of a particular danger. Consequently they are owed a lower duty.

Trespassers

Any person who enters the premises other than as a lawful visitor will do so as a trespasser. Frequently such trespassers will be children, and the courts have recognised that even trespassers need considerable protection from inherently dangerous things such as live railway lines.

Section 1(3) of the Occupiers' Liability Act 1984 extended a statutory duty of protection to trespassers. The occupier owes the duty to take **such care as is reasonable** to see that the trespasser is not injured. The duty arises if three conditions are met:

(a) The occupier knows or ought to know that the danger exists.
(b) The occupier knows or ought to know that the trespasser is in the vicinity of the danger.
(c) The risk is one against which the occupier could reasonably be expected to offer the trespasser some protection.

The effect of notices and signs

Notices posted by an occupier might offer protection against liability in one of two ways. First, they might turn a lawful visitor into a trespasser, thereby diminishing the extent of the duty owed. For example, if a householder posts a notice 'No hawkers, no circulars, no free newspapers' on his gate, then a hawker who would otherwise have entered as a lawful visitor will enter as a trespasser.

Second, notices which warn of a danger might provide the occupier with the defence of *volenti non fit injuria*. If a person enters premises despite a prominent notice stating that the premises are unsafe, he might well be deemed to have accepted the risk of injury. However, such notices have limitations. They are not much good at night time or as regards children who are too young to read them.

If the premises are used for the business purposes of the occupier then warning notices will be ineffective. The Unfair Contract Terms Act 1977 states that if the premises are occupied *'for the business purposes of the occupier'* then no notice or contract term can *'exclude or restrict his liability for death or personal injury arising from negligence'*. (A business occupier can, however, restrict liability for damage to goods if such a restriction is reasonable.) For example, a business which owned land on which there were large decaying chimneys would not protect itself against injury to trespassers merely by posting notices which warned of the danger. If the business does not also take reasonable care to see that trespassers are safe to use the land then it will break its duty under the 1984 Act, and the warning notice will be completely ineffective under the Unfair Contract Terms Act 1977. However, the notice might protect the business against damage to goods. If a trespasser ignored the notice and parked his car next to a decaying chimney then the business would not be liable for damage caused to the car, unless the court considered the notice's exclusion of liability to be unreasonable.

Defences

As with negligence, both *volenti non fit injuria* and contributory negligence are available as defences.

Strict liability

Strict liability is imposed by the rule in *Rylands* v *Fletcher*. The basis of the tort was explained by Blackburn J in the House of Lords in 1868:

> '*The person who, for his own purposes, brings on his land and collects and keeps there any thing likely to do mischief if it escapes, must keep it at his peril; and if he does not do so, is . . . answerable for all the damage which is the natural consequence of its escape.*'

Requirements of the tort

(a) The defendant must **bring something on to his land.**
(b) This must be a **non natural use** of the land.
(c) The thing must be **likely to do mischief** if it escapes.
(d) It must **escape** and cause damage.

Rylands v *Fletcher* (1868, House of Lords)

The defendant built a reservoir on his land. The water which accumulated in the reservoir entered old mine shafts and flooded the plaintiff's mine. It was not forseeable that this might happen.

Held The defendant was liable even though the damage was not forseeable. Building a reservoir and storing such a large quantity of water was an unnatural use of the land, satisfying (a) and (b). The water was likely to do mischief if it escaped, satisfying (c). The water did escape and cause damage, satisfying (d).

Defences

There are defences to strict liability, but this tort differs from other torts in that the duty is absolute and does not depend upon the defendant having been negligent. The defences are:

(a) That it was the **plaintiff's** fault that the thing escaped.
(b) That the escape was caused by an **Act of God** (see page 181).
(c) That the escape was caused by the **act of a stranger**. The stranger must not be an employee or an independent contractor working for the defendant.
(d) **Statutory authority**. The public utilities, such as the now privatised water authorities and the gas authorities, were created by statutes. The same statutes usually give the utilities generous protection in the event of their product escaping and causing damage.

Trespass to land

Any unauthorised **direct interference** with another person's land will amount to trespass to land. The tort can be committed not only by persons entering another's land, but also by depositing things onto it. If, for example, a business deposits rubbish onto someone else's land this will be a direct invasion of the land and will therefore amount to trespass to land.

Trespass can be committed underneath the ground or in the airspace above the land. Without the defence given by statutory authority, aeroplanes would commit trespass when they flew above a person's land and British Coal would commit a trespass when they mined underneath it.

The distinctions between trespass to land, private nuisance and strict liability are somewhat arbitrary. To summarise, to be liable under strict liability a dangerous thing brought on to the land must **escape** from the land. Private nuisance is an **indirect** interference with another's use and enjoyment of his land. Trespass to land is a **direct** invasion of the other person's land.

Trespass to the person

There are three forms of trespass to the person:

(a) **Battery** is the infliction of unlawful force on another person. If one person unlawfully hits another this will amount to battery.

(b) **Assault** occurs when a person is made to feel reasonably frightened that he is about to be battered. For example, it would be an assault to point a loaded gun at a person.

(c) **False imprisonment** consists of wrongfully depriving another person of his personal liberty. It is not necessary that the plaintiff is locked up. If a shop prevents a customer from leaving the premises, in the mistaken belief that the customer has been shoplifting, this would amount to false imprisonment.

Assault and battery are also crimes; false imprisonment is not.

Trespass to goods

A person commits **conversion**, a form of trespass to goods, if he denies another person his right to possess those goods. Usually the person suing will be the owner. A person whose goods were damaged or destroyed could sue the perpetrator for conversion.

A person can be liable for conversion even though he has acted innocently. If a thief steals a car and sells it to an innocent purchaser, this purchaser will be liable in conversion even though he did not know that the car was stolen. (He will therefore have to return the car to its owner.)

Damages are available for conversion, but if the goods still exist unharmed the plaintiff usually just wants his goods back. If the goods diminish in value before the court case is heard then the plaintiff will probably ask for damages.

IBL Ltd v *Coussens* (1991, House of Lords)

The plaintiff company bought two cars, an Aston Martin and a Rolls Royce, for the use of their managing director. When the managing director was dismissed he refused to return the cars. He was offered the chance to buy the cars but refused the offer. Two years later, when the case was decided, the company did not want the cars back, they wanted damages.

Held The company were entitled to damages to compensate them for what the cars were worth to the company when the director was dismissed.

Defamation

Defamation is the publication of a statement which would tend to lower the plaintiff in the opinion of right-thinking members of society generally.

The statement must be published, and this merely means that it must be made known to at least one other person. It does not need to be published commercially, i.e. appear in print.

Libel involves publication in some permanent form. Most libels are written, but they can also take the form of a film, a cartoon or a work of art.

Slander involves publication in a transient form. Usually this is speech, but it can include gestures.

Libel is the more serious form of defamation and can be sued upon without proving economic loss. In recent years juries have awarded massive damages for libel. Slander can be sued upon only if financial loss is proved.

If a bank wrongly dishonours a trader's cheque the trader can sue for defamation without proving loss. The smaller the amount of the cheque which was dishonoured the greater the defamation, and the larger the damages are likely to be.

ACTIVITY QUESTION 8.1

A chemicals manufacturer has committed the following five torts:

Tort 1 It left an uncovered pool of lethal chemical near a broken down fence. Young children broke through the fence and were killed by exposure to the chemical.

Tort 2   It deposited toxic waste slurry on the land of a neighbouring manufacturer.

Tort 3   It emitted noxious fumes which caused injury to a local farmer's sheep.

Tort 4   One of the manufacturer's delivery lorries spilt oil on a main road, causing a car following behind to crash.

Tort 5   Several barrels of highly toxic chemicals rolled downhill out of the manufacturer's premises on to a farmer's field, causing damage to crops.

Decide which tort has been committed in each case.

Statutory control of business: responsibility to individual citizens

If an individual is injured by the activities of a business then a remedy can usually be found within the law of tort. However, this judge-made law cannot always keep pace with the speed of technological change, and so the State has needed to legislate. The Data Protection Act provides a good example of such statutory protection.

The Data Protection Act 1984

Computers have become a fact of life in the past thirty years. Every day more information is stored on computer disks. The Data Protection Act regulates the storage of such information by requiring that it is registered. As the vast majority of businesses now store computerised data, the protection conferred by the Act is becoming increasingly significant.

The Definitions

Data means information recorded in a form in which it can be processed by equipment operating automatically in response to instructions given for that purpose. This definition rules out hand-written files, but a recently adopted new directive will extend it to hand-written files in 1997.

Personal data means data consisting of information which relates to a living individual who can be identified from that information. The individual must then be alive and must be capable of being identified. Names obviously identify people, but so do national insurance numbers, employee codes and bank account numbers. Opinions about the individual are included, but the data user's intentions about the individual are not. For example, if an employer had a computerised record that an employee 'should graduate next year' this would count as personal data. A statement that 'we intend to promote the employee next year' would not.

Data subject means a living individual who is the subject of personal data. Companies are not included.

Data user means a person who holds data, and this would include a company. The data user is not necessarily the person who owns or operates the computer, but he must control the use and content of the data. This means that he must be the one who decides what data are stored, whether they are amended and to what use they are put.

Processing, in relation to data, means amending, augmenting, deleting or rearranging the data or extracting the information constituting the data. This definition would include printing data, because in order to do this the information must be 'extracted' and therefore 'processed'.

Registration

Data users who hold personal data must apply for registration with the Data Protection Registrar. The following information must be registered:

(a) Who the data user is and how an individual may make a subject access request.
(b) The personal data held and the purpose for which they are held.
(c) From where the data user may obtain the information contained in the data.
(d) To whom the data user may disclose the information.
(e) Any overseas countries to which the data user may transfer the personal data.

The register is a public document which can be inspected free of charge.

It is a criminal offence to hold personal data without registering. Registered data users commit an offence if they knowingly or recklessly fail to keep their register entry complete and up to date. The maximum penalty for these offences is an unlimited fine.

The data protection principles

There are eight data protection principles. The last is concerned with security and applies only to computer bureaux. The first seven apply to all data users.

The first principle

'The information to be contained in personal data shall be obtained, and personal data shall be processed, fairly and lawfully.'

The second principle

'Personal data shall be held only for one or more specified and lawful purposes.'

The third principle

'Personal data held for any purpose or purposes shall not be used or disclosed in any manner incompatible with that purpose or those purposes.'

The fourth principle

'Personal data held for any purpose or purposes shall be adequate, relevant and not excessive in relation to that purpose or those purposes.'

The fifth principle

'Personal data shall be accurate and, where necessary, kept up to date.'

The sixth principle

'Personal data held for any purpose or purposes shall not be kept for longer than is necessary for that purpose or those purposes.'

The seventh principle

'An individual shall be entitled –
(a) at reasonable intervals and without undue delay or expense –
    (i)   to be informed by any data user whether he holds personal data of which that
        individual is the subject; and
    (ii) to access to any such data held by a data user; and
(b) where appropriate, to have such data corrected or erased.'

The eighth principle

'Appropriate security measures shall be taken against unauthorised access to, or alter-ation, disclosure or destruction of, personal data and against accidental loss or destruction of personal data.'

Individual rights

Individuals have four rights in respect of personal data held about them by others.

The subject access right

This gives the individual the right to be told whether the data user holds any personal data relating to him and, if so, to be supplied on request with a copy of the information.

The request must be in writing and a fee, not exceeding £10, can be charged for supplying the information.

A right to take action for compensation

If an individual suffers financial loss or physical injury because of a data user holding incorrect information about him, he may bring a court action to recover damages. The action is pursued in the ordinary civil courts.

It is a defence for the data user to show that he took all reasonable care to ensure that the personal information was accurate.

A right to have incorrect personal data corrected or erased

A data subject can apply for a court order requiring that incorrect personal data should be erased or corrected. Only matters of fact can be regarded as incorrect. Opinions cannot therefore be incorrect. However, the court can order the erasure or correction of an opinion if it was based on inaccurate facts.

Complaint to the Registrar

An individual who feels that any of the data principles or any provisions of the Act have been breached may complain to the Registrar. As long as the complaint has some substance the Registrar must pursue it. The Registrar usually aims for an agreed solution. His powers to prosecute for offences committed under the Act can be useful in securing such a solution. In addition to the power to prosecute, the Registrar can issue three types of notice:

(a) An **enforcement notice** directs a registered person to take specific steps to comply with the eight principles.
(b) A **de-registration notice** removes from the register all or part of any entry.
(c) A **transfer prohibition notice** prohibits the transfer of personal data overseas.

The Registrar must notify the complainant of any action he proposes to take, and the result of it.

The exemptions

The following categories of data are not required to be registered under the 1984 Act:

(a) Personal data held by an individual for personal, family or recreational affairs.
(b) Personal data used only for calculating wages and pensions, keeping accounts, or keeping records relating to the payment of purchases and sales.
(c) Personal data of members in members' clubs, if the member in question consents.
(d) Personal data which the law requires to be made public or which is exempt on the grounds of national security.

ACTIVITY QUESTION 8.2

Which of the following would be regarded as personal data under the Data Protection Act?
(a) An unauthorised biographer's word-processed notes on his deceased subject.
(b) An unauthorised biographer's hand-written notes on a living subject.
(c) A company's computerised personnel records.
(d) A library's computerised file on library users. The file shows which books are currently on loan.

Further activity question 8.2

Which one or more of the data protection principles would be broken in the following cases?
(a) An employer refuses to let employees see their computerised personnel records.
(b) An employer allows a private detective to copy employees' personnel records onto his own computer disk.
(c) A department store's computerised record of customers' accounts is used in a mail-shot which tries to sell a new product.
(d) The information on census forms is transferred onto a computer and then sold to a marketing agency.
(e) A credit agency's computerised file shows that Mr Smith, identified by his credit reference number, has defaulted on a loan. In fact, the credit reference number is incorrect, and Mr Smith has never defaulted.

Statutory control of business: environmental responsibility

In recent years an enormous number of statutes have imposed environmental controls on business. There are far too many of these statutes for us to be able to examine them in detail.

The major pieces of legislation are the Environmental Protection Act 1990, and the Water Resources Act 1991. The Environmental Protection Act made such radical changes that it has had to be phased in gradually. Some parts of the Act are still not in force.

Statutory control of the environment is enforced by specialist environmental protection agencies, such as the Department of the Environment, Her Majesty's

Inspectorate of Pollution, the National Rivers Authority and Local Authorities. The Government envisages that eventually one body, the Environment Agency, will take over the various functions of the other agencies.

Most of the statutes concerned impose strict liability on the business. The attitude of the courts can be seen from the leading case:

Alphacell Ltd v *Woodward* (1972, House of Lords)

A company's settling tanks overflowed into a river. The company was found guilty of causing a polluted substance to enter the river, contrary to the River (Prevention of Pollution) Act 1951, even though it had not been negligent and did not know that the pollution had taken place. In the case Lord Pearson said: '*Mens rea is generally not an ingredient in an offence of this kind which is in the nature of a public nuisance.*'

Further activity questions 8.3

1 Why are the laws on environmental pollution not stricter? Are they strict enough? What would be the consequences of insisting that all businesses were completely clean, quiet and safe? How would such rules affect businesses in your area?

2 In the American case on page 177, where the fast food manufacturer had to pay $2.7 million for serving its coffee too hot, it is easy to spot the winners – not only the lady who was burnt by the coffee, but also her lawyer, who would take a large percentage of the winnings. The loser looks like the fast food chain. But ultimately who pays for decisions such as this? In what ways does this make American society different? Which system is preferable?

3 Was it fair to convict Alphacell Ltd even though they had not been negligent and were ignorant that they had caused the pollution? In what way might the conviction adversely affect Alphacell?

TASK 8

1 Try to think of ways in which local businesses might commit the following torts:

(a) Negligence.
(b) Private nuisance.
(c) Public nuisance.
(d) Occupiers' liability.
(e) Strict liability.
(f) Trespass to land.
(g) Trespass to the person.
(h) Trespass to goods.
(i) Defamation.

For example, you might decide that a local supermarket could commit trespass to the person by wrongly arresting a suspected shoplifter. Try and think of realistic examples of all the other torts.

Write a report, indicating the ways in which your college could commit the torts and what steps they might take to ensure that they do not incur liability.

2 Write a report for your college management, indicating:

(a) what steps they must take to ensure that their computerised records comply with the requirements of the Data Protection Act, and
(b) the consequences which could follow from failure to comply with the Act.

9 Legal responsibility to providers of finance

Most businesses rely on outsiders to provide some of their finance. Subject to the controls of the Consumer Credit Act, which are considered later in this chapter, the providers of finance can lend the money on any terms which they see fit. If the business wants the loan it must agree to these terms. This matter, and the types of security generally required, were considered in Chapter 4. Here we need to examine the special position of companies.

Companies: shareholders and providers of finance

Shareholders have a stake in the company, and in effect they own the company. They do not own the company's assets; these are owned by the company itself. However, all shares carry rights, and if there are surplus assets after dissolution of the company these assets will be owned by some or all of the shareholders.

We cannot say that **all** shareholders will have a right to the assets on dissolution, because a company can allow for different classes of shares, each class having its own rights.

For example, article 2 of Table A provides:

'Subject to the provisions of the Act and without prejudice to any rights attached to existing shares, any shares may be issued with such rights or restrictions as the company may by ordinary resolution determine.'

Under an article such as this it would be possible to create a class of shares which did not have a right to vote at company meetings, or which did not have any right of ownership in the company's assets on dissolution.

Types of shares

The most common classification is into ordinary shares and preference shares.

Preference shares

The articles and memorandum will define the precise rights attaching to preference shares, and obviously these rights will vary from company to company. Generally the rights of preference shares will be as follows.

Preference shareholders, like ordinary shareholders, have **no right to a dividend** every year. However, if preference shares are not paid a dividend in one year they carry a **cumulative** right to a dividend the following year. This means that the preference share dividend which was not paid in the previous year must be paid before any dividend is paid on ordinary shares.

Preference shares are usually paid a **rate of interest per annum** as a dividend. For example, the articles might stipulate that preference shares carried a dividend of 12 per cent per annum.

Preference shares will carry the **same voting rights** as other shares. (However, articles commonly provide that preference shares do not carry a vote, except when their dividend is in arrears or when the motion proposes to alter their special rights.)

On dissolution the preference shareholders usually have the right to have their shares **repaid in full before the ordinary shares** are repaid at all.

If, after winding up, there is a surplus of assets this will be divided among the shareholders. Whether or not the preference shareholders are entitled to participate in this division will depend on what the articles say.

Ordinary shares

Dividends on ordinary shares are not expressed as an annual percentage, but are **dependent on the profits** available for distribution. Dividends can only be paid out of profits, but shareholders have no right to a dividend even if a profit is made. The directors might decide to reinvest the money in the company rather than declare a dividend. However, if a majority of shareholders disapproved of this they could pass a resolution to remove the directors.

Ordinary shares usually carry **full rights to vote** at any company meeting. However, it is possible that a company will have more than one type of ordinary share and that the different types will carry different voting rights. In *Holt* v *Holt* (1991), for example, the class A ordinary shares carried 10,000 votes per share, whereas the class B ordinary shares carried only one vote per share.

Varying the class rights of shares

If a company's shares are divided into classes (for example, preference shares and ordinary shares, or ordinary class A and ordinary class B) the company might want to alter the rights attached to one class or other.

Section 125 of the Companies Act 1985 does allow for such a variation. It also states that if the procedure for varying class rights is contained in the memorandum or articles then this procedure must be followed. (For most alterations 75 per cent of the class of shareholders whose rights are being altered must agree.)

Section 127 allows holders of at least 15 per cent of the type of shares affected to apply to the court to have the alteration cancelled. They must not have voted for the alteration and must apply within 21 days of the vote.

Other types of shares

Employee shares

Section 743 of the 1985 Act defines these as shares created for the benefit of employees of the company or their close relatives.

The Government encourages the issue of such shares. It is thought that allowing employees to share in the profits which they help to create motivates the workforce and harmonises employer/employee relations.

Rights issues

Section 89 of the 1985 Act provides that if a company offers ordinary shares for sale it must first offer them to the members in proportion to their existing shareholding. Such an issue of shares is called a rights issue. (Private companies may exclude this section in their memorandum or articles, public companies may not.)

Like other share issues, rights issues are primarily a means of raising capital. In the past a rights issue was often seen as a sign of financial trouble. Shareholders were in effect told that if they did not put more money into the company they would lose everything when it went into liquidation. But in recent years many PLCs have offered rights issues as a means of rewarding shareholders. The new shares are often offered at a substantial discount on the market price.

Bonus issues

Here the company uses its reserves to pay for new shares and then issues these to members in proportion to their existing shareholding.

Redeemable shares

These shares are issued with a redemption date. On that date the company must buy the shares back. They are useful, therefore, when a company needs a short-term injection of capital.

Debentures

It is possible that the members of a company will contribute all the capital which the company needs. However, most companies also borrow money, either as a loan or by buying goods on credit. Providers of either type of credit are likely to want security for the money they are owed. If the security is given by the company, rather than by the directors or shareholders, it is known as a debenture.

The Companies Acts have never defined a debenture. The following definition, made by Chitty J in *Levy* v *Abercorris Slate and Slab Co* (1887), is widely accepted:

> *'In my opinion a debenture means a document which either creates a debt or acknowledges it, and any document which fulfils either of these functions is a debenture.'*

The person who lends the money will want his debenture to be backed up by security. The company can give this security by granting a charge, a mortgage, over some or all of its assets. If the debt is not repaid the lender will be able to sell the mortgaged assets and take what is owed. Companies can give two types of charges: fixed charges and floating charges.

Fixed charges

As security a company may grant a fixed charge on certain assets. In effect this means that it mortgages those assets to the creditor (the debentureholder). Consequently, the company will not be able to dispose of the property charged without the permission of the debentureholder.

For example, A Co Ltd wants to borrow £10,000 from the bank. The bank lends the money but takes a fixed charge on the company's three delivery vans. As long as the company is repaying the loan as agreed it will retain possession of the vans and can use them in the ordinary way. The company cannot sell the vans though without the bank's permission. Furthermore, if the company fails to repay the debt the bank can sell the vans, deduct what it is owed, and hand over any remainder to the company.

All charges must be registered with the company and with the Registrar of Companies. If a charge is not registered it will be invalid. However, the debentureholder will still be able to sue as an unsecured creditor.

Floating charges

A company may grant more than one fixed charge on any particular asset. Let us assume that a few years ago B Co Ltd borrowed £40,000 from the bank and granted a fixed charge over the company factory, currently worth £200,000. If the company now wanted to borrow a further £20,000 from a different creditor then that creditor would be quite happy to register a second fixed charge on the company factory. If the company does not repay its debts then the factory could be sold by the creditors. The bank would always be entitled to its £40,000 first because it was the first charge registered. But the sale of the factory would easily realise enough to repay the second chargeholder.

If, however, there were no assets on which a fixed charge could be secured the creditor might be prepared to accept a floating charge. This means that the creditor would take some or all of the company's property, both present and future, as security.

A floating charge does not prevent the company from selling the assets over which it is granted. It is particularly useful then when a company has a good deal of money tied up in raw materials, stock in trade or book debts.

Example   Let us assume that C Co Ltd, which manufactures computers, has already granted a fixed charge over all those assets which it does not need to sell – assets such as its factory and its company cars. Let us further assume that the company has a warehouse stocked with computers ready for sale, that it is owed money by various creditors and that it has a large stock of materials from which it makes the computers. None of these remaining assets could be the subject of a fixed charge without crippling the company's activities. The company would not be able to sell the computers already manufactured, or work the raw materials into computers, without the permission of the fixed chargeholder. If such permission was granted the chargeholders would then lose their security.

But the finished computers, the money owed and the raw materials are worth a great deal. A creditor might well therefore take a floating charge over these assets, happy in the knowledge that if the company did not repay him he could recoup his loan by calling in the charge, selling the assets charged, and deducting what he was owed from the proceeds.

The contract which created the floating charge would state that the company would use the assets charged only in its normal course of business, and that the company would not grant a fixed charge over any such assets.

A floating charge does not provide the cast-iron security of a fixed charge. It is up to the creditor to ensure that it provides adequate security for the loan.

Crystallisation

A company can continue to sell assets over which a floating charge has been granted, up until the time of 'crystallisation'. So in the example just considered, C Co Ltd could still sell the finished computers even though they were the subject of a floating charge. But when crystallisation occurs the floating charge will become a fixed charge attaching to the assets of the company at that time. This, of course, will mean that the company is no longer free to dispose of the assets.

Crystallisation occurs automatically:

(a) When a receiver is appointed.
(b) When the company goes into liquidation.
(c) When the company ceases to carry on business.
(d) On the occurrence of an event which the contract stipulated would lead to automatic crystallisation. (The contract would have been made when the charge was created. It might, for example, state that if the company created another charge over the same class of assets then the first charge should crystallise.)

Crystallisation may also occur when the debentureholder gives notice that he is converting the floating charge into a fixed charge. (This can be done only if the contract which created the charge allows for it.)

ACTIVITY QUESTIONS 9.1

1 A large bicycle manufacturing company wants to borrow money. To do this it will need to issue debentures.
   (a) Over what types of assets might it issue a fixed charge?

(b) Over what type of assets might it issue a floating charge?

(c) Which type of charge would give the lender the greater security?

(d) What precautions should be taken by (i) the manufacturer and (ii) the lender?

2 A friend of yours runs a small company and is in need of capital. The company is prepared to raise the capital by issuing ordinary shares, preference shares or debentures. In which way would you be most willing to contribute if:

(a) You were sure that the company would prove to be extremely successful?

(b) You thought that the company might face severe difficulties?

Further activity questions 9.1

1 Complete the following table to show the rights which usually attach to shares and debentures.

The rights of shareholders and debentureholders

	Ordinary shareholders	Preference shareholders	Debenture-holders
On dissolution, do they own the company's surplus assets? (Yes/No/Maybe)			
Entitled to vote at company meetings? (Yes/No/Maybe)			
Are they paid interest? (Yes/No)			
Relative priority on dissolution (Paid 1st/2nd/3rd)			

2 Compare the rights of ordinary shareholders, preference shareholders and debentureholders. Are preference shares more similar to ordinary shares or to debentures?

Types of credit transactions

Credit is an everyday fact of commercial life. It is not usual for commercial organisations to pay cash, or to pay in advance, when making a business deal. Whenever payment is deferred some sort of credit will have been provided. The principal methods of supplying credit are considered below.

Loans

A loan is the most fundamental form of credit. If a loan is made a creditor lends money to a debtor so that the debtor can buy goods or services. The debtor agrees to repay the money, with interest, over a period of time.

The creditor is usually not connected with the transaction he is financing. A bank, for example, may lend money to enable a business to buy new machinery. The contract between the business and the supplier of the machinery is nothing to do with the bank. The bank merely lends the money. Creditors are, however, likely to want **security** for the money they lend.

If the debtor is a company the creditor will probably register a **charge** over the company's assets, as explained earlier in this chapter. If the debtor is a partnership or a sole trader the creditor may take a **mortgage** of property. The property mortgaged does not need to be business property; it might well be the house of the sole trader or of one of the partners. If the loan is not repaid the creditor will be able to repossess the property (sell it and take the amount still owed).

Alternatively the creditor may be willing to accept a **third party guarantee** of the loan. The guarantor would then be liable to repay the loan if the debtor defaulted.

Security for a loan is not always necessary. Sometimes a bank will allow an **overdraft** without requiring security. An overdraft is a form of loan whereby customers can overdraw their bank accounts (take more money out of the account than has been deposited into it) on the understanding that money will be deposited later. There will be a limit above which the customer may not overdraw.

The rate of interest on an overdraft is usually higher than on a bank loan. However, the customer can clear his overdraft as soon as he wishes, and if the account is overdrawn for only a short time he might not pay much interest.

Large overdrafts are a risky way for a small business to borrow money as the bank can insist that they be repaid at any time.

The Consumer Credit Act 1974, which is considered later in this chapter, does apply to loans.

Hire purchase

Under a hire-purchase agreement a creditor hires goods for a fixed period, with an option to buy the goods for a nominal sum at the end of that period. This can be demonstrated by considering the case of a motorist who is acquiring a car on hire purchase by making 36 monthly instalments of £250 each. For the first 35 months the motorist is paying the money to hire the car, which remains the seller's property. With the thirty-sixth payment the motorist buys the car, which then becomes his property. At no stage does the motorist make a commitment to continue with the agreement for the full 36 months.

Usually a third party finances the deal, although the customer might not be aware of this. If the finance is provided by a third party, the hire-purchase agreement takes the form of a triangular transaction as shown in Fig 9.1:

(a) The dealer sells the goods to the finance company.
(b) The finance company makes the hire-purchase agreement with the customer.
(c) There may be a collateral contract between the dealer and the customer. (The meaning of this is considered shortly.)

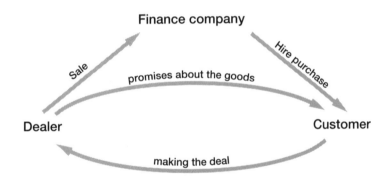

Fig 9.1 Hire-purchase agreement: triangular transaction

Hire purchase presents difficulties when the goods do not match the description given to them by the dealer. It would seem that the customer has no rights. His contract was not with the dealer but with the finance company (who did not apply the description). However, two forms of help are offered to the customer. First, as long as the hire-purchase agreement is a **regulated agreement**, the Consumer Credit Act 1974 will make the dealer the **agent** of the finance company.

An agreement will be a regulated one if two conditions are met:

(a) The customer is **not a company**.
and
(b) The **credit is for less than £15,000**.

As we shall see later in this chapter, if the finance company is made the agent of the dealer it will be equally responsible for any misrepresentation or breach of contract by the dealer.

Second, the courts might be willing to find a **collateral contract** between the dealer and the customer. The following case shows an example of a collateral contract in a triangular transaction:

Andrews v *Hopkinson* (1957)

The plaintiff visited a motor dealer to look at second-hand cars. He took a vehicle on hire purchase, through a finance company, because the dealer told him, 'It's a good little bus. I would stake my life on it. You will have no trouble with it'. In fact the vehicle had defective steering. This caused an accident in which the plaintiff was badly injured. As this case pre-dated the Consumer Credit Act 1974 the plaintiff seemed to have no remedy. (The finance company was not liable for the dealer's statements, and there appeared to be no contract between the dealer and the customer.)

Held The dealer was liable on the collateral contract which he made with the plaintiff. This collateral contract was created when the plaintiff agreed to take the vehicle on hire purchase (thus benefiting the defendant) and the defendant promised that it was 'a good little bus' (thus benefiting the plaintiff).

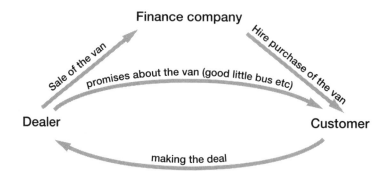

Fig 9.2 *Andrews* v *Hopkinson*: collateral contract

To some extent collateral contracts are a fiction, invented by the court to do justice in a particular case. However, they can be useful when no other remedy is available. Since the Consumer Credit Act 1974 came into force the court will need to find a collateral contract only if the hire-purchase agreement is not regulated by the Act. (Because the customer is a company, or the credit is over £15,000.)

The Consumer Credit Act applies to hire-purchase agreements. The Sale of

Goods Act 1979 will not apply until the goods are finally purchased, by which time it will be too late to have much effect. However, the Supply of Goods (Implied Terms) Act 1973, as amended by the Consumer Credit Act 1974, implies terms very similar to those which the Sale of Goods Act implies into contracts for the sale of goods. (See the table on page 169.)

Conditional sales

A conditional sale is a sale in which ownership of the goods stays with the seller until the buyer has paid the full price for the goods. The buyer usually takes immediate possession of the goods. For example, a garage might make a conditional sale of a delivery van to a florist. The terms of the contract might provide that the florist is to pay for the van in 36 monthly instalments. The florist will take immediate possession of the van, but the van will remain the property of the garage until all the instalments have been paid.

Where the goods are to be paid for by instalments a conditional sale is very similar to hire purchase (except that in hire purchase the buyer does not commit himself to completing the payments).

One important difference between a conditional sale and hire purchase is that the Sale of Goods Act 1979 applies **immediately** in the case of a conditional sale. The Act will not apply to hire purchase until the sale is actually made with payment of the final instalment.

The Consumer Credit Act 1974 does apply to conditional sales.

Credit sales

Under a credit sale ownership of the goods passes to the buyer immediately, and the seller extends credit to the buyer. For example, a mail order catalogue firm might sell a coat to a customer under a credit sale. The coat becomes the customer's property as soon as the sale is made. The mail order firm gives the customer credit, and the customer is obliged to pay the price of the coat under the credit terms specified in the contract.

Credit sales are commonly used where the goods supplied have a low second-hand value, there being no point in the seller retaining ownership if the goods are worth very little.

Both the Sale of Goods Act 1979 and the Consumer Credit Act 1974 will apply to credit sales.

Hire and rental agreements

A person who rents goods gives possession of the goods in return for regular payments. He does not agree to sell the goods. Hire is very similar, but is usually for a longer period.

The Sale of Goods Act 1979 does not apply to rental agreements, but the Supply of Goods and Services Act 1982 does.

The Consumer Credit Act 1974 applies to both hire and rental agreements, although in fact no credit is supplied.

Pledge

Goods are pledged when possession of them is given to a lender as security for a loan. When the debtor repays the loan he is given the goods back. If the debtor does not repay the creditor can sell the goods.

Easily transportable goods of high value are suitable to pledge, often to a pawnbroker. For example, a person who wanted to borrow £100 might pledge a camera worth £1,000 to a pawnbroker. As long as the debtor repays the £100 with interest within a certain time the pawnbroker will return the camera. If the debtor does not repay the debt then eventually the pawnbroker will be able to sell the camera and take what he is owed from the proceeds.

Neither the Sale of Goods Act nor the Supply of Goods and Services Act applies to pledges, but the Consumer Credit Act does.

Trade credit

Immediate payment for goods is not the norm in commercial life. Just as the newsagent delivers newspapers before he is paid for them, so businesses informally accept deferred payment for goods and services which they supply. This is a form of credit, but for policy reasons the Consumer Credit Act 1974 does not apply to such transactions.

If the credit relates to a sale of goods then the Sale of Goods Act 1979 will apply. If it relates to the supply of a service then the Supply of Goods and Services Act 1982 will apply.

ACTIVITY QUESTION 9.2

In the transactions described below, company A has agreed to supply machinery to company B. The seven transactions described provide one example of each of the following types of credit: trade credit; a loan; hire purchase; a conditional sale; a contract of hire; a credit sale; and an overdraft. Match the transactions to the various types of credit. You might, for example, think that (a) was an example of a hire purchase.

(a) Company B takes possession of the machinery, but ownership is not to pass to company B until it has paid all 36 instalments of the price. At the outset company B commits itself to buying the machine and making all 36 payments.

(b) Company B hires the machinery and takes possession of it. If Company B continues to hire the machinery for the full 36 months, it is to be given an option to purchase the machinery for a nominal price. Company B does not commit itself to hiring for the full 36 months.

(c) Along with the machinery, company A sends an invoice which requests payment in full within 28 days.

(d) Company B has agreed to pay £1,000 a month for the use of the machinery until it has filled an order. After that the machinery will be returned to company A.

(e) Company B's bank has agreed that company B can pay for the machinery by writing a cheque for £10,000. The company bank balance stands at £2,300.

(f) Company B's bank has credited the company account with £10,000 so that the machinery can be bought. Company B is to repay this money by paying £560 a month for two years.

(g) Company B takes immediate possession of the machinery and gets immediate ownership of it. The contract of sale says that the price is to be paid by 12 monthly instalments of £1,000 each.

Further activity question 9.2

Complete the following table, indicating:

(a) Whether the creditor and the supplier are the same person.

(b) Whether the customer gets immediate ownership of the goods supplied.

(c) Which of the following statutes govern the transaction: Consumer Credit Act, Sale of Goods Act, Supply of Goods and Services Act, Supply of Goods (Implied Terms) Act.

To help you get started, some of the table has already been completed.

	Loan to buy goods	Goods on HP (triangular transaction)	Conditional sale of goods	Credit sale of goods	Hire/rent of goods	Trade credit for goods or services
Creditor and supplier of goods the same person?		*No*				
Does the customer get immediate ownership of the goods?	*Not applicable*			*Yes*		
Which statutes apply?			*SGA CCA*			*SGA (goods) SGSA (services)*

The Consumer Credit Act 1974

This landmark piece of legislation has created a framework for the control of credit and hire transactions. The Act exercises this control in two ways. First, it makes **general regulations**, which apply to all creditors. Second, it **regulates individual credit agreements**.

An outline of the Act's effect can be seen from Fig 9.3.

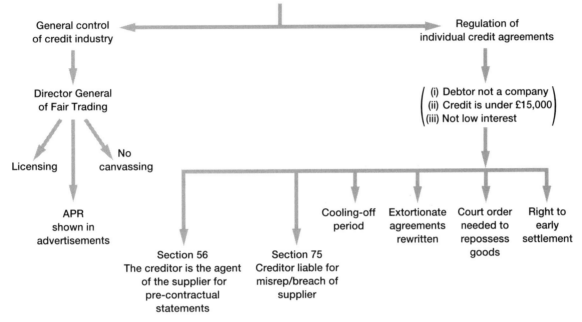

Fig 9.3 Effect of the Consumer Credit Act 1974

General control of the credit industry

The Director General of Fair Trading

The Director General of Fair Trading controls the credit industry through a system of licensing and supervision.

Almost all providers of credit need to hold a **licence**. Anyone providing credit without a licence will commit a criminal offence and will not be able to enforce his credit agreements without an order from the Director General.

Licences will not be granted to those with criminal offences relating to dishonesty, or to those who have traded unscrupulously.

The Director General of Fair Trading is not only in charge of licensing, he also keeps an eye on the whole credit industry.

Advertising and canvassing

The advertising of credit is strictly controlled under regulations passed by the Secretary of State. These regulations are complex and vary with different types of advertisements. One important requirement is that all advertisements clearly show the **APR** (the Annual Percentage Rate) of interest. This rate is calculated according to a strict formula.

By reference to the APR, a debtor can immediately see what the true rate of interest is. (Most creditors also include other rates of interest in their advertisements. It is interesting to notice the difference between these rates and the APR.)

Canvassing to take credit is outlawed. (A person is canvassed to take credit if he is approached to do so, without having asked to be approached, anywhere except the lender's place of business.)

The regulation of individual credit agreements

The Consumer Credit Act 1974 implies very important rules into **regulated credit agreements**. An agreement will be regulated if two conditions are satisfied:

(a) The debtor is not a company.
(b) The credit supplied (or the rent to be paid) is less than £15,000.

It is important to note that it is **the credit** which must be less than £15,000. The credit does not include any part of the price which was paid in cash. Nor does it include interest.

Example   A machine is sold for £5,000 down plus £20,000 payable over three years. £6,000 of the £20,000 is interest. This is still a regulated agreement. The credit is only £14,000 even though the total price is £25,000. (Cash £5,000, credit £14,000, interest £6,000.)

Mortgages to buy houses are not regulated agreements if the mortgage was given by a non profit-making organisation such as a building society, insurance company, local authority or charity. If the mortgage was provided by a bank the agreement will be a regulated one if the credit was less than £15,000.

Low interest agreements are also exempted. An agreement is a low interest agreement if the APR is either below 13 per cent or lower than 1 per cent above the current base rate (the rate of interest used by the High Street banks as a basis for their lending rates).

ACTIVITY QUESTION 9.3

Are the following regulated agreements?

(a) A company borrows £12,000 from its bank to buy a new computer system.

(b) Mrs Aziz buys a new car for £26,000. The car dealer allows Mrs Aziz £5,000 for her old car. Total interest to be paid, at an APR of 16 per cent, is £5,000.

(c) Miss Brown buys a house for £30,000. She paid £20,000 cash (with the proceeds of the sale of her old house). She took a mortgage of £10,000 from the bank where she works. The mortgage was granted at the special employees' rate of 6 per cent interest.

(d) A self-employed builder buys a new van on hire purchase. The builder traded in his old van and under the hire-purchase agreement has to pay £320 a month for 36 months. The APR is 18 per cent.

(e) Mr Benjamin borrows £1,000 from the bank, at 21 per cent APR, to pay for an exotic holiday.

Protection given under a regulated agreement

Dealer is agent of the creditor

As we saw when we considered *Andrews* v *Hopkinson*, there are often three parties involved in a credit transaction. Particularly in contracts of hire purchase, it is common for the dealer in the goods to arrange a triangular transaction involving a finance company. (See Fig 9.1 on page 203.)

In such a triangular transaction the customer makes the credit agreement with the finance company and not with the dealer. Before the Consumer Credit Act 1974, unless a collateral contract could be implied, the customer had no remedy in respect of false claims which the dealer made about the goods.

Section 56 of the 1974 Act now gives the customer statutory protection. It provides that if the supplier of goods makes any claims before the contract is made then he makes these as **agent** of the creditor who finances the transaction. This liability applies to **terms and representations** and cannot be excluded.

The effect of section 56 can be demonstrated by considering how it would apply to *Andrews* v *Hopkinson*. It will be remembered that in that case the dealer said that the van was 'a good little bus,' but that the customer made the deal with the finance company who made no claims about the van. Section 56 would make the dealer the agent of the finance company as regards claims made about the van. Therefore, the finance company would be as liable as if it had made the claim itself.

If the agreement was not a regulated one (because the credit was over £15,000 or the creditor was a company) then section 56 would not apply. However, a court might still find a collateral contract, as it did in *Andrews* v *Hopkinson*.

Creditor responsible for dealer's misrepresentations and breaches of contract

Section 75 of the Act protects a customer who uses credit supplied by a third party. It provides that the creditor is liable for any misrepresentation or breach of contract made by the dealer if:

(a) the contract was a commercial transaction relating to the supply of a single item with a cash price between £100 and £30,000; and
(b) the credit is given either under a credit card or under an arrangement between the dealer and the creditor.

This section is particularly useful when the supplier has become insolvent before the contract has been performed. When Laker Airways went into liquidation customers who had paid cash for their tickets were left with no remedy. Those who had paid any amount of the ticket price with their credit cards could sue the credit card companies for the whole of their ticket price.

Notice that section 75 will apply only if the cash price of **any single item** was more than £100. If a customer bought five different items, at £90 each from the same supplier, the provider of credit would not assume any liability under section 75. But if the cash price of any single item is between £100 and £30,000 then the creditor is fully liable in respect of that particular item, no matter how small the credit advanced.

Notice also that section 75 does not apply where the customer has arranged his own credit in advance. It would apply to purchase with a credit card but would not apply where a customer overdraws his bank account, or took out a bank loan, to make the purchase.

Cooling-off period

A debtor who signs a regulated agreement anywhere other than at the creditor's place of business is given a cooling-off period by sections 67–74 of the Act. During this period the debtor can cancel the whole deal, giving back what he gained and escaping from all liability. For example, if a salesman calls at Mrs Benjamin's house and persuades her to make a credit deal to have the house double-glazed then she has the right to cancel the agreement. But if Mrs Benjamin had made the deal at the double-glazing firm's place of business then she would not have such a right.

This cooling-off period lasts for five days after the customer received his second copy of the credit agreement. (This second copy must be delivered to the customer within seven days of his making the deal.)

Early settlement

Section 97 of the 1974 Act gives the debtor a right to require the creditor to say how much would have to be paid to clear the debt.

Section 94 gives the debtor a right to clear the debt at any time (and therefore save on future interest payments). This right cannot be excluded.

Repossession of the goods

We have seen that in hire-purchase contracts and conditional sales ownership remains with the seller until all the instalments have been paid. If the debtor breaks his contract then the seller will want to repossess the goods.

Section 90 of the Act requires the seller to get a court order to repossess if the buyer has paid at least one-third of the total purchase price of the goods.

Extortionate terms

Sections 137–40 give the court the power to rewrite credit agreements which they consider to be grossly extortionate. Generally it will be an exceptionally high rate of interest which will make a credit agreement extortionate. If the court does rewrite such an agreement it will usually do no more than substitute a lower rate of interest.

Effectiveness of the Act

We have seen that the Consumer Credit Act 1974 confers very real advantages on debtors who make regulated agreements. Furthermore, there is no doubt that the courts are willing to apply the Act when asked to do so. However, it appears that many poorer debtors remain ignorant of their rights.

A report of the Policies Studies Institute, 'Moneylenders and their Customers', published in December 1994, found that there were 1,200 licensed credit firms, employing 27,000 house-to-house collectors. The APR in the credit agreements ranged from 105 per cent to 481 per cent. Not surprisingly, the report concluded that most customers paid little attention to the APR, even though this had to be disclosed in contracts. Instead the customers were concerned about the amount borrowed, the amount charged, and the amount which had to be repaid each week. Many customers said they liked the discipline of making a weekly payment.

It would seem that the Consumer Credit Act 1974 could help many of these debtors, but only if they are aware of the rights which the Act confers and willing to enforce those rights.

ACTIVITY QUESTION 9.4

How can the Consumer Credit Act 1974 help the following creditors?

(a) Shabana used her credit card to buy a carpet for £400 and a bedside lamp for £22. The purchase price of both items was deducted from her account. The store from which she bought went into liquidation before the goods were delivered.

(b) Bill has a number of credit arrangements. He is buying his furniture on hire purchase (APR 24 per cent), he is paying for his double-glazing over three years (APR 22 per cent) and has an overdraft (APR 18 per cent). Recently Bill inherited £10,000. He has invested this sum in a building society, but the rate of interest he receives on his building society account is only 6 per cent.

Further activity question 9.4

How can the Consumer Credit Act 1974 help the following creditors?

(a) Last year Cheryl had her house double-glazed and a conservatory built. She is paying the price of £3,500 by instalments over three years. The APR is 17 per cent. She is disappointed to find that the double-glazing is not nearly as effective as the salesman claimed. She contacted the double-glazing firm who told her that they have no liability for their salesmen's statements. They also point out that they don't even have a contract with Cheryl. A triangular transaction was arranged and Cheryl in fact bought the double-glazing from a finance company. The finance company say that they cannot be responsible for claims made by the salesmen of another company.

(b) David, an elderly gentleman, sometimes gets confused. It seems that yester-day a salesman arrived, uninvited, at David's home and that David agreed to have stone cladding put on his Mock Tudor house. The cost was to be £2,000, spread over two years. The APR is 15 per cent. David now realises that the stone cladding would spoil the appearance of his house. He is considering ringing the cladding firm up to say that he will pay the £2,000 but does not want the cladding.

TASK 9

A private language college operates as a company limited by shares. All of the shares are owned by the four founders of the college. The college wants to expand, in particular to acquire a new building and to have the use of 20 new computers.

Write a report for the college management, indicating:

a) How the college might get the money to buy the new building. This part of the report should explain the rights of the lenders and the matters they are likely to consider before lending the money.

b) The various ways in which the computers might be acquired without paying the full price immediately. The rights of providers of finance should be explained.

10 Legal responsibility to employees

The interrelationship between employer and employee

The relationship between employer and employee is a contractual one. As we have already seen, contracts are made by the process of offer and acceptance. This is as true of employment contracts as it is of other contracts. One party, usually the employer, offers a set of terms and the other party accepts.

However, the common law and various Acts of Parliament impose duties on both employers and employees. These duties cannot be bypassed by the contract of employment.

The basic principles of employment law are covered in Mandatory Unit 4. In this chapter we expand upon these principles.

How employment law has developed

In the nineteenth century contracts of employment were regarded in much the same way as any other contracts. The judges believed in the notion of **freedom of contract**, which held that sane adults were free to make any contracts they wished. As Dickens and other writers illustrated, employers were in a position ruthlessly to exploit their employees. Indeed, many employers saw their workers as just another raw material to be exploited to the fullest possible extent. In the days before the welfare state, workers were faced with the choice of finding an employer, no matter how bad his terms, or going to the workhouse. Their freedom to make such contracts of employment as they wished was largely illusory.

Throughout most of this century employees have become increasingly protected. This protection was given by the courts, which implied terms into contracts of employment, and by statutes which laid down minimum standards of employer behaviour.

Terms implied by the courts

Over the years the courts have developed certain terms which they will automatically imply into contracts of employment. Some of these terms impose duties on the employer, some on the employee. It is however beyond the scope of this book to consider the large number of cases which created these implied terms.

Duties imposed on the employer

(a) To pay the amount agreed.
(b) To treat employees with respect and trust.
(c) To meet safety requirements.
(d) To give employees time off for public duties (such as being a magistrate).
(e) To indemnify employees for expenses incurred in performing their work.

Duties imposed on employees

(a) To be ready and willing to work.
(b) To use reasonable care and skill.
(c) To obey lawful orders.
(d) To look after the employer's property.
(e) To act in good faith.

Statutory intervention

Written particulars

A contract of employment is made in the same way as any other contract. One party makes an offer and the other party accepts. There is no need for either the offer or the acceptance to be in writing.

However, the Employment Protection (Consolidation) Act (EPCA) 1978 requires the employer to give the employee written particulars of the terms of his contract within two months of the commencement of the employment. These written particulars must state the following details:

(a) The parties' names.

(b) The date when the employment commenced.

(c) Whether any employment with a previous employer is to count as continuous employment.

(d) The rate of pay and how it is calculated.

(e) The terms and conditions covering hours of work, holidays, sick pay and pension schemes.

(f) The amount of notice either side must give to end the employment.

(g) The job title.

(h) Any disciplinary rules which apply to the employee.

(i) Whether the employment is contracted out of the state pension scheme.

It is important to realise that these written particulars do not create the contract of employment. The contract will have been created when one party accepted the other's offer, and this will usually have been before the statement of written particulars is issued.

The written particulars do, however, provide very strong evidence of what the terms of the contract are. Furthermore, if the employer states that the particulars are the terms of the contract, and the employee accepts this, then they will become the terms of the contract, even if they differ from what was originally agreed. (A new contract will have been formed; the employer made a new offer and the employee accepted it.)

Discrimination

The Equal Pay Act 1970

This Act deals with all matters **governed by the contract of employment** (such as rates of pay and conditions at work), whereas the Sex Discrimination Act 1975 (see below) deals with matters **outside the contract of employment** (such as refusing to employ a person in the first place).

The Equal Pay Act 1970 is not therefore confined to pay alone. It also covers matters such as sick pay, mortgage schemes, rent allowances, and indeed any other matter governed by the contract of employment.

The Act requires that if a woman does 'like work' or 'work rated as equivalent' to that of a man in the same employment then her conditions of service should be no less favourable than those of the man.

Work rated as equivalent means that a properly conducted job evaluation scheme has found the work to be equivalent. **Like work** means that the work is broadly similar. It does not need to be identical.

Capper Pass Ltd **v** *Lawton* (1976)

A woman who cooked 10–20 lunches for directors wished to be compared to two male assistant chefs who cooked 350 lunches for the workforce. The directors ate in one sitting, whereas the assistants had to prepare six sittings a day, two at breakfast, two at lunch, and two at tea. The woman worked 40 hours a week, the two assistants worked 45 and were supervised by a head chef.

Held The work was broadly similar and so the woman was entitled to the same rate of pay as the men.

It should be noted that Article 119 of the Treaty of Rome says that EC members must '. . . *ensure and subsequently maintain the application of the principle that men and women should receive equal pay for equal work*'. This article makes disputes about equal pay 'European cases' and means that the final court of appeal in such cases is no longer the House of Lords but the European Court.

Remedies under the Act

The complainant takes the case to an industrial tribunal. If the tribunal upholds the complaint it can award damages and arrears of pay, which may be backdated for up to two years.

The Sex Discrimination Acts 1975 and 1986

The original Sex Discrimination Act, the 1975 Act, is concerned with discrimination on the grounds of a person's sex or marital status. It is still in force and made three types of discrimination unlawful:

(a) **Direct discrimination**. This arises where a person is refused a job because of his or her sex. For example, in *Batisha* v *Say* (1977) a woman was refused a job as a cave guide because 'it is a man's job'.

(b) **Indirect discrimination**. This arises where a condition which can be fulfilled by one sex only is imposed. For example, an advertisement for a bus driver which stated 'must be a keen amateur boxer,' would amount to indirect discrimination.

(c) **Victimisation**. A person must not be treated less favourably than other employees as a result of having brought proceedings under the Equal Pay Act or the Sex Discrimination Acts.

Methods of discrimination

The Sex Discrimination Act 1975 mentions five types of discriminatory acts:

(a) **Making discriminatory arrangements for the purpose of determining who shall be employed**. This would include asking questions of the women which were not asked of the men. Questions such as, 'what arrangements have you made in the event of your having children?' could be discriminatory, although not all such questions are.

(b) **Offering discriminatory terms of employment**. The Equal Pay Act 1970 deals with the terms of the employment themselves. The Sex Discrimination Act 1975 deals with **offering** inferior terms on the grounds of a person's sex. For example, if a woman finds that she is paid less than the men with whom she does like work she could sue under the Equal Pay Act 1970. A new female employee who is **offered** the job at a lower rate than the men's could sue under the Sex Discrimination Act 1975.

(c) **Refusing or deliberately omitting to offer employment because of a person's sex**. It should be noted that this statute can apply to men just as much as to women. In *Munro* v *Allied Suppliers* (1977), for example, it was held to be discrimination when a man was not taken on as a cook because the female employees said that they would not work with him.

(d) **Offering better access to promotion, training, transfer, or any other benefit, facilities or services**.

Peake v Automotive Products (1977 Court of Appeal)

Automotive Products employed 3,500 men and 400 women in their factory. Men and women were paid the same. Both sexes finished their work at 4.25 pm, but the women were allowed to leave immediately, whereas the men could not leave before 4.30. This was a tradition of 30 years standing, and was designed to avoid a crush at the factory gates. A male factory worker complained.

Held This was not discrimination. Lord Denning said the Act was not meant to obliterate all the chivalry and courtesy which men might be expected to show women.

(e) **Dismissing a person or subjecting him to any other detriment.**

Maclean v Paris Travel (1976)

A company did not employ married couples. A female employee was sacked when she announced that she intended to marry the assistant manager.

Held This was discrimination.

Exceptions

The Acts do not apply to:

(a) work done wholly or mainly outside the UK;

(b) jobs performed in private households, if these need to be done by a man because of the closeness of contact with the person living in the house.

Permissible discriminations

The Sex Discrimination Acts do allow for certain permissible discriminations. It is possible to discriminate in favour of one or other sex if this is necessary for one of seven reasons:

(a) The need to preserve decency.

(b) The essential nature of the job calls for authentic male or female characteristics (excluding physical strength and stamina).

(c) The job is a live-in job where the employer cannot reasonably provide facilities for both sexes.

(d) The nature of the establishment where the work is done requires that one sex or other is employed. For example, certain jobs in prisons and hospitals need to be performed by men, and others need to be performed by women.

(e) The job is a social work job providing personal services, the nature of which requires that it is held by a person of a particular sex.

(f) The job involves going to countries which might object to the employee's sex.

(g) The job is one of two held by a married couple.

Enforcement of the Act

A person with a complaint under either statute makes the complaint to an **industrial tribunal** within three months of the act complained of. First a conciliation officer will try to resolve the dispute. Only if the parties cannot agree to a settlement will a tribunal hear the case. If the tribunal finds that the complaint was justified it can give three types of remedy:

(a) **Declare a violation of the complainant's rights**. Here the tribunal would merely declare that there has been discrimination and that this has violated the complainant's rights.

(b) **Award compensation**. The industrial tribunal can award damages to compensate the complainant for losses suffered as a result of the discrimination.

(c) **Order the employer not to discriminate in the same way in the future**. If the employer does not comply with such an order, damages already awarded may be increased.

The Race Relations Act 1976

The Race Relations Act 1976, which modelled itself on the Sex Discrimination Act 1975, outlawed three types of racial discrimination:

(a) **Direct discrimination**. A person is directly discriminated against if he is treated less favourably than another person would be treated on the grounds of his race.

Owen and Briggs v *James* (1982)

In response to an advertisement in the *Huddersfield Daily Examiner*, a black woman applied for a job as a typist. She was not employed. Later she saw another advertisement worded slightly differently. She applied again, not realising that the advertisement was for the same job. Again she was refused and the employer told her not to come back. Later the same day the employer took on a white woman. The white woman could only do 35 words per minute shorthand; the black woman could do 80.

Held This was direct discrimination.

(b) **Indirect discrimination**. Indirect discrimination occurs when a person is unjustifiably asked to comply with a requirement which persons of his race would find harder to fulfil than would others.

 Hussein v Saints Complete House Furnishers (1979)

A small firm of household furnishers was in the habit of taking on employees through the City Careers Service. They asked for a new employee, but stated that they would not interview applicants from Liverpool City Centre because if they did employ such people their unemployed friends hung around the shop. Fifty per cent of Liverpool City Centre residents are black, compared with 2 per cent of other Liverpool residents.

Held This was indirect discrimination.

(c) **Victimisation**. A person cannot be treated less favourably than other employees as a result of his having taken any action under the Act.

Type of discrimination outlawed

The 1976 Act outlaws discrimination on racial grounds, which it defines as meaning on the grounds of **colour, race, nationality or ethnic or national origins**.

An ethnic group would be one which regards itself as distinct on the grounds of its history and culture. For example, *Gwynedd County Council* v *Jones* (1986) held that the Welsh are a distinct ethnic group. Other examples of ethnic groups would include Bosnians, Jews, Sikhs and Scots.

The Equal Pay Act 1970 and Sex Discrimination Act 1975 distinguished between matters inside the contract of employment and matters outside the contract. The Race Relations Act 1976 makes no such distinction and covers both types of discrimination. The Act also outlaws discriminatory advertisements.

Exceptions

Some **genuine occupational qualifications** are allowed. For example, an employer can employ a person of a particular race if this is necessary for one of the following reasons:

(a) To promote authenticity in a work of drama or entertainment.
(b) To create an authentic work of art.
(c) To give authenticity to places where food and drink are served.
(d) To employ social workers who are concerned with the welfare of racial groups.

Enforcement of the Act

Individuals can complain to the industrial tribunal within three months of the discriminatory act. The tribunal can declare the complainant's rights, award compensation and order the employer not to discriminate in the future.

The **Commission for Racial Equality** also has the power to enforce the Act. If it suspects that a person or a business is discriminating racially it can investigate the matter and serve a notice ordering that the discrimination ceases. If there is any further discrimination within a five-year period the Commission can get an injunction to force compliance with its order.

Disabled persons

The Disabled Persons (Employment) Act 1944 requires employers who employ at least 20 employees to ensure that at least 3 per cent are registered disabled persons.

Persons with criminal records

The Rehabilitation of Offenders Act 1974 allows people whose convictions have become **spent** to deny that they have ever been convicted. Furthermore, if a person is dismissed because of a spent conviction this will amount to unfair dismissal.

A conviction becomes spent after a length of time which varies with the severity of the sentence passed. The times are:

Over 2½ years' imprisonment	Never spent
6 months–2½ years	Spent after 10 years
Less than 6 months	Spent after 7 years
Youth custody	Spent after 7 years
Fined/community service order	Spent after 5 years
Detention centre	Spent after 3 years
Probation/binding over	Spent after 1 year
Care/supervision order	Spent after 1 year
Absolute discharge	Spent after 6 months

ACTIVITY QUESTIONS 10.1

1 Under which statute could a woman seek a remedy if:
  (a) She was refused a job on the grounds of her sex?
  (b) She was paid less than a man doing the same work for the same employer, on the grounds of her sex?
  (c) She was refused a job because of her ethnic origin?

2 Can a man be a victim of sex discrimination?

3 What is the significance of an offender's conviction becoming spent?

Further activity question 10.1

Read the following discrimination cases and decide:

(a) Under which statute the complaint was brought.

(b) Whether you think the complainant won.

The actual decisions are available at the end of this chapter.

Noble v David Gold and Son Ltd (1980, Court of Appeal)

Both women and men worked in the employer's warehouse. The women did light work, such as sorting and packing books. The men did heavier work such as loading and unloading. Three women claimed that they should be paid the same as the men.

Held

Hayward v Cammell Laird Shipbuilders Ltd (1986, House of Lords)

A female caterer wished to be compared to male painters and joiners. As apprentices the caterers, painters, thermal insulation engineers and joiners had all been paid the same rate. After the apprenticeship the caterer was paid a lower hourly wage, although she had better conditions on holidays, meal breaks and sick pay. She applied to be paid the same hourly wage as the men.

Held

Brooks v Ladbroke Lucky Seven Entertainment (1977)

Ladbrokes dismissed a gambling club employee when they discovered that he had a conviction. They did not know that the conviction was spent and argued that the nature of the work would have justified dismissal anyway. The man claimed unfair dismissal.

Held

Zarczynska v Levy (1979)

A part-time barmaid claimed that she had been told not to serve black customers. She objected to this and was dismissed. Although she had not been dismissed on the grounds of her own race, she claimed that she had been dismissed on racial grounds.

Held

Noone v North West Thames Regional Health Authority (1988, Court of Appeal)

A Sri Lankan doctor, who had obtained her initial qualification in Sri Lanka, applied for a job as a consultant microbiologist. Her qualifications and experience seemed far better than those of any of the other candidates but she was not given the job.

Held

Redundancy

Employees under the age of 65, who have at least two years' continuous employment since reaching the age of 18, are entitled to a lump sum payment if they are dismissed on the grounds of redundancy.

When is a dismissal redundancy?

A dismissal will be due to redundancy if it arose wholly or mainly because:

(a) The employer has ceased to carry on the business in which the employee was employed.
(b) The employer has ceased to carry on the business in the place where the employee was employed.
(c) The kind of work which the employee does either has diminished or is expected to diminish.

Suitable alternative employment

If the employer offers suitable alternative employment the employee must take this or forfeit the right to a redundancy payment. However, if the alternative employment is not suitable the employee can refuse it and still claim to have been made redundant.

Taylor v Kent CC (1969)

A 53-year-old, who had been headmaster of a school for 10 years, was made redundant when his school was merged with another school. He was offered alternative employment as a supply teacher at his headmaster's salary. He declined the offer.

Held He was made redundant. The alternative employment was not suitable.

Redundancy payments

Most people who are made redundant are surprised at how little they receive. Over the past few years the newspapers have contained numerous accurate accounts of miners and others receiving payments in excess of £30,000. These employees were not receiving a statutory redundancy payment. Their contracts of employment contained terms which entitled them to enhanced redundancy rates.

If employees' contracts do not contain a special term giving them more (and most contracts do not) then the amount the employees will receive is calculated as follows:

- For every year of continuous employment between the ages of 18 and 21 the employee is entitled to half a week's wages.
- For every year of continuous employment between 22 and 41 the employee is entitled to one week's wages.
- For every year of continuous employment between 42 and 65 the employee is entitled to one and a half week's wages.
- The maximum number of years which can be taken into account is 20. This means the maximum payment is $20 \times 1.5 \times £205 = £6,150$.
- The wages used in the calculation will be the weekly wages currently received, with a maximum weekly wage of £205.
- Employees who are over 64 have their payment reduced by one-twelfth for every month by which they are over 64. So a man who is age 64 years and nine months would have his payment reduced by $\frac{9}{12}$, i.e. 75 per cent.

A couple of examples should demonstrate how the payment is calculated:

Example 1   Alice, who is 28 years old, is made redundant. She earns £180 a week and has five years' continuous employment. During the whole period of her continuous employment Alice was between the ages of 22 and 41. She is therefore entitled to one week's wages for every year worked, and her redundancy payment will be $5 \times £180 = £900$.

Example 2   Ada, who is 62, is made redundant after 30 years' continuous employment. Her weekly wage is £350. Ada is entitled to a payment for 20 of her

30 years. She has been employed for 20 years since she reached the age of 42. Therefore each of those years will be paid at one and a half weeks' wages. Her weekly wage will be reduced to the maximum permissible, £205. Ada will therefore receive $20 \times 1.5 \times £205 = £6,150$.

Unfair and wrongful dismissal

If employees are dismissed they may be able to sue their employer for either unfair or wrongful dismissal. These are quite separate matters.

Unfair dismissal is a statutory remedy which gives the dismissed employee a right to a fixed payment.

If employees sue for wrongful dismissal they are simply suing for breach of contract. The employees' contracts of employment will give them an entitlement to a certain amount of notice. If they have been dismissed without having been given this notice the contract will have been broken and the employees will therefore be entitled to damages.

Unfair dismissal

Full-time workers who have two years' continuous employment since reaching the age of 18 have the right not to be unfairly dismissed. A recent European Court case extended these rights to all part-time workers. The basis of this decision was that it was sex discrimination not to give part-timers equal rights as the vast majority of part-time workers are women.

What is a dismissal?

The EPCA 1978 states that an employee is dismissed if:

(a) The employer terminates the contract, with or without notice.
(b) A fixed-term contract ends and is not renewed.
(c) The employee terminates the contract on the ground of the employer's unreasonable conduct (constructive dismissal).

In *Western Excavating Ltd* v *Sharp*, Lord Denning explained the meaning of constructive dismissal:

> *'If the employer is guilty of conduct which is a significant breach going to the root of the contract . . . then the employee is entitled to regard himself as discharged*

from any further performance. . . . He is constructively dismissed. The employee is entitled in those circumstances to leave at the instant without giving any notice at all, or, alternatively, he may give notice and say that he is leaving at the end of the notice.'

When is a dismissal unfair?

'Unfair' has a technical meaning here. The EPCA 1978 says that all dismissals are unfair unless the employer can justify the dismissal on one of the following five grounds:

(a) The employee's **capability or qualifications** to do the job.
(b) The employee's **conduct**, inside or outside the employment.
(c) That the employee was made **redundant**.
(d) That it would be **illegal** to keep the employee on in the job.
(e) **Some other substantial reason** which would justify the employee's dismissal.

The last category is necessary to prevent the list of reasons from becoming too rigid. Usually the reason is a commercial one.

Wilson v Underhill School Ltd (1977)

Teachers were awarded a national pay rise. The school at which the applicant was employed was in financial difficulties and could not meet the award in full. All the other teachers agreed to forgo some of their pay rise. The applicant would not agree to this and so she was dismissed.

Held The dismissal was fair.

Remedies

(a) **Reinstatement**. If the industrial tribunal orders reinstatement then the employee must be treated as if he had never been dismissed. He will therefore get his old job back and recover back-pay for any time that he has not been allowed to work. In practice reinstatement is rarely ordered.

(b) Re-**engagement**. Here the employee is not given his old job back, but the employer is ordered to give him a similar job.

(c) **Compensation**. The basic award is calculated in the same way as a redundancy payment. However, the contributory negligence of the employee might reduce the award. For example, if a person whose award has been calculated at £6,000 was found to have been 25 per cent to blame for the dismissal, his damages would be reduced to £4,500.

There might also be a compensatory award which would cover matters such as loss of earnings, loss of pension rights and damages for the manner of dismissal. The maximum for this is £11,000, and it can be awarded in addition to the basic award.

ACTIVITY QUESTIONS 10.2

1 An employee is dismissed for the following reasons. Which of the reasons would mean that the employee was made redundant?
(a) Because the employer is going out of business.
(b) Because the employee was convicted of drinking and driving.
(c) Because the employee became too ill to do the job properly.
(d) Because the employer no longer did the type of work which the employee was employed to do.
(e) Because the employer is transferring his business to a new site several hundred miles away.

2 What would be the size of a redundancy payment made to the following redundant employees?
(a) A 40-year-old, with ten year's continuous employment, who earns £180 a week.
(b) A 62-year-old, with ten year's continuous employment, who earns £450 a week.

Further activity question 10.2

In each of the following cases the employee claimed to have been unfairly dismissed and the employer denied this. We have seen that there are only five grounds on which a dismissal can be fair. In each of the cases therefore the employer argued one of these five. Read the cases and try to decide:

(a) on which ground the employer sought to justify the dismissal;
(b) whether or not the dismissal was judged unfair.

The actual decisions are available at the end of this chapter.

International Sports Ltd v *Thompson* (1980)

Over the previous 18 months the applicant had been absent from work for about 25 per cent of the time. She always provided a medical certificate to cover her absences. She suffered from various complaints, including 'dizzy spells, anxiety and nerves, bronchitis, virus infection, althruigra of the left knee and dyspepsia and flatulence'. The employer's medical advisor said that there was no point in examining her because the complaints were all unconnected and none of them amounted to a chronic illness. After a warning, the applicant was dismissed.

Held

Tayside Regional Council v *Macintosh* (1982)

The applicant was employed as a vehicle mechanic. The job advertisement said that it was essential that he held a driving licence, and at the interview he confirmed that he did. The contract of employment did not mention this requirement. He was banned from driving and his employers dismissed him.

Held

Thomson v *Alloa Motor Co Ltd* (1983)

A petrol pump attendant was picked up from work by her husband. She was learning to drive and took the wheel. While driving away she crashed into a petrol pump. The damage to the pump was so extensive that the employer would have no option but to sue the applicant. She was dismissed without notice.

Held

Moore v *C & A Modes* (1981)

A section leader at a C & A store, with 20 years' experience, was allegedly caught shoplifting at a nearby Woolworth store. She admitted the offence to a security officer and signed a statement to that effect. Later she denied the shoplifting, saying that at the time she had been absent-minded because she needed a holiday, because it was a hot day and because she had a lot on her mind. C & A dismissed her.

Held

Mathieson v Noble and Sons Ltd (1972)

A salesman was disqualified from driving. At his own expense he arranged for a chauffeur to drive him around until his disqualification was over. His employer was not prepared to give this arrangement a try and sacked him.

Held

O'Brien v Prudential Assurance Co (1979)

The applicant was a district insurance inspector who would need to visit clients' homes. When he had applied for the job he had not revealed that he had a history of severe mental illness which had required treatment with strong drugs as well as periods in hospital. Since 1972 he had not been treated with any drugs other than those in common use. None of these drugs was connected with his mental illness. When the company discovered his medical history it dismissed him, even though he had an excellent work record.

Held

Wrongful dismissal

An employee is **summarily** dismissed when he is dismissed without notice. The employee's behaviour might justify such a dismissal, in which case he will have no remedy. But if an employee is summarily dismissed without a good reason then his contract of employment, which will entitle him to a period of notice, will have been broken. The employee can then sue the employer for breach of contract, and such an action is known as an action for wrongful dismissal.

How much notice?

The contract of employment will usually state the amount of notice required. In addition, every employee is entitled to a reasonable period of notice, the length of which will depend upon a variety of factors, such as the nature of his position and his length of service with the employer.

The EPCA 1978 lays down that employees are entitled to a **minimum** of one week's notice for every year of continuous employment (up to a maximum of 12 weeks).

If an employee is summarily dismissed for a justifiable reason he may well have forfeited his right to notice. (His breach of the contract of employment would have to be so bad that the employer would be justified in calling the contract off.)

A person on a fixed-term contract who is dismissed when the contract ends is not wrongfully dismissed. (He could, however, have been unfairly dismissed.)

Wrongful dismissal is not a great deal of use to many employees because their notice entitlement is not long enough to result in large damages. It can be very useful to those who are highly paid and who are entitled to long periods of notice.

In *Shove v Downs Surgical PLC* (1984), for example, a chairman of a company had a contract of employment which entitled him to 30 months' notice. He was summarily dismissed and his wrongful dismissal damages, even after mitigation, came to £84,300. (£53,000 was for loss of wages. Other headings were: withdrawal from the company life insurance scheme, loss of private health benefits, loss of the use of a company car, and loss of fees from a consultancy business he was setting up.)

When we study the remedies for breach of contract we will see that the purpose of contract damages is to put the injured party in the position he would have been if the contract had been performed as agreed. The injured party will be able to claim for any forseeable loss which resulted from the breach of contract. Such losses might include the type of matters claimed for in *Shove v Downs Surgical PLC*, as well as rather more obvious matters. A doorman, for example, would be able to claim the loss of tips which would otherwise have been earned.

The industrial tribunal can award £25,000 damages for wrongful dismissal. (In addition to the £11,000 basic award for unfair dismissal.) If the wrongful dismissal claim is for more than £25,000 it must be pursued through the ordinary courts.

Other remedies are available for breach of contract. These are considered in Chapter 15.

ACTIVITY QUESTIONS 10.3

1 What is the minimum notice entitlement of an employee who has been continuously employed for:
   (a) 3 years.
   (b) 10 years.
   (c) 32 years.

2 What are the major differences between unfair dismissal and wrongful dismissal?

Further activity question 10.3

Work out the amount of wrongful dismissal damages and the amount of the basic award for unfair dismissal in the following cases. Assume that the employee was both unfairly and wrongfully dismissed, and that the contract of employment contained no term specifically spelling out the period of notice.

(a) Farzana, a 20-year-old waitress with two years' continuous employment, who earns £120 a week.

(b) Gerry, a 42-year-old painter with one year's continuous employment, who earns £180 a week.

(c) Brian, a 58-year-old football club manager with a three-year fixed-term contract worth £2,000 a week. He was dismissed with six months of the contract yet to run.

(d) Alex, a 50-year-old doorman with 18 years' continuous employment, who earns a basic wage of £120 and picks up about as much again in tips.

(e) John, a 34-year-old farmworker with 14 years' continuous employment, who earns £160 a week. As a result of being dismissed John suffers a nervous breakdown and spends his £4,000 savings on alternative medicines.

The Health and Safety at Work etc. Act 1974

This major piece of legislation imposed the following duties on all employers:

(a) To provide and maintain safe plant and safe systems of work.
(b) To make sure that articles and substances are used, handled and stored safely.
(c) To provide the information, instruction and supervision necessary to make sure that employees are safe at work.
(d) To keep the workplace in a safe state and to make sure that there is a safe way in and a safe way out.
(e) To make sure that there is a safe working environment.

Employers with more than five employees must also issue a **written statement** which sets out health and safety policy and how it is being enforced.

Enforcement

The Act imposes **criminal** sanctions on employers. Those who break it can be fined or imprisoned.

Local authorities appoint inspectors to check that the Act is being complied with. These inspectors have very wide powers, including the right to enter premises at any reasonable time, take away samples or articles, and to dismantle unsafe equipment.

Common law health and safety

The Health and Safety at Work etc. Act 1974 uses the criminal law to try to create safe working conditions. The **civil** law also protects employees. If an employee is injured at work he may be able to sue the employer for the tort of negligence.

Paris v Stepney Borough Council (1951, House of Lords)

Paris was employed on vehicle maintenance. His employers knew that he had the use of only one eye. While lying underneath a vehicle and hammering a bolt, his good eye was injured by a shard of metal. He claimed that his employers, who had told him to do the work, were negligent in not supplying him with goggles.

Held The employers were liable. Lord Oaksey said that the standard required of employers was *'the care which an ordinary prudent employer would take in all the circumstances'*. The employer had failed to achieve this standard.

Damages for negligence can be very substantial. The prospect of having to pay damages could be more of a deterrent to an employer than the possibility of conviction under the Health and Safety at Work etc. Act 1974. The employer ought to be insured against injuries to employees. But if the insurance company has to pay damages as a result of the employer's negligence it is likely to increase the employer's premiums.

The employer's common law duty is usually split up into three parts:

(a) **To provide safe plant and appliances**. This would include all machinery supplied.

Bradford v Robinson Rentals (1967)

In very cold weather a 57-year-old van driver was asked to drive 400 miles in an unheated van. He protested to his employers but was ordered to make the journey anyway. As a result he suffered frostbite to his hands and feet.

Held The employer was liable.

(b) **To provide a safe system of work.**

Barcock v Brighton Corporation (1949)

The plaintiff was employed as a labourer and after four years became a fitter. He acquired some knowledge of electrical matters on the job but was never given any training. He was employed to test electricity substations and devised his own method of doing this. The method was unsafe and contrary to several regulations. While testing a substation he was injured.

Held The employer was liable.

(c) **To provide reasonably competent fellow employees**. An employer has a duty to take reasonable care to provide reasonably competent fellow employees.

 ### *Hudson v Ridge Manufacturing Co Ltd* (1957)

An employee, who frequently played practical jokes, injured the plaintiff by grabbing him from behind and wrestling him to the ground. The plaintiff's wrist was broken and he sued the employer. The practical joker was 'not over-intelligent,' and had frequently indulged in skylarking and horseplay, such as tripping up fellow workers.

Held The employer was liable.

If the accident is caused solely by the fault of the employee who is injured then the employer will not have been negligent.

Furthermore, if the employee's negligence is partly to blame for his own injuries then, under the Law Reform (Contributory Negligence) Act 1945, his damages will be reduced to the extent which the court thinks fit.

If the employee consented to taking the risk which injured him the employer will have a complete defence. This is called *volenti non fit injuria*, and is considered in Chapter 13. Employees who are injured as a consequence of not using safety equipment or not following safety procedures are often defeated by *volenti*. However, an employer who knows that his employees are misbehaving in this way has a duty to take reasonable steps to ensure that they do use the equipment and follow the procedures.

The employer will have the defence of *volenti non fit injuria* if the employees' continue to ignore safety measures despite the employer's efforts to ensure that they follow them.

 ### *MacWilliam v Sir William Aroll & Co Ltd* (1962)

Experienced steel erectors were provided with safety harnesses but never used them. The employer took the harnesses away so that they could be used on another site. One of the steel erectors was killed when he fell 70 feet from a scaffold.

Held The employer was not liable. He was negligent in not providing the safety equipment, but this negligence had not caused the employee's death because the employee would not have used the equipment even if it had been provided.

ACTIVITY QUESTIONS 10.4

1 Which one of the following matters would not be contained in the written particulars which employers must give to employees?
  (a) Whether previous employment is to count as continuous employment.
  (b) The amount of pay and the way in which it is to be calculated.
  (c) The amount of notice required to end the employment.
  (d) The employer's equal opportunities policy.

2 John, aged 64 years and six months, has been made redundant after 40 years' continuous employment. His weekly wage is £300. How much will John's statutory redundancy payment be?
  (a) £15,000.
  (b) £9,000.
  (c) £6,150.
  (d) £3,075.

3 Deirdre's employer made sexual advances towards her. When Deirdre complained the employer was so abusive that Deirdre immediately quit the job. Which one of the following statements is true?
  (a) There has been no dismissal. Deirdre left the job.
  (b) Deirdre can claim that she has been constructively dismissed.
  (c) Deirdre can claim that she has been made redundant.
  (d) Deirdre is in breach of her contract of employment.

TASK 10

Using decided cases where possible, prepare notes for a presentation to be made to the Albanian students. The presentation should show an example of:

(a) The Equal Pay Act.
(b) The Sex Discrimination Act.
(c) The Race Relations Act.
(d) The Rehabilitation of Offenders Act.
(e) A case of unfair dismissal
(f) A case of wrongful dismissal.
(g) A case of redundancy.

Where it is not possible to use decided cases, examples should be used.

Case decisions

There follow the actual decisions in the cases set out at pages 225 and 231.

Noble v David Gold and Son Ltd

The complaint was brought under the Equal Pay Act 1970.

Held The applicant lost because the work was not broadly similar to that done by the men. Therefore it was not 'like work'.

Hayward v Cammell Laird Shipbuilders Ltd

The complaint was brought under the Equal Pay Act 1970.

Held The applicant won. Her work was broadly similar to that done by the men.

Brooks v Ladbroke Lucky Seven Entertainment

The complaint was made under the Rehabilitation of Offenders Act 1974.

Held The dismissal was unfair. The employer should have investigated the nature of the conviction and the sentence passed.

Zarczynska v Levy

The complaint was brought under the Race Relations Act 1976.

Held This would have amounted to a dismissal on racial grounds. (In fact though she lost the case because the tribunal did not believe her story.) Similarly it was stated that if a white woman was banned from a pub for coming in with a black man she too would have been discriminated against on racial grounds.

Noone v North West Thames Health Authority

The complaint was made under the Race Relations Act 1976. (It could also have been made under the Sex Discrimination Act 1975.)

Held the employer was guilty of racial discrimination.

International Sports Ltd v Thompson

The employer's argument was that the employee was not capable of performing the job.

Held The dismissal was fair. There had to come a time when the employer was justified in saying that he had had enough.

Tayside Regional Council v Macintosh

The employer argued that the applicant was not capable of doing the job.

Held The dismissal was fair. The employee knew that holding a current driving licence was a requirement of the job.

Thomson v Alloa Motor Co Ltd

The employer argued that the applicant's conduct justified her dismissal.

Held The dismissal was unfair. The accident had no bearing on the applicant's ability to do the job.

Moore v C & A Modes

The employer alleged that the conduct outside the employment justified dismissal

Held The dismissal was fair. The employee should have been very aware of the harm which shoplifting could cause to a retail store.

Mathieson v Noble and Sons Ltd

The employer argued that the employee was not capable of doing the job.

Held The dismissal was unfair. The employer should have given the scheme a go to see how it worked out.

O'Brien v Prudential Assurance Co

The employer argued that the applicant was not capable and qualified to do the job.

Held The dismissal was fair because he had to go to people's houses and an incident could not be risked.

11 Legal responsibility to shareholders and directors

Shareholders (members)

People become members of a company by acquiring shares in the company. Section 352 of the Companies Act 1985 requires that every company keeps a register of members, giving their names, addresses, and details of their shareholding. Members of the company may inspect this register free of charge. Non-members also have a right to inspect it, but they must pay a small fee.

The Companies Acts have never defined a share, but the classic definition was given by Farwell J in *Borland's Trustees* v *Steel Bros & Co Ltd* (1901):

> *'A share is the interest of a shareholder in the company measured by a sum of money, for the purpose of liability in the first place, and of interest in the second.'*

This definition mentions both liability and interest (rights).

We saw in Chapter 3 that the only **liability** of a shareholder in a limited company is to pay the full purchase price of his shares if called upon to do so. Once this amount has been paid he has no further liability.

The shareholder's **rights** are spelt out by the company's articles. Usually these rights would include a right to attend meetings, to vote at meetings and to receive a dividend if one is declared.

Becoming a shareholder

A person can become a member of a company in three ways:

(a) By subscribing for shares when the company is formed.
(b) By buying shares, either from the company or from an existing member.
(c) By inheriting shares from a member who has died.

Ceasing to be a member

A person ceases to be a member when his name is removed from the company register. His name will be removed when he dies, or when he gives away or sells his shares.

Until a shareholder's name is removed he remains a member of the company.

Musselwhite v Musselwhite & Son Ltd (1962)

Members of a company who had sold their shares to others were not informed of a company meeting. The names of the selling members had not been removed from the company register, although the contracts to sell the shares had been made. The selling shareholders were not informed of the meeting because the directors thought that they were no longer shareholders.

Held The members who had sold their shares remained members because their names were still on the company register. (The consequence of this was that the meeting was invalid as some members of the company had not been informed of it.)

Effect of the articles

As we have seen, the articles of association make the internal rules of the company.

Section 14 of the 1985 Act says that both the memorandum and the articles bind the members and the company as if they had been signed and sealed by each member.

The effects of section 14 are threefold:

(a) The company is bound to every individual member in his capacity as a member.
(b) Every member is bound to the company.
(c) Each member is bound to every other member.

It is necessary to look at each of these in more detail.

The company is bound to every individual member in his capacity as a member

Pender v Lushington (1877)

The articles of a company provided that every 10 shares commanded one vote, but that no member should be entitled to more than 100 votes. A shareholder who held more than 1,000 shares transferred some of these to Pender so that the shares could use their full voting power. The chairman of the company, Lushington, refused to accept the votes of Pender's shares.

Held The shares had been properly transferred and so not to accept Pender's votes was a breach of his rights as a member of the company.

However, the articles only make a contract between the company and a member who is acting **in his capacity as a member.**

All of us act in many capacities. For example, when a judge tries a case he acts in his capacity as a judge, when he votes at a General Election he acts in his capacity as a voter, when he buys from a shop he acts in his capacity as a consumer.

Shareholders will not be able to sue the company on the articles unless they are suing in their capacity **as a shareholder**.

Eley v Positive Life Assurance Co Ltd (1876, Court of Appeal)

Eley was a member of a company and the articles provided that he should be the company solicitor for life. The company dismissed Eley from the post of company solicitor and he sued, claiming that the articles gave him a contractual right to stay in the job.

Held Eley lost. The articles only made a contract between the company and members acting in their capacity as members. Eley was not suing in his capacity as a member, he was suing in his capacity as a dismissed employee.

Every member is bound to the company

The company can insist that the members abide by the rules in the articles.

Hickman v Kent Sheep Breeders Association (1915)

The articles provided that any dispute between members and the company had to be referred to arbitration. The company wanted to expel Hickman, and he applied to the court for an injunction to prevent this.

Held The injunction could not be granted. The articles provided that disputes had to be settled by arbitration, and therefore the company could insist that this rule was binding on all the members.

Each member is bound to every other member

The articles constitute a contract between each member and every other member.

Rayfield v Hands (1960)

An article stated: '*Every member who intends to transfer his shares shall inform the directors, who will take the said shares equally between them at a fair value . . .*'. Rayfield asked the three directors to purchase his shares, but they refused to do so.

Held The directors, as members, were under a contractual obligation to buy Rayfield's shares.

As the articles have contractual force, their importance can hardly be overstated. Obviously, then, the power to alter them is vitally important. This power lies with the members. They can change the articles by passing a **special resolution** at a company meeting.

Company meetings

There are two types of company meetings: annual general meetings and extraordinary meetings.

Annual general meeting (AGM)

An annual general meeting must be held once every **calendar** year and within 15 months of the last one. For example, if X Co Ltd held its 1995 AGM on 1 June, it would have to hold its 1996 AGM before 1 September.

Since the Companies Act 1985, a private limited company can dispense with the requirement to hold an AGM. However, any member of the company has the right to insist that an AGM is held.

Furthermore, section 376 provides that if 5 per cent of the members with voting rights give the company six weeks notice of a resolution which they propose to move at the AGM, then the company must give notice of the resolution to all its members.

Extraordinary general meetings (EGM)

All meetings other than the AGM are extraordinary general meetings. Most articles provide that the directors have the right to call an EGM. (For example, article 37 of Table A provides this.)

Section 368 of the 1985 Act provides that, no matter what the articles say, 10 per cent of voting members with fully paid-up shares can compel the directors to call an EGM. They do this by presenting a signed requisition, which states the object of the meeting, to the directors. The directors then have 21 days in which to call a meeting. If they do not do this then the members who presented the requisition can call the meeting themselves.

Notice of meetings

Section 369 says that all members must be given 21 days' written notice of an AGM. (This period can be reduced if **all** the members entitled to attend and vote agree to the reduction.)

Section 369 requires only 14 days' notice of an EGM, but the period remains 21 days if a special resolution is to be proposed.

The written notice must explain the nature of any business which is not ordinary business, as well as the date, the place and the time of the meeting. If a special or extraordinary resolution is proposed the text of the resolution must be specified in full.

Conduct of meetings

A meeting must have a quorum of members. In all but single member companies the quorum will be set at two members. This means that if only one member turns up to the meeting it will be inquorate and therefore invalid. Proxies do not count towards a quorum; only members are counted.

A meeting only needs to be quorate at its commencement. Once the meeting has begun the number present may fall below the quorum.

There must be a chairman to preside over the meeting. The chairman's job is to ensure that the meeting follows the procedure set out in the agenda.

Voting

Usually a vote is taken by a show of hands. Each member has one vote, regardless of how many shares he holds. However, if any member demands a poll then each voting share will carry the voting rights conferred on it by the articles.

Section 373 says that this right to demand a poll cannot be excluded by the articles.

Proxies

A member who does not attend the meeting can ask a proxy to attend and vote for him. The proxy does not need to be a member.

A **general proxy** gives a discretionary power to vote.

A **special proxy** requires that the vote be cast as instructed.

Minutes

Minutes of company meetings and board meetings must be kept, and must be available for inspection by members.

Resolutions

As we shall see, it is the directors who manage a company. But to appoint directors, or remove them, or to do other acts which can only be done by the members themselves, a resolution must be passed at a company meeting.

Table 11.1 shows the different types of resolutions and the kinds of business for which they are required.

Table 11.1 Company resolutions

Type	Ordinary	Extraordinary	Special
Proposed by	Board of Directors	Board of Directors	Board of Directors
Majority needed	Over 50% of those present and voting	75% of those present and voting	75% of those present and voting
Proxies allowed?	Yes	Yes	Yes
Notice of meeting	21 days if at AGM 14 days if at EGM	21 days if at AGM 14 days if at EGM	21 days at AGM or EGM
Type of business	Any business for which Companies Act or articles don't require special or extraordinary resolutions To remove the directors To resolve not to sue directors who have used their powers irregularly	To initiate a creditor's voluntary winding up when the company is insolvent	To initiate a member's voluntary winding up To vary the rights of classes of shares Alteration of memorandum or articles To change from a public company to a private company or vice versa
Formalities	Minutes kept No need to register	Minutes kept Registered with Registrar within 15 days	Minutes kept Registered with Registrar within 15 days

The company secretary

Section 283 of the 1985 Act requires every company to have a company secretary. The secretary may also be a director, but if there is only one director he may not be the secretary.

The secretary's duties are to look after the administration of the company. His tasks would include keeping the company register up to date, sending information to the Registrar of Companies, arranging meetings, sending notice of meetings and resolutions to members, and keeping up to date with legislation which affects the company.

The company secretary has a limited power to bind the company, but only as regards the type of **administrative** contracts which a company secretary could be expected to make.

ACTIVITY QUESTIONS 11.1

1 How do people become members (shareholders) of a company?

2 What percentage of a company's voting shares must a person hold:
  (a) To be able to pass an ordinary resolution without the votes of other shareholders?
  (b) To be able to pass a special resolution without the help of other shareholders?
  (c) To make sure that any special resolution can be defeated?

3 Do the rules in a company's articles of association create a contract between one member of a company and another?

4 What is the function of a company secretary?

Further activity questions 11.1

1 Ace Ltd has five shareholders, A,B,C,D, and E, all of whom own 20 per cent of the shares. A and B are the only two directors. C wants to see the articles altered so that shareholders can sell their shares only to the company. D, who is much older than the others, is very much opposed to this. A, B and E are open to persuasion on the matter.
  (a) Explain what support C will need in order to achieve the change.
  (b) Assuming that the necessary support will be gained, explain how much notice of the resolution must be given, and how the voting will take place.

2 E wants to call an EGM of Ace Ltd to propose a resolution to dismiss A as a director. Both A and B are opposed to this.
  (a) Can E insist that an EGM is called?
  (b) Once a company meeting is held, what support will E need to dismiss A as a director?

3 (a) An EGM of Ace Ltd has been called, but only A, E and C's proxy turn up. Five minutes after the meeting starts A, who does not like the way things are going, leaves. A claims that all votes passed after his departure are invalid as the meeting was inquorate. Is this correct?
  (b) D has sold all of his shares in Ace Ltd to B, but D's name is still on the company register. D is not informed of a company meeting. How will this affect resolutions passed at the meeting?

4 Athena Ltd held its last AGM on 5 November 1994. Assuming that the company has not elected to dispense with next year's AGM, what is the latest date on which it could be held?
  (a) 5 November 1995.
  (b) 31 December 1995.

(c) 5 February 1996.

(d) 5 November 1996.

5 What percentage of votes is required to pass a resolution to remove a director?

(a) 50 per cent of all the members of the company.

(b) 50 per cent of those members present and voting.

(c) 75 per cent of all the members of the company

(d) 75 per cent of those members present and voting.

Directors

Appointment and removal

Unless the articles provide otherwise, directors are appointed by an **ordinary resolution** at a company meeting.

Public companies must have two directors, but private companies need only one. Usually the directors of a company also own shares in the company. (Often they own a majority of the shares.) However, there is no requirement that a director should also be a member of the company.

No matter what the articles might say, a director can always be removed by an **ordinary resolution** of which the members have been given **special notice**. (This means that the company has been given 28 days' notice and the members 21 days' notice.)

However, on the vote to remove a director the shares of the director whose removal is proposed might have enhanced voting power.

Bushell v Faith (1970, House of Lords)

The 300 shares in a company were owned equally by a brother and two sisters, all three of whom were also directors. The articles provided that in any resolution to remove a director that director's shares should carry three votes per share. The two sisters wanted to remove their brother as a director. At a general meeting the sisters voted for removal, the brother voted against. The sisters claimed that the resolution had been passed by 200:100. The brother claimed that it had been defeated by 200:300.

Held The article giving the enhanced voting rights was perfectly valid. Therefore the resolution to remove the brother from the board had been defeated by 300 votes to 200.

Remuneration

Directors are not automatically entitled to any remuneration. But if, as is usual, they have a contract which gives them a salary then they will be able to sue for compensation if the contract is broken.

Directors' powers

The powers of the directors are contained in the articles of association.
Article 70 of Table A is fairly typical:

'Subject to the provisions of the Acts, the memorandum and the articles and to any directions given by special resolution, the business of the company shall be managed by the directors who may exercise all the powers of the company . . .'

The directors then are usually given very wide powers to manage the company. As long as they stay within these powers, they need not obey resolutions passed by the members.

ASCFS Co Ltd v *Cuninghame* (1906, Court of Appeal)

One of the articles gave the directors the power to sell the company property on whatever terms they thought fit. At a general meeting of the company a resolution was passed, ordering the directors to sell company property to a new company. The directors did not approve of the terms of the contract and refused to sell.

Held The directors were within their rights. Whether or not to sell was a question for them and not for the shareholders.

Collins MR *'It is by the consensus of all the individuals in the company that these directors became agents. . . . It is not fair to say that a majority at a meeting . . . [can] alter the mandate of the agent. The minority must also be taken into account.'*

However, it must be remembered that a majority of the shareholders have very considerable powers. Subject to a *Bushell* v *Faith* clause in the articles, they can always vote the directors out of office. Furthermore, if three-quarters of the shareholders decide to do so, they can change the articles. Such a change could either alter the powers of the directors or remove any *Bushell* v *Faith* clause. But these changes would apply only in the future. The articles cannot be changed retrospectively.

Directors as agents

The directors are the agents of the company, and a company can act only through its directors. As long as a director acts within his authority then, like other agents, he will incur no personal liability.

Section 35 of the 1985 Act says that if a contract is made between the Board of Directors and a person acting in good faith, then the contract will always be binding on the company. This is so even if the Board exceeded its powers, or even if the directors had not followed proper company procedures.

TCB Ltd v Gray (1987, Court of Appeal)

A company called Link borrowed money from TCB Ltd and issued a debenture as security for the loan. The debenture was approved by Link's Board of Directors, and following the Board's instructions it was signed by a solicitor who was not a director. Link's articles stated that debentures would be valid only if they had been signed by a director. Link therefore argued that the debenture was invalid.

Held The debenture was valid. The Board had failed to follow the correct procedures, but section 35 gave protection to TCB Ltd because they had dealt with the company in good faith.

Holding out

If a company gives the impression that a person has the authority to make a transaction then the company will be bound by such a transaction, whether or not the person who made it really did have such authority. This is known as holding out. The company is said to have held out that the person had authority.

Freeman & Lockyer v Buckhurst Park Properties Ltd
(1964, Court of Appeal)

A company was formed to buy and resell an estate. The directors had the power to appoint a managing director but they never did so. One of the directors, Mr Kapoor, acted as if he had been appointed managing director. The other directors knew this but did nothing about it. Kapoor asked architects to do work on behalf of the company. When the architects sued the company for their fees the company argued that Kapoor had no authority to employ architects and therefore the contract was not binding on the company.

Held A managing director would usually have authority to employ architects. The company had given the impression that Kapoor was managing director. Therefore, as regards people dealing with the company in good faith, Kapoor had the authority to bind the company as if he really was managing director. The company had held him out to have such powers to bind the company, so he did have such powers.

ACTIVITY QUESTIONS 11.2

1 Assuming that a company's articles give no power to do so, how can directors be prematurely removed from office?

2 Are directors automatically entitled to a salary?

3 How can a person be 'held out' to be a director. What consequences could follow from this?

Further activity questions 11.2

1 Old Joe Bloggs owns all the shares in a company. He wants to leave his shares to his three children, equally. Joe wants all of his children to be directors and he wants to ensure that they all remain directors for as long as they want.
   (a) Will it be possible for Joe to ensure that his three children all have the right to remain as directors?
   (b) If Joe had five children, could he still ensure that any group of four could not gang up on any one director?

2 David is the managing director of Goliath Ltd. There are three other directors, but David has always made whatever decisions he considered necessary and then informed the others at Board meetings. Goliath's articles used to provide that the managing director could make any contracts up to the value of £20,000. Recently the articles were changed so that contracts worth more than £5,000 had to be authorised by the full Board.

Yesterday David saw what seemed like a good business opportunity for the company. He therefore ordered goods worth £17,000 on the company's behalf. The supplier of the goods had made many similar contracts with the company through David. The other directors are convinced that the £17,000 contract is a bad one and are refusing to honour it. Assuming that the supplier of the goods acted in good faith:
   (a) Can the company refuse to honour the contract?
   (b) Would your answer be different if the contract had been for £32,000?

3 A is the sole director of a company in which he owns 15 per cent of the shares. The articles contain a *Bushell* v *Faith* clause saying that in any motion to remove A as director his shares should carry 10 votes per share. A ordered goods despite an ordinary resolution telling him not to do so.

(a) Can the 85 per cent of the shareholders pass a resolution to remove A as a director?

(b) Is there any way in which the 85 per cent can remove A's authority?

Director's duties

Fiduciary duties

A director stands in a **fiduciary** position to the company, and is therefore in a position of great trust. The implications of this are contained in the classic speech of Lord Cranworth in *Aberdeen Railway Co* v *Blaikie Bros* (1854):

> 'The Directors are a body to whom is delegated the duty of managing the general affairs of the Company. . . . Such agents have duties . . . of a fiduciary nature. . . . And it is a rule of universal application, that no one, having such duties to discharge, shall be allowed to enter into engagements in which he has, or can have, a personal interest conflicting, or which possibly may conflict, with the interests of those whom he is bound to protect.'

There are two separate aspects of the fiduciary duty owed by directors:

(a) The directors must exercise their powers for the benefit of the company as a whole.

(b) There must be no conflict between the directors' interests and the interests of the company.

Re W & M Roith Ltd (1967)

A director of a company, who was also the controlling shareholder, was in a poor state of health. He renewed his contract with the company without revealing his health problems. The new contract made very generous pension provisions for the director's widow in the event of the director's death. Shortly after making the agreement the director died. His widow claimed on the pension.

Held The company did not have to pay. If the company had known of the director's health problems it would not have agreed such generous pension provisions. When the director had made the contract he had not been intending to benefit the company as a whole, but intending to benefit his wife.

Regal (Hastings) Ltd v *Gulliver* (1942, House of Lords)

Regal Ltd owned a cinema. It wanted to acquire two more cinemas so that it could sell all three as a going concern. A subsidiary company was formed to make the purchase. The sellers of the cinemas would not go ahead with the deal unless the subsidiary company had at least £5,000 paid-up share capital. Regal could provide only £2,000 of the money which the subsidiary needed. The directors of Regal therefore personally subscribed for a further 3,000 £1 shares in the subsidiary. At the conclusion of the whole business the shares in the subsidiary were sold for £3.80 each. Both Regal and its directors had therefore made a handsome profit.

Held The directors had to account to Regal for the profit they had made. It was only because they were directors of Regal that they gained the opportunity to make the profit.

Guinness plc v *Saunders* (1990, House of Lords)

The full board of Guinness formed a sub-committee of three directors to arrange a takeover bid for another company. One of these three, W, successfully arranged the takeover. The sub-committee agreed to pay W £5,200,000 for his services.

Held This payment could be set aside because, under the company's articles, only the full board of directors had the power to award payment to a director.

Non-fiduciary duties

The directors have other duties besides the fiduciary ones.

Care and skill

Directors owe a duty of care and skill to the company. The standard expected is that of a reasonable man looking after his own affairs. Generally this standard is not very high. However, if a director is employed in his professional capacity then a higher standard will be expected.

Duties to employees

Section 309 of the 1985 Act says that directors should have regard to the interests of the company's employees. The section seems to be a rather vague statement of intention, and if there is any conflict between the interests of the company and the interests of the employees the directors must put the company's interests first.

Creditors

If a company becomes insolvent the assets of the company are regarded as belonging to the creditors rather than to the shareholders. The liquidator will be able to prohibit the directors from acting in certain ways. If the directors ignore these instructions they can become personally liable.

Effects of breach of duty

A director will not be liable to the company for the act of his co-directors if he did not know of the act and should not have suspected it. This is because the other directors are neither his employees nor his agents.

If directors are liable together they are jointly and severally liable. This means that if a director is sued and ordered to pay damages he will be entitled to a contribution from the others.

Even if the directors do exceed their powers or use them irregularly the shareholders may still ratify their acts at a general meeting.

Bamford v Bamford (1970, Court of Appeal)

The company was in danger of being taken over. To avoid this the directors issued an extra 500,000 shares to a business which distributed the company's products. This might have been contrary to the articles. (This point was never decided.) The shareholders approved the issue of the shares by passing an ordinary resolution at a general meeting.

Held Even if the directors had irregularly exercised their powers, the ratification by the shareholders made the contract a good one, and absolved the directors from all liability.

Harman LJ '*Directors can, by making a full and frank disclosure and calling together the general body of the shareholders, obtain . . . forgiveness of their sins; and . . . everything will go on as if it had been done right from the beginning. I cannot believe that this is not a commonplace of company law. It is done every day. Of course, if the majority of the general meeting will not forgive and approve, the directors must pay for it.*'

Section 727 of the 1985 Act allows the court to grant to relief to a director in breach of his duty if the director *'acted honestly and reasonably and ought fairly to be excused'*.

Control of the company

The voting shareholders control the company. If a shareholder has more than 50 per cent of the voting shares then he can pass any ordinary resolution. A shareholder with 75 per cent of the shares can pass any extraordinary or special resolution. Similarly, shareholders who between them can muster over 50 per cent or 75 per cent can exercise the different types of control.

These percentages can be vitally important when a person is considering investing in a company. Let us look at an example. If B invites A to form a company with him, and suggests that A takes 49 per cent of the shares while B takes 51 per cent, then their ownership of the company is almost equal. However, their control of the company is very far from equal, and A should be very wary about accepting such a proposition. However, A would at least have some degree of 'negative control,' in the sense that he could block a special resolution. If A was offered only 25 per cent of the shares he would in effect have no control at all.

If two shareholders each have 50 per cent of the shares then they will both have negative control. Neither will be able to force through any resolution without the consent of the other. This might sound an ideal way to run a company owned by two people – and while the shareholders get on with each other it probably is – but if complete deadlock is reached then the court may well wind up the company (if either party so requests) on the ground that this is just and equitable.

In *Re Yenidge Tobacco Co Ltd* (1916), the court wound up a profitable company because the two shareholder/directors, Mr Weinberg and Mr Rothman, had reached complete deadlock. As Lord Cozens Hardy MR said:

'Certainly, having regard to the fact that there are only two directors who will not speak to each other, and no business which deserves the name of business in the affairs of the company can be carried on, I think the company should not be allowed to continue.'

A minority shareholder is, of course, in an even worse position than a 50 per cent shareholder in complete deadlock. (One can imagine how Weinberg would have felt if he had owned 49 per cent of the shares to Rothman's 51 per cent.)

The position of the minority shareholder is not improved by the **rule in *Foss* v *Harbottle*,** which states that if a wrong is done to a company then only the company has the right to take action. The case itself illustrates the problems which this can cause for minority shareholders.

Foss v *Harbottle* (1843)

Two members of a company sued five directors who had sold land to the company for more than it was worth.

Held The shareholders had no right to sue. If the directors had wronged the company then only the company could sue in respect of that wrong. (The company was most unlikely to do this because it was controlled by the very directors who had cheated it!)

The rule in *Foss* v *Harbottle* is a logical extension of *Salomon* v *Salomon*. That case decided that a company is a separate legal person. It follows that if a company is wronged it alone has the power to sue.

The rule has the advantage of preventing multiple actions; if every shareholder in every company was able to sue for any perceived wrong to the company then there would be an enormous number of potential court cases. However, the rule could obviously be very unfair to minority shareholders, and now both the courts and statute offer protection to the minority.

Protection of minority shareholders

The rule in *Foss* v *Harbottle* is still perfectly valid, but a number of other rules now protect minority shareholders.

Protection from the courts

The courts will protect a minority shareholder in three situations:

(a) Where there is a fraud on the minority.
(b) Where the personal rights of a member have been infringed.
(c) If the act done is *ultra vires* or illegal.

Fraud on the minority

Fraud on the minority covers so many types of underhand behaviour that it is impossible to define. But the following cases have been held to amount to fraud on the minority.

Cook v Deeks (1916, Privy Council)

Cook was one of four directors in a construction company. The company had often done profitable business with the Canadian Pacific Railway Company. When a new contract was being negotiated with the railway, the other three directors made the contract in their own names rather than in the company name. The three directors (who owned 75 per cent of the shares) then passed a resolution that the company had no interest in the new contract. Cook claimed that the resolution was ineffective and that the benefit of the contract should go to the company.

Held Cook won. The other three directors had committed a fraud on the minority.

Clemens v Clemens Bros Ltd (1976)

Clemens had 45 per cent of the shares in a company and her aunt had 55 per cent. The articles provided that if either shareholder wished to sell her shares, the other had the right to buy them. Clemens therefore had negative control of the company, and if she outlived her aunt would eventually have total control. The aunt and four non-shareholders were directors. These five proposed to increase the number of shares so that Clemens's holding fell to 24.5 per cent. The aunt used her shares to pass the resolution.

Held The resolution was void. It was a fraud on the minority, its real purpose being to deprive Clemens of her control of the company.

Daniels v Daniels (1978)

A company's controlling shareholders and directors, Mr and Mrs Daniels, caused the company to sell land to Mrs Daniels for less than it was worth. The plaintiff, a minority shareholder sued.

Held The agreement should be set aside.

Where the personal rights of a member have been infringed

An example of this has already been given, in *Pender* v *Lushington* (page 242), where the company refused to give Pender's shares one vote for every 10 shares held. This was held to be invalid because Pender was a member, and not to give him voting rights would have infringed his rights as a member.

If the act done is *ultra vires* or illegal

In Chapter 5 we saw that a company will not be granted a certificate of incorporation until it has registered a memorandum and articles of association with the

Registrar of Companies. We also saw that the memorandum concerns the relationship between the company and outsiders.

The most important clause in the memorandum is the **objects clause**. This clause states the capacity of the company (what contracts the company is capable of making). If the company does any act which is outside the objects clause that act is *ultra vires* (beyond the powers of) the company, and therefore void. Because such an act is void it cannot be ratified, even by a unanimous vote of the members of the company.

This common law approach was designed to protect two groups of people:

(a) subscribers to the company, who would know what their money would be spent on;

(b) people contracting with the company, who would know the exact extent of the company's powers.

People dealing with the company could, of course, insist upon examining the company's memorandum before entering into any contracts. It is rather unlikely that many contractors would actually do this. However, even if they did not, they were given **constructive** notice of the memorandum, which means that they were deemed to have read and understood it.

So a contractor who had actually read the memorandum would have actual notice of the company's capacity, and a contractor who had not read the memorandum would have constructive notice, which is equally valid.

Far from protecting such contractors, the *ultra vires* rule could be very unfair to them.

Re Jon Beauforte Ltd (1953)

A company's memorandum authorised it to carry on the business of making costumes and gowns. The company decided to go into the completely different business of making veneered panels. Consequently the company made contracts with builders to build a new factory, and with merchants to supply veneers and coke. The company went into liquidation. The builder and the merchants sued on their contracts.

Held Neither the builder nor the merchants succeeded. All of the contracts were *ultra vires* and all of the contractors had constructive notice of this.

It was a condition of Britain's entry into the European Community that this rule was changed. The European Communities Act 1972 made the change initially, and the present law is now contained in the Companies Act 1985, section 35 which provides:

'In favour of a person dealing with a company in good faith, the power of the board of directors to bind the company, or authorise others to do so, shall be deemed free of any limitation under the company's constitution.

For this purpose –

(a) a person "deals with" a company if he is a party to any transaction or other act to which the company is a party;

(b) a person shall not be regarded as acting in bad faith by reason only of his knowing that an act is beyond the powers of the directors under the company's constitution; and

(c) a person shall be presumed to have acted in good faith unless the contrary is proved.'

ACTIVITY QUESTIONS 11.3

1 In *Re Jon Beauforte*, the builder and the merchants were not paid because their contracts with the company were *ultra vires*. What made the contracts *ultra vires*?

2 In what way did the *ultra vires* rule protect shareholders?

Further activity questions 11.3

Read section 35 carefully, and then answer the following questions:

1 In whose favour does the section apply?
  (a) Only a person dealing with the company in good faith.
  (b) Only the company.
  (c) Both the company and a person dealing with it in good faith.

2 If the directors decide on a transaction, what can a third party in good faith assume? Can this assumption be made regardless of whether or not the third party has read the objects clause?

3 Does the third party dealing with the company need to prove that he acted in good faith, or does the company need to prove that he did not?

4 Applying section 35, how would *Re Jon Beauforte* be decided today?

5 The facts of *Ashbury Railway Carriage Co Ltd* v *Riche* (1875, House of Lords) were as follows: The company's objects clause stated that it had the capacity to make railway carriages and wagons. The company took over a concession to build a railway line in Belgium, and employed Mr Riche to do the actual construction. The contract to build the railway was *ultra vires*, but all the shareholders voted to ratify it. Later the company repudiated the contract and Mr Riche sued on it, saying that it was binding on the company.
  (a) How was the case decided in 1875?
  (b) How would it be decided today?

Statutory protection of minority shareholders

The Insolvency Act 1986

A court can wind a company up under sections 122 to 124 of the Insolvency Act 1986 on the ground that it is just and equitable to do so. Even a single shareholder can petition the court to do this.

Sections 459 to 461 of the Companies Act 1985

Any member may petition the court on the ground that the affairs of the company are being, or have been or will be conducted in a manner which is unfairly prejudicial to the members generally or to particular members.

If the court agrees that the conduct is unfairly prejudicial it can:

(a) Order the company to behave in a certain way in the future.
(b) Prevent the company from doing certain acts.
(c) Order the company to sue for a wrong done to it.
(d) Order the majority or the company to buy the shares of the minority.
(e) Make any order which it sees fit.

Re HR Harmer Ltd (1958, Court of Appeal)

Harmer had a successful business dealing in postage stamps. He formed a company to take the business over. His two sons were, like him, life directors. Harmer retained voting control of the company although his sons held most of the shares. When Harmer was 88 his sons asked the court for relief on the grounds that he completely ignored their wishes, running the company as if he still owned all of it. He had made bad business decisions, employed private detectives to watch the staff and countermanded resolutions passed by the Board.

Held The court ordered that Harmer should be made president of the company for life (without any special powers) and be paid a salary. They also ordered him not to interfere in the company's business otherwise than in accordance with the valid decisions of the Board of Directors.

Re Nuneaton Borough Athletic Football Club (1991)

The company was authorised to issue only 2,000 £1 shares. The petitioner had bought 24,000 shares, although these had never been validly created. He had therefore paid a good deal of money for shares which did not exist.

Held The owner of the 2,000 validly created shares should transfer 1,007 of them to the petitioner at a fair price. However, it was a condition that the petitioner should repay the very large loans which the owner of the 2,000 shares had made to the club.

Re Sam Weller and Sons Ltd (1990)

The petitioner owned 42.5 per cent of the shares in a company which was controlled by his uncle, Sam Weller. The company had not increased its dividend in 37 years, despite being prosperous in recent years. In 1985 out of net profits of £36,000 it had paid only £2,650 in dividends.

Held This could amount to unfair prejudice.

> Peter Gibson J *'It is asserted by the petitioners that the sole director is conducting the affairs of the company for the sole benefit of himself and his family, and that while he and his sons are taking an income from the company, he is causing the company to pay inadequate dividends to the shareholders . . . (whose interests may be not only prejudiced by the policy of low dividend payments, but unfairly prejudiced).'*

ACTIVITY QUESTIONS 11.4

1 If directors abuse or exceed their powers, can the shareholders absolve the directors from liability?

2 What is the rule in *Foss* v *Harbottle*?

3 Why do minority shareholders need protection from the courts and from statute?

Further activity questions 11.4

1 In the following cases fraud on the minority was alleged. Consider the facts of each case and decide whether or not the directors' actions amounted to fraud on the minority. The actual decisions are available at the end of this chapter.

Menier v Hooper's Telegraph Works (1874, Court of Appeal)

E Limited (E) had 5,325 shares, and H Limited (H) owned 3,000 of these. E had won a concession from the Portuguese Government to lay a transatlantic cable from Portugal to Brazil. H was to manufacture the cable. H then found that it could make more money by laying the cable for another company, and managed to persuade the Portuguese Government to transfer the cable-laying concession to this other company. To prevent E from suing, H used its 3,000 shares to wind up E.

Held

Pavlides v *Jensen* (1956)

A minority shareholder in a company brought an action against the directors, alleging that they had sold a mine for far less than it was worth, and that this therefore amounted to fraud on the minority. The directors did have the power to sell the mine and there was no suggestion that they had been fraudulent or dishonest. However, the directors had committed an error of judgement and they had been negligent in selling the mine.

Held

Alexander v *Automatic Telephone Co* (1900, Court of Appeal)

All the subscribers to a company paid 6*d* per share. The five directors, who owned 75 per cent of the shares, passed a resolution that all shareholders who were not directors should pay a further 2*s* 6*d* per share. Two of these directors (who had voted for the resolution) later claimed that this amounted to fraud on the minority.

Held

2 Bilco has two shareholders. Bill owns 750 shares and Connie, his wife, owns 250. Bill and Connie are not getting on too well and there is talk of a separation. Connie's brother, Jim, who feels that pressures of company business are contributing to Bill's problems, has offered to buy 500 of Bill's shares. The company is worth £50,000 and Jim has offered to pay £25,000. He is only prepared to buy the shares if he is made a director. Is Jim's offer reasonable in financial terms?

3 In recent years a great deal of publicity has attached to the enormous salaries paid to the directors of privatised companies. Could these directors' fees amount to a fraud on the minority shareholders? Assuming that most shareholders in the privatised companies disapprove of such large fees, how is it that they continue to be paid?

TASK 11

Explain to the Albanian students visiting your college:

(a) Who runs a company.

(b) What powers the shareholders in a company have.

(c) The legal duties imposed on directors of companies.

(d) How the minority shareholders in a company are protected.

(e) The consequences of a company making a contract which is *ultra vires*.

Case decisions

There follow the actual decisions in the cases set out at page 261.

Menier v Hooper's Telegraph Works

Held H had committed a fraud on the minority and had to account for profits made to E Ltd.

Pavlides v Jensen

Held The action failed. Being negligent is not the same as being fraudulent.

Alexander v Automatic Telephone Co

Held The directors' actions did amount to fraud, and they too were compelled to pay the 2*s* 6*d* per share.

12 Legal responsibility to partners

The main risk of being in partnership is that a partner can become liable to outsiders as a result of the actions of his fellow partners. This aspect of partnership liability is therefore considered before partners' legal relationship with each other.

Partners' liability to outsiders

The firm's liability in contract

Section 5 of the Partnership Act 1890 explains the partnership's liability under contracts made by individual partners. This section takes the form of one very long sentence, and if it is read as a whole it can be difficult to understand. But if the section is broken down into its component parts it becomes relatively straightforward. First, though, it is necessary to reproduce section 5 in its entirety:

> '*Every partner is an agent of the firm and his other partners for the purpose of the business of the partnership; and the acts of every partner who does any act for carrying on in the usual way business of the kind carried on by the firm of which he is a member bind the firm and his partners, unless the partner so acting has in fact no authority to act for the firm in the particular matter, and the person with whom he is dealing either knows that he has no authority, or does not know or believe him to be a partner.*'

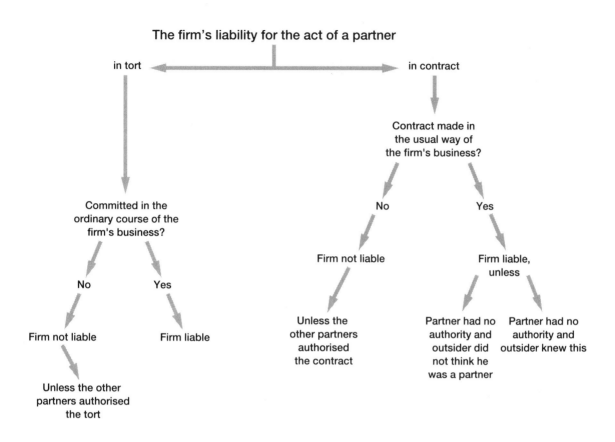

The firm's liability for the act of a partner

Fig 12.1 Liability of a firm in contract and tort

'Every partner is an agent of the firm and his other partners for the purpose of the business of the partnership . . .'

An agent has the power to make contracts on behalf of a third party, his principal. Shop assistants, for example, are agents; they sell goods which belong not to themselves, but to the shops for which they work. Once a contract with a customer has been made, it is binding on the shop, not on the shop assistant. Similarly, purchasing clerks and salesmen are agents. It is not their own goods which they buy and sell. So when the opening clause of section 5 states that partners are agents of the firm and of their other partners, this is of enormous significance.

This means that no matter how disastrous a contract a partner makes, his fellow partners will be completely bound by the contract. If there are not enough partnership assets to honour the contract then this liability will extend to each partner personally.

This agency of the partner applies only to contracts made *'for carrying on in the usual way business of the kind carried on by the firm of which he is a member'*. This is a very important limitation. The firm will not be bound by all contracts made by a partner. It will be bound only if the contract was the type of contract which the firm would usually make in the course of its business.

For example, if a partner in a firm of accountants ordered office furniture or a new computer these contracts would be binding on the firm. But if the partner ordered a new sports car this contract would not be binding on the firm; it is not in the usual way of business for a firm of accountants to order sports cars.

'. . . unless the partner so acting has in fact no authority to act for the firm in the particular matter, and the person with whom he is dealing either knows that he has no authority, or does not know or believe him to be a partner.'

The final clause of section 5 allows for situations where a partner will not be the agent of the firm, even as regards goods which were ordered in the usual way of the firm's business.

It can be seen that there are two requirements here. First, the partner must have had no authority to act for the firm in the way that he did. Second, the person with whom he dealt must either have known this, or must have thought that the partner was not in fact a partner in the firm.

For example, let us assume that the articles of firm ABC say that partner C has no authority to buy supplies on the firm's behalf. If C does buy supplies on the firm's behalf the firm will be liable unless:

(a) the supplier knows that C has no authority to buy; or
(b) the supplier does not know or believe C to be a partner in the firm.

Contracts not made in the ordinary course of business

Section 7 deals with contracts which are **not** made in the ordinary course of the firm's business:

> *'Where one partner pledges the credit of the firm for a purpose apparently not connected with the firm's ordinary course of business, the firm is not bound, unless he is in fact specifically authorised by the other partners; but this section does not affect any personal liability incurred by any individual partner.'*

Again, it might be helpful to break this section down.

Section 7 begins: '**Where one partner pledges the credit of the firm for a purpose apparently not connected with the firm's ordinary course of business, the firm is not bound** . . .'. For example, in a firm of accountants, DEF, partner D orders a new snooker table for the firm. Under section 7 this contract would not be binding on the firm because it is not in the ordinary course of business for a firm of accountants to need a snooker table.

Section 7 continues: '. . . *unless he is in fact specifically authorised by the other partners . . .'*. So the contract to buy the snooker table would be binding on the firm if E and F had authorised D to order it.

The final clause of section 7 says: '... *but this section does not affect any personal liability incurred by any individual partner*'. This merely means that the one who made the contract (in this case D when he ordered the snooker table) will be personally liable whether the other partners are liable or not.

ACTIVITY QUESTIONS 12.1

1 If one of the partners in a firm of dentists orders a new dental chair, without the knowledge or permission of his fellow partners, will the partnership be bound by the contract?

2 Would the partnership still be bound if one of the other partners had told the supplier of the chair that the partner who ordered the chair had no authority to order such goods on behalf of the partnership?

3 Would the partnership of dentists be bound if one of the partners, without authority, ordered a new fur coat for the partnership?

Further activity question 12.1

Using sections 5 and 7, decide whether or not the firm was bound in the following cases. The actual decisions are available at the end of this chapter.

Mercantile Credit Co Ltd v Garrod (1962)

Parkin and Garrod were partners in a firm which carried on the business of repairing cars and letting lock-up garages. The partnership deed stated that neither partner had authority to buy or sell cars. Parkin, without Garrod's permission, sold a car to Mercantile Credit for £700. Parkin did not in fact own the car and Mercantile Credit claimed their £700 back. Garrod was much wealthier than Parkin and so Mercantile Credit sued Garrod, arguing that the partnership, and all members of the firm, were liable on the contract to sell the car.

Held

Bond v Gibson (1808)

G and J were in partnership together making harnesses for horses. J bought a great number of bits, which would be used to make bridles. The seller, B, thought that the bits were being purchased on behalf of the partnership, but in fact G knew nothing about them. As soon as J got the bits he pawned them and took off with the money. B claimed that G, as J's partner, was liable to him for the price.

Held

The firm's liability for a partner's torts

In Chapter 13 we shall consider types of liability, and we shall see that liability can arise in many different ways.

The question here is whether the partnership as a whole is liable if one partner commits a tort. Let us assume, for example, that partner G in the firm GHI accidentally crashes his car into a bus, injuring several passengers. Can the injured passengers sue H and I as partners of G? Or are they restricted to suing G alone?

Section 10 of the Partnership Act 1890 provides the answer:

'Where, by any [tort] . . . of any partner acting in the ordinary course of the business of the firm, or with the authority of his co-partners, loss or injury is caused to any person not being a partner in the firm . . . the firm is liable therefor to the same extent as the partner [who committed the tort] . . .'

It can be seen that the partnership is liable for a partner's torts only if *either*:

(a) the tort was committed **in the ordinary course of the firm's business**; *or*
(b) the other partners **authorised the tort**.

So a firm of accountants would be liable for a partner who stole money which he had been given to invest for a client. (Investing money would be in the ordinary course of the firm's business, and stealing money would amount to the tort of conversion.) But the firm would not be liable for a partner who lost his temper and battered a client (unless the other partners had authorised him to do this!).

 ### *Hamlyn* v *Houston & Co* (1903, Court of Appeal)

Partners in Houston & Co were encouraged to get information on rival firms by all legal means. One of the partners went further and bribed a clerk in a rival firm into giving information. As a result the rival firm suffered loss and it sued Houston & Co for the tort of inducement to break a contract.

Held The firm was liable under section 10. It was within the ordinary course of the firm's business to obtain information about rival firms.

> *Collins* MR *'If it was within the ordinary course of the business of the partnership to obtain this information by legitimate means, it was within the scope of Houston to obtain it, and the firm is liable if it is obtained by unlawful means.'*

If we have another look at the case of partner G, who crashed into the bus, we can now decide whether or not the other partners are liable. They will be liable if G was driving on the firm's business (if he was going to see one of the firm's clients or fetching goods for the firm), but they will not be liable if G was driving on his own account (if he was going home after work or driving to visit friends).

Liability by 'holding out'

A person 'holds himself out' to be a partner if he leads third parties to believe that he is a partner. If a third party gives credit to the firm as a consequence, then the person who held himself out to be a partner will be liable as if he really was a partner. Section 14 of the Partnership Act 1890 provides:

> *'Every one who by words spoken or written or by conduct represents himself, or who knowingly suffers himself to be represented, as a partner in a particular firm, is liable as a partner to anyone who has on the faith of any such representation given credit to the firm . . .'*

Note that the person can hold himself out as a partner by *'words spoken or written or by conduct'*.

If the representation is made by a third party the person represented as a partner will not be liable unless he *'knowingly suffers himself to be represented, as a partner'*.

Tower Cabinet Co Ltd v Ingram (1949)

Christmas and Ingram were partners in a firm of furnishers called Merry's. After Ingram's retirement Christmas ordered goods using old partnership notepaper. This notepaper contained the names of both Ingram and Christmas. Ingram did not know that Christmas had used the notepaper and the supplier of the goods had never dealt with the firm when Ingram was a partner. The suppliers were not paid for their goods. Having sued the firm and won, they claimed the money from Ingram.

Held Ingram was not liable under section 14 because he had not knowingly allowed himself to be represented as a partner. If he had known that Christmas had used the notepaper then Ingram would have been liable.

> Lynskey J *'Before the company can succeed in making Mr Ingram liable under this section (section 14) they have to satisfy the court that Mr Ingram, by words spoken or written or by conduct, represented himself as a partner. There is no evidence of that. Alternatively, they must prove that he knowingly suffered himself to be represented as a partner. . . . it is impossible to say that Mr Ingram knowingly suffered himself to be so represented.'*

ACTIVITY QUESTIONS 12.2

1 While at work, a partner in a firm of dentists negligently performs a tooth extraction. This causes the patient to become seriously ill with an infected jaw. Is the partnership liable for the partner's negligence?

2 While on a skiing holiday, a partner in a firm of dentists negligently collides with a fellow skier, causing serious injury. Is the partnership liable for this?

3 What risk does a person run by allowing outsiders to believe that he is a partner?

Further activity question 12.2

Using sections 10 and 14, decide whether or not the firm was bound in the following cases. The actual decisions in the cases are available at the end of this chapter.

Blyth v *Fladgate* (1891)

S, a partner in a firm of solicitors, made a loan on behalf of a client. The loan was secured by a mortgage on a house. However, S was negligent in that he did not ensure that the house was worth at least as much as the loan. In fact the house was worth considerably less, and the clients lost a lot of money. The clients sued the firm, saying that all the partners were liable for S's tort (negligence).

Held

Arbuckle v *Taylor* (1815)

A partner in a firm believed that an outsider had stolen property belonging to the firm. He brought a private prosecution which failed. The outsider then sued all the partners for the tort of malicious prosecution.

Held

D & H Bunny Ltd v *Atkins* (1961)

A and N told the credit manager of a company that they had decided to go into partnership together. Believing this, the manager let N have goods on credit. In fact no partnership ever existed between A and N. The company sued A for the price of the goods.

Held

Suing a partnership

It is possible to sue a partnership in the firm's name. (This is merely a rule of convenience and does not detract from the principle that a partnership has no legal personality of its own.)

A writ can be served on any of the partners, or it can be sent to the firm's principal place of business.

If a plaintiff wins judgment against a firm then the firm must pay out of its assets. If there are insufficient assets to meet the debt then all partners are personally liable.

If judgment is enforced against one of the partners he will be able to claim a contribution from his fellow partners.

Partners will usually have to contribute in equal shares, but this is not necessarily so. The Civil Liabilities (Contribution) Act 1978 says that each partner must contribute the amount which the court considers 'just and equitable'.

Partners' legal relationship with each other

The partnership agreement, if there is one, will form a contract between all of the partners. They will all therefore be bound by the provisions of the agreement.

Usually the agreement will state that most issues can be resolved by a simple vote. If this is the case then each partner will have one vote and the majority will get their way. (Of course many partnership agreements do not say this; they might state that one partner's vote is to count more than another's, or that certain partners are to have a veto.)

Changes requiring unanimous consent

No matter what the partnership agreement says, a unanimous vote is required to alter the partnership agreement, to admit a new partner, or to vary the partnership business.

Altering the partnership agreement

Section 19 of the Partnership Act 1890 provides as follows:

'The mutual rights and duties of partners, whether ascertained by agreement or defined by this Act, may be varied by consent of all the partners, and such consent may either be express or inferred from a course of dealing.'

Variation of the agreement must be by *'consent of all the partners'*. This therefore implies that the decision to change must be unanimous. A majority of partners will not be able to force a minority to accept changes in the partnership agreement.

However, the section also says that an agreement to change can be *'inferred from a course of dealing'*. This makes it plain that changes can be made without any express agreement if all the partners behave as if the change had been agreed. So if some partners see that their fellow partners are acting contrary to the partnership agreement they should put a stop to this. If they do not, they will run the risk that the agreement will become altered by inference.

An example was given by Lord Eldon in *Const* v *Harris* (1824):

'If in a common partnership, the parties agree that no one of them shall draw or accept a bill of exchange in his own name, without the concurrence of all the others, yet, if they slide into a habit of permitting one of them to draw or accept bills, without the concurrence of the others, this court will hold that they have varied the terms of the original agreement in that respect.'

New partners

Section 24 (7) of the Act plainly states: *'No person may be introduced as a partner without the consent of all existing partners.'*

Varying the partnership business

Section 24 (8) is again quite clear: *'. . . no change may be made in the nature of the partnership business without the consent of all existing partners.'*

Apart from these areas where unanimity is required, the partnership agreement can make whatever rules the partners please.

Implied rules of the partnership

When we studied formation of partnerships we saw that the partners do not need to make any formal agreement. **Section 24** of the Partnership Act 1890 therefore lays down a number of rules which will apply if no agreement has been made, or if the agreement made does not cover the situation.

It is important to remember that these provisions contained in section 24 are to apply only if the partners have not made their own agreement to the contrary on the matters concerned.

The rules contained in section 24 are as follows.

Capital and profits

Section 24(1) states that all partners are entitled to share equally in the firm's capital and profits, and all must contribute equally to losses of capital. So if A and B go into partnership together and do not agree anything about profits and losses then they will share these equally. (In most partnerships this will not be the case – there will be an agreement to the contrary.)

If A put £10,000 capital into the firm, and B put in only £1,000 then on dissolution they would not share the capital equally. It would be implied that as they had contributed capital in the ratio 10:1 they should share what capital remains in the same ratio. However, A and B would share profits equally.

Indemnity

Section 24(2) states that if a partner incurs any expense in the ordinary and proper conduct of the firm's business, the firm must indemnify that partner in respect of the liability incurred.

For example, if partner A in firm ABC suddenly has to travel abroad on the firm's business then the firm must pay the expenses which A incurs.

Interest on capital and advances

Section 24(4) tells us that a partner is not entitled to any interest on **capital** which he has contributed to the partnership. But if he advances any money beyond the amount of capital he agreed to contribute this is treated as a **loan** to the partnership. Section 24(3) provides that interest on such loans should be paid at a rate of 5 per cent per annum. (It is of course quite likely that partnership agreements will make other rules, particularly about the rate of interest.)

Management

Section 24(5) provides that every partner may take part in the management of the firm. The partnership deed might however state that partners do not have an equal right to manage.

If the deed went further and excluded one partner from management that partner could apply to have the firm wound up on the just and equitable ground. Such an exclusion of the right to manage would run contrary to the very definition of a partner as a person who *'carries on a business in common . . .'*.

Remuneration

Section 24(6) says that no partner is entitled to any salary for taking part in the business.

(Again, it is very common for partnership agreements to provide that partners should be paid salaries. If salaries are paid this will obviously reduce the amount of profit available to be shared by the partners.)

Disputes about ordinary matters

Section 24(8) makes two provisions. First, it states that the nature of the partnership business may not be changed without the consent of all of the partners. Second, it states that differences about ordinary matters connected with the partnership business can be resolved by a simple majority.

So a majority of the partners in a firm of car dealers could take the decision to move to new premises. The decision to move into a new type of business, such as selling videos, would have to be unanimous.

Partnership books

Section 24(9) says that the partnership books are to be kept at the firm's place of business, and that every partner may have access to them, when he thinks fit, and inspect and copy any of them.

Expulsion of partners

Under section 25: *'No majority of the partners can expel any partner unless a power to do so has been conferred by express agreement between the partners.'*

This express agreement may well be contained in the partnership agreement. It is fairly common for an article in a partnership deed to lay down that a partner can be expelled for breaking the partnership rules. Even if this is the case, the partners must exercise the article in good faith. They cannot use it unjustifiably to expel a partner.

The duty of good faith

Partners are agents of their fellow partners and therefore owe each other a duty of the utmost good faith. Sections 28 to 30 of the 1890 Act spell out three important consequences of this: that partners must render true accounts and information, that they must account for profits, and that they must not compete with the firm.

Rendering true accounts and information

Under section 28: *'Partners are bound to render true accounts and full information of all things affecting the partnership to any partner or his legal representatives.'*

Law v Law (1905, Court of Appeal)

Two brothers, W and J, were partners in a manufacturing business in Halifax. J ran the firm while W lived in London and took little part in the firm's affairs. J bought W out for £21,000, but later W discovered that the business was worth far more than J had led him to believe.

Held The court set aside W's agreement to sell his share of the partnership. J had not put W in possession of all material facts relating to the partnership's assets.

Accounting for profits

Section 29 provides:

> *'Every partner must account to the firm for any benefit derived by him without the consent of the other partners from any transaction concerning the partnership, or from any use by him of the partnership property name or business connection.'*

If a partner makes any personal profit as a consequence of his being a partner he must hand this profit over to the firm.

Bentley v Craven (1853)

Bentley and Craven were in partnership together in a firm which bought and sold sugar. Craven was the firm's buyer and was therefore occasionally able to buy sugar at a greatly reduced price. On one occasion he was offered a consignment of sugar at well below the wholesale price. He bought this sugar himself and then sold it to the firm at the going wholesale rate.

Held Craven had to account to the firm for this secret profit. That is to say he had to pay the profit he had made to the firm. He had used a partnership asset (his position in the firm) to make the profit.

Competing with the firm

Section 30 of the Act states:

> *'If a partner, without the consent of the other partners, carries on any business of the same nature as and competing with that of the firm, he must account for and pay over to the firm all profits made by him in that business.'*

This section is similar to section 29. The difference is that under section 30 the partner is liable merely as a result of competing with the firm. He does not need to use partnership property or assets. Under section 29 a partner is liable for misusing partnership property or assets. He does not need to be competing with the firm.

Note that it is permissible for partners to compete with the firm or use the firm's assets to make a profit as long as the other partners consent to this.

ACTIVITY QUESTIONS 12.3

1 In a firm of six partners, five partners want the partnership agreement to be changed and one partner does not. Can the five insist that the agreement is changed?

2 How will the profits of a partnership be shared if there is no express agreement about the matter?

3 If a partner incurs expenses while at work on partnership business, will the partnership have to reimburse him?

4 Are partners automatically entitled to a salary?

5 A partner competes with the firm without telling his fellow partners. What will happen to profits he makes?

Further activity question 12.3

Decide the outcome of the following cases. The actual decisions are available at the end of this chapter.

Trimble v Goldberg (1906, Privy Council)

G, T and B went into partnership to buy and resell land and shares belonging to a South African. T went out to South Africa and bought all the land and the shares on behalf of the partnership. The shares were in a company called Sigma Syndicate, and while in South Africa T also bought land belonging to Sigma Syndicate. When G found out about this purchase he sued T, claiming the benefit of the purchase for the partnership.

Held

Hogar Estates Ltd v Shebron Holdings Ltd (1980)

H and S were in partnership as land developers. S offered to buy H out, explaining that the land had been refused planning permission. After the offer to buy was made, but before the contract was drawn up, S found out that he was highly likely to get planning permission in the future. He did not reveal this to H, who went ahead with the sale. When H found out what had happened he sued to have the agreement set aside.

Held

Pathirana v Pathirana (1967, Privy Council)

R and A were agents of Caltex (Ceylon) Ltd, selling petrol from a service station owned by Caltex. They began to fall out and A gave three months' notice of dissolution of the partnership. R, without A's knowledge, sent notice of this dissolution to Caltex and asked them to transfer the agency into his name alone. Caltex did this and R ran the business alone, but otherwise as before. A sued R for a share of the profits.

Held

Limited partnerships

It is not possible for all of the partners in a firm to have limited liability in the same way that all the shareholders in a limited company have limited liability. It is however possible for one or more of the partners to have limited liability under the Limited Partnership Act 1907. However, there must always be at least one general partner who has unlimited liability.

Every limited partnership must register with the Registrar of Companies, giving the following information:

(a) The firm name.
(b) The general nature of the business.
(c) The principal place of business.
(d) The full name of each of the partners.
(e) The date of commencement, and the length of time for which the business is entered into.
(f) A statement that the partnership is limited, and the description of every limited partner.
(g) The sum contributed by every limited partner, and whether paid in cash or otherwise.

There must then be two classes of partner in a limited partnership:

(a) **General partners**, who manage the business and have unlimited liability.
(b) **Limited partners**, who contribute a certain amount of capital and are not liable beyond this amount. They are **not allowed to take part in the management** of the business and are not agents of the firm. If a limited partner does take part in management he will lose his limited liability.

ACTIVITY QUESTIONS 12.4

1 Can a partnership have limited liability?

2 Can one of the partners have limited liability?

3 Can all of the partners in a firm have limited liability?

Further activity questions 12.4

1 A partner in a firm of general practitioners orders a new carpet for the surgery. The other partners are furious about this because they bought a new carpet, from a different shop, six months earlier. Which one of the following is true?

   (a) The firm is liable for the price of the new carpet under section 5.
   (b) The firm is liable under section 7.

(c) The firm is not liable under section 5 or section 7 because only one partner, without the authority of the others, made the contract.

2 A partner in a firm of solicitors orders a very expensive telescope, saying that it is for the partnership. His fellow partners did not authorise the contract and are refusing to be bound by it. Which one of the following statements is true?

(a) The firm is liable under section 5.
(b) The firm is liable under section 7.
(c) The firm is not liable under section 5 or section 7, but the partner who made the order is personally liable.

3 A partner in a firm of builders, while drunk, drives the firm's van through a customer's greenhouse. Which of the following is true?

(a) The firm is liable if the partner was at work when he did it.
(b) As it was the firm's van, the firm is liable whether the partner was at work or not.
(c) The firm is not liable under any circumstances. It is not within the usual course of business to drive vans through greenhouses.

4 A, B and C are in partnership. No agreement has been made as to how profits or capital are to be shared. At the outset A contributed £10,000 capital, B £5,000 and C £1,000. Which of the following is true:

(a) Profits should be shared equally and (on dissolution) so should capital.
(b) Profits should be shared equally, but capital should be shared unequally.
(c) Profits and capital should be shared in the proportion to which capital was contributed.

5 D, E and F are in partnership. F is sometimes very extravagant and the partnership deed forbids him to buy anything on the firm's behalf. If F does buy goods, which of the following is true?

(a) The firm will always be liable.
(b) The firm will be liable if the goods were in the usual course of business, as long as the supplier did not know of the prohibition.
(c) The firm will be liable if the goods were in the usual course of the firm's business, even if the supplier did know of the prohibition.

6 G, a partner in GHI Fruit and Vegetables, impulsively makes the following contracts in the firm's name. By which of them would his partners be bound?

(a) He takes out an unnecessary bank loan for the firm.
(b) He orders a new computer game for H's son's 21st birthday.

(c) He orders a top of the range computer to help with the firm's accounts.

(d) He orders a new and unnecessary delivery van.

(e) He orders a ton of ripe bananas.

TASK 12

The Albanian students visiting your college are keen to understand the risks which a partner assumes.

Using a medical partnership as an example, write a report indicating:

a) The extent to which one partner can be liable for goods ordered by another partner.

b) The extent to which a partner can be liable for another partner's torts.

c) What duties the partners will owe to each other.

d) Whether any partner can limit his potential liability.

Case decisions

There follow the actual decisions in the cases set out at pages 267 and 277.

Mercantile Credit Co v Garrod

Held The firm was liable under section 5, despite the prohibition as to buying and selling cars. An outsider would have thought that it was in the usual course of the firm's business to buy and sell cars, and therefore a contract to sell a car would be binding on the firm.

Bond v Gibson

Held G was liable. Purchasing bits would be a normal part of the firm's business.

Blyth v Fladgate

Held All the partners in the firm were liable. S had committed the tort in the ordinary course of the firm's business.

Arbuckle v Taylor

Held The other partners were not liable for the tort. It was not within the ordinary scope of the firm's business to bring criminal proceedings against outsiders.

D & H Bunny Ltd v Atkins

Held A was liable even though the firm never came into existence. A had held himself out to be a partner, and was therefore liable as if he was a partner.

Trimble v Goldberg

Held G's action failed. It was not within the scope of the firm's business to buy the land belonging to Sigma Syndicate. Nor did buying the land amount to rivalry with the firm.

Hogar Estates Ltd v Shebron Holdings Ltd

Held The agreement was set aside. S had broken his fiduciary duty even though he had not made a misrepresentation and could not be proved to have been dishonest.

Pathirana v Pathirana

Held A was entitled to a share of the profits. Section 29 applied because R had used his business connections to acquire the agency for himself.

13 Types of business liability: civil and criminal/contract and tort

In chapter 1 we outlined the essential differences between civil and criminal liability, and compared contractual liability with liability in tort. In this chapter we examine these matters in more detail.

Civil and criminal liability

The burden of proof in civil and criminal law

The burden of proof is concerned with the degree to which a case must be proved. The criminal law demands one burden of proof and the civil law another.

Criminal law

In **criminal cases** the prosecution must prove all the elements of the crime **beyond a reasonable doubt**.

Woolmington v DPP (1935, House of Lords)

The accused was charged with murder after he shot his mother-in-law with a double barrelled shotgun. His defence was that he had not intended to shoot her. The accused's wife had gone to live with the mother-in-law and the accused said that he took the gun around to the mother-in-law's house, threatening to shoot himself if his wife did not return. He claimed that the gun had gone off accidentally, killing the mother-in-law. The trial judge said that the jury should convict the accused of murder unless he could prove that his story was true. They did convict him, and his appeal went to the House of Lords.

Held The conviction for murder was overturned. The trial judge had misdirected the jury. The prosecution should have proved, beyond a reasonable doubt, that the accused's story was not true.

> Lord Sankey *'Throughout the web of the English criminal law one golden thread is always to be seen – that it is the duty of the prosecution to prove the prisoner's guilt. . . . If . . . there is a reasonable doubt . . . the prosecution has not made out the case and the prisoner is entitled to an acquittal.'*

Civil law

In **civil cases** the plaintiff will have to prove two things:

(a) that the facts he alleges are true; and
(b) that these facts give rise to liability.

For example, a plaintiff seeking damages on account of a car accident must prove:

(a) that it was the defendant's bad driving which caused the accident; and
(b) that such bad driving amounts to a tort.

The two things must be proved **on a balance of probabilities**, which means that the judge must think it more likely than not that they are true.

Analysis of a crime

The elements of a crime

Almost all crimes are made up of two elements, an *actus reus* (guilty act) and a *mens rea* (guilty mind). The prosecution must prove **both** beyond a reasonable doubt. This can best be understood by examining homicide. Although it would be most unusual for a person to commit homicide as a business activity, it is the crime which provides the best example of the principles of *actus reus* and *mens rea*. Once understood, these principles can then be applied to other crimes.

Homicide includes murder and manslaughter and the *actus reus* of both murder and manslaughter is the same. For both crimes the accused must voluntarily and unlawfully cause the death of another human being, either by doing some act or by omitting to do some act. The victim must die within a year and a day of the injury inflicted. It is the different *mens rea* of the two crimes which distinguishes them. The *mens rea* **of murder** is that the accused either intended to kill or intended to cause serious harm. The *mens rea* **of manslaughter** is that the accused was acting in a grossly negligent or reckless manner. (There are also several defences which reduce murder to manslaughter.)

So if an accused kills another person by shooting him with a gun, the *actus reus* of both murder and manslaughter is established. Which crime, if either, the accused will have committed will depend upon the accused's state of mind when he pulled the trigger.

If the accused intended to kill the victim or intended to cause serious injury then he will be guilty of murder. If the accused was grossly negligent, perhaps pointing the gun at a friend in the belief that it was unloaded, then he will be guilty of manslaughter.

If the accused has neither *mens rea* he will not be guilty of either offence. If, for example, he shot the victim on a firing range, not knowing that the victim was hiding behind one of the targets, he would not be guilty of murder, manslaughter, or any other crime.

ACTIVITY QUESTIONS 13.1

1 To establish that a defendant has committed a crime, the prosecution must prove that the defendant committed the *actus reus* of that crime while having the *mens rea* of the same crime. What is meant by:

(a) The *actus reus*?

(b) The *mens rea*?

(c) To what extent must the prosecution prove these two things?

2 (a) To win a civil case, what two things must the plaintiff prove?

(b) To what extent must the plaintiff prove the two things?

Further activity questions 13.1

1 Theft is defined by section 1 of the Theft Act 1968, which states that a person is guilty of theft if he '*dishonestly appropriates property belonging to another with the intention of permanently depriving the other of it*'. A person '*appropriates*' property if he deals with it as if he were the owner of it. (By walking off with it, for example, or destroying it.) Which of the following parts of the definition relate to the *actus reus* of the crime, and which relate to the *mens rea*?

(a) *dishonestly*

(b) *appropriates property belonging to another*

(c) *with the intention of permanently depriving the other of it.*

2 Section 15 of the Theft Act 1968 says that a person will be guilty of obtaining by deception if he '*by any deception dishonestly appropriates property belonging to another, with the intention of permanently depriving the other of it*'. Break the words of this definition down into the *actus reus* and the *mens rea* of the crime.

Actus reus and *mens rea* must coincide

A person can only be guilty of a crime if he commits the *actus reus* of that crime at the same time as he has the *mens rea*. A person who today accidentally ran over his enemy would not be guilty of murder on account of his having unsuccessfully attempted to run him over yesterday. Such a person would have had the *mens rea* of murder yesterday and have committed the *actus reus* today, but that is not enough. The two must coincide.

Similarly, an accused must intend to commit the *actus reus* in the manner in which he did commit it. If an accused was driving around to his enemy's house, with the intention of shooting him dead, he would not be guilty of murder if he accidentally ran over his enemy on the way.

The doctrine of **transferred malice** holds that a person can be guilty of a crime even if the outcome of his actions was not quite what he expected. For example, if A shoots a gun at B intending to kill him, but misses and kills C, he will still be guilty of murder. He is guilty because he had the *mens rea* for murder at the same time as he had the *actus reus* for murder. Transferred malice will apply only where a person has the *actus reus* and *mens rea* of **the same crime**.

R v Pembliton (1874)

The accused and his friends had been thrown out of a pub. They then fought with a crowd of people. After the fight the accused threw a large stone at the people he had been fighting with, intending to hurt them. The stone missed the people, but broke a large window. The accused was charged with maliciously damaging the window.

Held He was not guilty of this offence. He had the *actus reus* of malicious damage to property (he broke the window) but he did not have the *mens rea* (he did not intend to break it). Nor would he have been guilty of maliciously wounding the people he threw the stone at. He had the *mens rea* for that crime, but not the *actus reus*.

R v Latimer (1866)

The accused had a fight with another man in a pub. Having got the worst of the fight, the accused went out into the pub yard. He came back into the pub with his belt in his hand and swung it at the man with whom he had been fighting. The belt only grazed this man, but it bounced off him and severely wounded the woman he was talking to. The accused was charged with maliciously wounding the woman.

Held The accused was guilty of malicious wounding. He had committed the *actus reus* of that crime (by wounding the woman) at the same time as he had the *mens rea* (by intending to wound the man).

Parliament has created a number of offences which do not require *mens rea*. These tend to be public welfare offences, where it is thought that the public are best protected by imposing criminal liability on businesses. There are too many of these offences to list them all here. However, the attitude of the courts can be understood by studying one of them.

Smedleys Ltd v *Breed* (1974, House of Lords)

In the seven-week canning season Smedleys canned three and a half million tins of peas in one factory. One tin was found to contain a caterpillar, which was similar to a pea in size, weight, colour and density. Eating the caterpillar would not have been injurious to health. Smedleys were charged under section 2(1) of the Food and Drug Act 1955 with selling food which is not of the substance demanded by the purchaser.

Held Smedleys were guilty despite the fact that they had taken all reasonable care in the preparation of the food.

Further activity question 13.2

Smedleys were convicted of a crime even though they did not know they had committed it and had taken all reasonable precautions to avoid committing it.

(a) What do the courts and Parliament hope to achieve by imposing strict liability in this way?

(b) Is it fair to businesses?

(c) Would manufacturers behave differently if *mens rea* had to be proved for crimes such as the one for which Smedleys were convicted?

Liability in contract and liability in tort

In Chapter 1 we defined a tort as *'a civil wrong which is not a breach of contract'*. We noticed that this definition makes it plain that civil liability can be classified into two types: liability arising in contract, and liability arising in tort.

We also saw that liability under a contract is voluntarily undertaken whereas tortious liability is imposed by the courts, and noted the different purposes of contract damages and tort damages.

By examining the major tort, the tort of negligence, it is possible to appreciate these differences more fully and to introduce concepts, such as forseeability and defences, which apply to most torts.

Negligence

In order to establish negligence the plaintiff must prove three things:

(a) That the defendant owed him a duty of care.
(b) That the defendant breached that duty.
(c) That forseeable damage resulted from the breach.

The duty of care

Donoghue v *Stevenson*
(1932, House of Lords)

The plaintiff's friend bought a bottle of ginger beer and gave it to the plaintiff. After the plaintiff had drunk some of the ginger beer she discovered the remains of a decomposed snail in the bottle. This gave her gastro-enteritis and caused her to suffer nervous shock. She could not sue the retailer of the ginger beer because

she had no contract with the retailer. Instead she sued the manufacturer of the ginger beer, claiming that the manufacturer owed a duty of care to his customers.

Held (3:2) The plaintiff won. Manufacturers owe a duty of care to see that their customers are not injured by their product.

> Lord Atkin '*You must take reasonable care to avoid acts and omissions which you can reasonably forsee would be likely to injure your neighbour. Who, then, in law is my neighbour? The answer seems to be – persons who are so closely and directly affected by my act that I ought reasonably have them in contemplation as being so affected when I am directing my mind to the acts or omissions which are called in question.*'

Using this famous '**neighbour speech**,' the courts have established certain **duty situations**. For example, it is well established that road users owe a duty of care to other road users and pedestrians. Similarly, manufacturers and repairers owe a duty to their customers.

When a new situation arises the courts will go back to Lord Atkin's speech and decide whether a duty is owed under the 'neighbour principle'. For example, in *Spring* v *Guardian Assurance PLC* (1994, House of Lords) it was decided that employers owe a duty of care to employees when they are preparing references. If they break this duty by giving an unjustifiably bad reference the employee can sue.

Breaching the duty

Merely owing a duty of care is not enough to give rise to an action for negligence. Every time a person gets into a car he owes a duty of care to many people. He is not liable to be sued by such people unless he injures them by breaching the duty which he owes them.

A duty of care will be breached if the defendant does not take the care which a reasonable man would take. This is an **objective** standard; it is no defence that the defendant was doing his incompetent best. Notice the contrast with criminal law here – most *mens rea* demand that the accused deliberately does wrong.

A higher standard of care is expected of professional people. They must show the degree of care which a reasonably competent person in that profession would show.

A defendant will not breach the duty if he could not have foreseen that his action would cause injury.

Roe v *Minister of Health* (1954, Court of Appeal)

In 1947 the plaintiff was paralysed by an anaesthetic used by the defendant. The anaesthetic was kept in glass ampoules which were stored in disinfectant. Traces of disinfectant had seeped through the glass ampoules and into the anaesthetic.

Held The defendant was not liable because in 1947 no one knew that fluid could permeate glass. Of course a hospital would have been liable if a similar accident had occurred after this fact had become known. The court, Denning LJ said, *'must not look at the 1947 accident with 1954 spectacles'*.

In deciding whether or not a duty has been breached the court will consider four factors:

(a) The **likelihood of harm**.
(b) The **potential seriousness of damage**.
(c) The **cost of prevention**.
(d) The **usefulness of the defendant's actions**.

The first two factors are weighed against the second two. If the first two are greater than the second two, then the duty will have been breached: if they are smaller, it will not. This sounds rather complicated, but two cases illustrate that it is relatively straightforward.

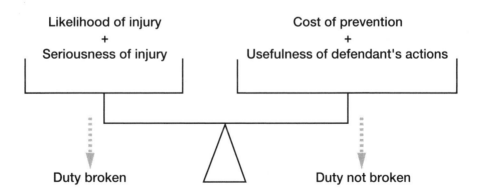

Fig 13.1 Duty of care: factors to be taken into account

Bolton v *Stone* (1951, House of Lords)

A cricket ball was hit right out of the ground and struck and injured the plaintiff. The ball cleared a 7 foot high fence built on a 10 foot high bank. The plaintiff was 22 yards beyond the fence, about 100 yards from the wicket. About half a dozen balls had been hit out of the ground in the previous 30 years.

Held The duty was not broken. A and B (the likelihood of harm and the potential seriousness of damage) were much smaller than C and D (the cost of preventing the accident).

The usefulness of playing cricket was not much of a factor in this case. However, it was accepted that people need to take recreation and that cricket is a traditional type of English recreation.

Paris v *Stepney Borough Council* (1951, House of Lords)

The plaintiff, who had the use of only one eye, was told by his employers to hammer the underneath of a vehicle. He was not given protective goggles and lost the use of his good eye when this was pierced by a shard of metal.

Held The duty was broken. A and B (the likelihood of harm and the potential seriousness of damage) were much greater than C and D (the cost of preventing the accident and the usefulness of working without goggles).

The usefulness of the defendant's actions tends to be an important factor in cases where the defendant acted in an emergency.

Watt v *Hertfordshire CC* (1954, Court of Appeal)

A fire station received a call that a woman was trapped under a heavy vehicle about 250 yards away from the station. The officer in charge set off immediately, ordering that a lorry should be loaded with heavy lifting gear and that it should follow as soon as possible. The lifting gear was loaded on to the back of the lorry, but there was no time to lash it down. When the lorry braked one of the firemen travelling with the lifting gear was injured.

Held The fire authority was not negligent. The risk to the firemen had to be balanced against the end to be achieved.

> Denning LJ *'If this accident had happened in a commercial enterprise without any emergency, there could be no doubt that the [fireman] would succeed. But the commercial end to make profit is very different from the human end to save life and limb. The saving of life and limb justifies the taking of considerable risk.'*

ACTIVITY QUESTIONS 13.3

1 Is contractual liability voluntarily undertaken or imposed by the courts? What about liability in tort?

2 To establish the tort of negligence, what three things must the plaintiff prove?

Further activity question 13.3

Using the four factors which the courts take into account, decide whether or not the duty was broken in the following cases. Do not write your answers down as the actual decisions are available at the end of this chapter.

Miller v *Jackson* (1977, Court of Appeal)

A village cricket team had their pitch close to some houses. Balls were hit out of the ground fairly frequently. The plaintiff recorded 13 incidents between July 1972 and July 1975. The action was commenced after a cricket ball hit the hinge of a dining room window. A young child was sitting behind the glass (which did not break).

Held

Haley v *London Electricity Board* (1965, House of Lords)

Electricity Board workers dug a 60 foot trench in the pavement and left warning signs at both ends of the trench. They also laid a long-handled hammer across one end of the trench, and picks and shovels across the other. These precautions would have been quite sufficient for ordinarily sighted people. But the plaintiff, who was blind, tripped on the hammer and banged his head on the pavement. As a result of this accident he became almost totally deaf. The plaintiff was not himself negligent, his white stick passed over the hammer.

Held

Glasgow Corporation v *Muir* (1943, House of Lords)

The manageress of a tea room allowed two members of a picnic party to carry an urn of tea through the tea room. Access to the tea room could be gained only by passing through a small shop. As the picnickers passed through the shop one of them let go of the urn. Several gallons of boiling tea were spilt and some young children, who were in the shop buying sweets, were scalded.

Held

Latimer v *AEC Ltd* (1953, House of Lords)

During an abnormally heavy rain storm, the floor of a factory became flooded. This caused an oily cooling mixture to escape from a channel in the floor and mix with the water. As a result the factory floor became very slippery. The employer put down sawdust to make the floor less slippery. A workman was trying to load a heavy barrel on to a lorry in an area of the factory which had not been treated with sawdust. He slipped and injured himself.

Held

Res ipsa loquitor

As negligence is a civil action, the plaintiff must prove his case on a balance of probabilities. Sometimes he will not be able to prove in precisely what way the defendant was negligent. In *Donoghue* v *Stevenson*, for instance, the plaintiff would not have been able to prove exactly how the defendants were negligent in allowing the snail to get into the bottle of ginger beer.

Res ipsa loquitor ('the thing speaks for itself') can **reverse the burden of proof**, meaning that the defendant must prove that the damage was not caused by his failure to take reasonable care.

Res ipsa loquitor will apply only if three conditions are satisfied:

(a) The defendant must have been in control of the thing that caused the damage.
(b) The accident must be of a kind which would not normally happen without carelessness.
(c) The cause of the accident must be unknown.

Scott v *London & St Katherine Docks Co* (1865)

The plaintiff, a customs officer at work in the docks, was passing the defendants' warehouse when he was injured by six bags of sugar which fell on him. The plaintiff could not prove how this had happened.

Held *Res ipsa loquitor* applied and so the burden of proof was reversed. The defendants therefore had to prove that they had not been negligent. They were unable to do this, and so the plaintiff won.

Forseeable damage resulted from the breach of duty

A plaintiff can recover damages only if he can prove that the defendant's breach of duty **caused** his loss. Furthermore, he must prove that the loss was of a type which would **foreseeably** follow from the defendant's breach.

Causation

The plaintiff can recover damages only in respect of a loss which he can prove was caused by the defendant's actions. There must be a chain of causation between what the defendant did and the loss which the plaintiff suffered. This chain must not be broken by *novus actus interviens* (a new act intervening).

The Orepesa (1943, Privy Council)

A ship called 'The Orepesa' was negligently navigated and damaged another ship. The captain of the other ship decided to approach 'The Orepesa' in a lifeboat, to discuss the best way to save the ship. The lifeboat overturned in the heavy sea and several crew members were drowned. Their relatives sued the owners of 'The Orepesa'.

Held The owners of 'The Orepesa' were liable. The actions of the captain of the other ship did not break the chain of causation because they were reasonable under the circumstances.

Unreasonable actions will break the chain. So if one of the lifeboat crew had drowned after deciding to swim to 'The Orepesa' then the chain would have been broken and the owners of 'The Orepesa' would not have been liable for his death.

Foreseeability

The damage suffered by the plaintiff must be a **type of damage** which was forseeable. The extent of the damage does not need to be forseeable, nor does the precise way in which it arose.

Defences to negligence

Contributory negligence

This is not a complete defence, but reduces the damages payable to the plaintiff. Individual damages for personal injuries can run to over a million pounds, and any percentage reduction can amount to a great deal of money.

The Law Reform (Contributory Negligence) Act 1945, section 1 provides:

'Where any person suffers damage as the result partly of his own fault and partly of the fault of any other person . . . the damages recoverable . . . shall be reduced to such an extent as the court thinks just and equitable having regard to the claimant's share in the responsibility for the damage.'

Froom v Butcher (1975, Court of Appeal)

A motorist was injured by an accident which was not in any way his own fault. He suffered injuries to his head, chest and finger. If he had been wearing a seat belt (which in those days was not compulsory) the injuries to his head and chest would have been avoided altogether.

Held The damages in respect of the head and chest injuries were reduced by 25 per cent. The damages for injury to his finger were not reduced.

Now that it is compulsory to wear a seat belt the damages would probably be reduced to a far greater extent.

Volenti non fit injuria ('to one who volunteers no harm is done')

It is a complete defence to show that the injured person voluntarily assumed the risk which injured him. The defence is known by its Latin name, *volenti non fit injuria*, and often defeats employees who are injured as a result of not following safety procedures.

ICI Ltd v Shatwell (1965, House of Lords)

Shot firers were badly injured when they tested detonators without taking the proper safety precautions. They sued their employer, who did not know that the safety precautions had not been adopted.

Held The employer had a complete defence. The injured workers had voluntarily assumed the risk which injured them.

Damages

It has already been stated that the purpose of tort damages is to put the injured party into the position he would have been in if the tort had not been committed. However, if the plaintiff has suffered physical injuries it may not be possible to return him to the physical condition he was in before the tort was committed. Consequently, he may claim damages for pain and suffering, and loss of enjoyment of life, as well as for lost earnings. As a matter of policy, damages for mere 'economic' loss are not recoverable.

Spartan Steel & Alloys Ltd v *Martin & Co Ltd* (1972, Court of Appeal)

The defendant's employees damaged an electricity cable while digging up a road. This caused the plaintiffs' factory to be without electricity for 14 hours. Without electricity the plaintiffs could not maintain the temperature of molten metal in a mould. Consequently this metal had to be poured away. The plaintiffs claimed for the loss of the metal and also for 14 hours' lost production.

Held The loss of the molten metal was allowed. But the claim for lost production was classed as 'economic' loss and not allowed.

TASK 13

The Albanian students visiting your college want to know the difference in English law between civil and criminal liability. Yesterday you read in the paper of a hotel owner who not only stole a watch from a guest's room but who also served soup which gave several guests gastro-enteritis. Using the hotel owner as an example, explain:

a) What matters would need to be proved, and the extent to which these matters would need to be proved, in order to convict the hotelier of the crime of theft.

b) What matters would need to be proved, and the extent to which these matters would be needed to be proved, in order for the hotelier to be liable in negligence.

c) The purpose of convicting the hotelier of theft and the purpose of the guest suing in negligence.

d) Other ways in which a small hotel might be liable for negligence.

Case decisions

There follow the actual decisions in the cases set out at pages 291–2.

Miller v Jackson (1977)

Held The duty was broken because a serious accident was quite likely to happen. The risk of injury, and the potential seriousness of injury, outweighed the cost of prevention and the usefulness of the cricket club's activities. (However, in some ways this was almost a split decision. The court found that the defendants were liable for nuisance as well as negligence but refused to grant an injunction prohibiting further cricket matches, recognising that it was in the public interest that people should engage in sports such as cricket. The only remedy available was damages.)

Haley v London Electricity Board (1965)

Held The defendants were liable. The likelihood of injury was fairly high (blind people must walk up and down the pavement) and the injury was fairly serious. The cost of prevention (adequately fencing off the hole) was minimal. There was nothing useful in not fencing the hole.

Glasgow Corporation v Muir (1943)

Held The duty was not broken. A reasonable person could not have anticipated the damage to the children. The likelihood of injury was minimal.

Latimer v AEC Ltd (1953)

Held The employer was not liable. He had done all that could reasonably be expected of him, considering the risk involved (the likelihood of harm and the seriousness of injury). The cost of preventing the injury, shutting down the factory, was very high. Such a cost would be justified in some circumstances, but in this case it was not.

14 Types of business liability: vicarious/strict and fault based/common law and statutory

Vicarious liability

A person who is vicariously liable takes the blame for the fault of someone else. The concept is an ancient one. In the Middle Ages if a royal schoolboy misbehaved his 'whipping boy' was punished.

These days vicarious liability is placed on employers. They are vicariously liable for employees who commit torts during the course of their employment.

So if an employee, while performing his work, injures another person then both he and his employer will be liable. The employee will be personally liable and the employer will be vicariously liable.

The injured person is likely to sue the employer rather than the employee. (The employer ought to be insured, and should therefore have the assets to pay any damages awarded.)

Vicarious liability will only arise if two conditions are satisfied:

(a) The relationship between the boss and the worker was that of employer and employee.
(b) The employee committed the tort during the course of his employment.

Who is an employee?

A person who works for another may do so either as an employee or as an independent contractor. Sometimes it is easy to tell the difference between the two. College lecturers, shop assistants and bank managers are easily recognisable as employees. Window cleaners and jobbing builders are usually independent contractors. But other workers can be very difficult to categorise, and the courts have devised several tests to distinguish employees from independent contractors.

The control test

This test says that a worker is an employee if the boss controls not only **what** he does but also **how** he does it.

Walker v CPFC (1910)

A professional footballer signed a one-year contract with Crystal Palace Football Club. He was paid £3 10s a week and had to attend training every day at 10.30 am. While playing he was injured. If he was a 'workman' he could obtain compensation under a statute then in force. If he was an independent contractor the statute would not help him.

Held He was an employee, a workman. Not only did he have to do what he was told (train and play matches), but he also had to do this in the manner in which he was told to do it.

The trouble with this test is that it tends to regard all highly skilled workers as independent contractors. Most surgeons, for example, are employees of the health authorities for which they work. But the control test would tend to classify them as independent contractors. The health authorities exercise control in that they tell the surgeons what to do, but they do not tell the surgeons **how** to perform their operations (although they can insist that certain practices and procedures are followed).

The integration test

This test was created by Lord Denning, who said that *'under a contract of [employment], a man is employed as part of the business, and his work is done as an integral part of the business; whereas, under [an independent contract], his work although done for the business, is not integrated into it but is only accessory to it'*. Lord Denning made the same point more simply when he stated that employees are employed as *'part and parcel of the organisation'*.

If we apply the integration test to an obvious employee, a school teacher, and an obvious independent contractor, a roofer fixing the school roof for £600, we see that the test achieves the correct results. The teacher is employed as part and parcel of the business. His job is not confined to teaching his classes. He is concerned with the general welfare of the school and the students. He is an integral part of the organisation. But the roofer is not employed as part and parcel of the business. All that he cares about is that he gets the job done and gets paid for it. Apart from that he could not care whether the school prospers or not. His work is not done as an integral part of the business, it is only accessory to it.

We saw that the control test was not always satisfactory when applied to highly skilled workers. The integration test seems better to achieve the right results.

Cassidy v *Ministry of Health* (1951, Court of Appeal)

The plaintiff, a general labourer, was suffering from Dupuytren's contraction, which restricted the use of two of the fingers of his left hand. After an operation, his hand was kept rigid in a splint for 14 days. When the splint was removed the defendant's whole hand was useless.

Held The hospital was vicariously liable for the doctors and the nurses who treated the patient. They were all employees because they were all part and parcel of the hospital.

The multiple test

This test, created by Mackenna J in 1968, is currently the one which is most in favour with the courts. It says that a worker will be an employee if three conditions are satisfied:

(a) He agrees to provide **his own** work and skill in return for a wage or other payment.
(b) He agrees, expressly or impliedly, that he will be **under the control** of the person paying for his work.
(c) The rest of the terms of the contract are **consistent with** a contract of employment. (This would include matters such as who paid the worker's tax, what type of national insurance contributions he paid and who provided equipment.)

ACTIVITY QUESTIONS 14.1

1 What is meant by vicarious liability?

2 Why would a person injured by an employee generally prefer to sue the employer rather than the employee who injured him?

Further activity questions 14.1

1 Mackenna J formulated the multiple test in the following case. Read the facts of the case and decide which of the facts pointed towards a contract of employment and which pointed towards a contract for independent services. Then try to decide whether the court held the drivers to be employees or independent contractors. The actual decision is available at the end of this chapter.

Ready Mixed Concrete Ltd v *MPNI* (1968)

Drivers carried concrete for the company at their own expense and were paid for doing so by the mile. The drivers had to buy a lorry and paint it in the company's colours. The company provided hire purchase for this, but the drivers had to maintain, repair and insure their lorries. Drivers had to wear the company uniform and obey the company rules. They were not allowed to act as carriers except as specified in their contract with the company. The contract said that the drivers were independent contractors, and they could use substitute drivers if they were unable to work themselves.

Held

2 What would the outcome of the *Ready Mixed Concrete* case have been if the courts had applied:
(a) The control test?
(b) The integration test?

3 Use the three tests to decide whether the following workers are employees or independent contractors. Then complete the chart by writing either 'employee' or 'independent contractor' in the relevant boxes. Some of the boxes have been completed to get you started.
(a) Is a door to door salesman, paid commission only, an employee of the firm for which he works?
(b) Is a solicitor, selling a house for a client, an employee of the client?
(c) Is the chief solicitor of a local authority an employee of the authority?
(d) Is a postman an employee of the Post Office?
(e) Is a plumber, putting central heating in a house for £2,000, an employee of the householder?
(f) Is an actress starring in a film an employee of the film company?
(g) Is a driving instructor an employee of his pupil?

Test used / Worker	Control test	Integration test	Multiple test
Door to door salesman			
Solicitor acting for client	*Independent contractor*		
Chief solicitor			*employee*
Postman			
Plumber		*Independent contractor*	
Actress			
Driving instructor			

When is an employee in the course of his employment?

Employers are liable for the torts of their employees only if these torts were committed in the course of the employee's employment. If a bus driver, for example, crashes a bus while at work the bus company will be liable to people who are injured. If the same driver crashes his own car while driving to the supermarket the bus company will not be liable.

In many cases, as with the bus driver in the example above, it is easy to tell whether or not an employee is acting in the course of his employment. In other cases it is not so easy, and over the years the courts have developed the following rules:

(a) An employee will be acting in the course of his employment when he is doing what he was expressly or impliedly authorised to do.

Poland v John Parr and Sons (1927, Court of Appeal)

An employee wrongly believed that a boy was tampering with a bag of sugar on one of the employer's wagons. To protect the sugar, the employee slapped the boy who fell under the wagon. The boy suffered injuries which resulted in the amputation of his leg.

Held The employer was vicariously liable. The employee had implied authorisation to protect the employer's property.

(b) If an employee is authorised to do an act properly then the employer will be liable if the employee performs the act negligently.

This is obviously the case. If all employees performed their duties properly then it would be most unusual for cases of vicarious liability ever to arise. It is when employees perform their duties negligently that accidents happen.

Century Insurance Co v NIRTB (1942, House of Lords)

The driver of a petrol tanker, while emptying his tanker, lit a cigarette and threw away the match. This caused a huge explosion.

Held The employer was liable. The driver was employed to empty his tanker and that was what he was doing when he caused the explosion.

(c) If an employee commits the tort while doing some act which is designed to help the employer then the employer will be liable.

Kay v ITW (1967, Court of Appeal)

The assistant manager of a warehouse was authorised to drive small vans and cars. In order to make a space in the warehouse, he moved a large diesel truck belonging to another firm. He did not notice that the truck was in reverse, and when he started it up he ran over the plaintiff.

Held The employer was liable. The employee moved the truck so that he could get on with his work.

(d) If the employee does something entirely for his own benefit he is said to be 'on a frolic of his own,' and the employer will not be liable.

Hilton v Thomas Burton Ltd (1961)

In the middle of the afternoon, employees of a demolition contractor drove five miles from their place of work to visit a cafe. On the way back the driver crashed the firm's van and the foreman was killed. The employer did not mind the men using the firm's van to fetch refreshments.

Held The employer was not liable. The men were acting entirely for their own benefit and were therefore on a frolic of their own.

Liability for prohibited acts

If the employer prohibits the employee from performing certain acts then generally he will not be liable if the employee ignores the prohibition. But if the employer's prohibition is only as to the **manner of performing** an authorised act then he will remain liable. Two cases illustrate this distinction.

Iqbal v London Transport Executive (1973, Court of Appeal)

A bus conductor had been expressly prohibited from driving buses. The bus on which he worked was parked in such a way that it was causing an obstruction. The conductor was ordered to fetch an engineer to move the bus. He attempted to move the bus himself and caused an accident.

Held The employer was not liable. The conductor was acting outside the course of his employment because the thing he had been expressly forbidden to do (driving buses) was never part of his job.

Limpus v London General Omnibus Co (1862)

The defendants' bus driver obstructed a bus belonging to the plaintiff in order to prevent it passing. This caused injury to one of the plaintiff's horses and damage to his bus. The defendants had specifically ordered their drivers not to race with or obstruct other firms' buses.

Held The defendants were liable. The driver was in the course of his employment when he caused the accident. He had express authorisation to drive buses. The prohibition was only as to the manner of doing this. (If this were not the case then all transport firms could avoid liability for accidents caused by their drivers. They would merely need frequently to order the drivers to obey the highway code at all times.)

Defences

Both *volenti non fit injuria* and **contributory negligence** will be available to an employer who is sued on the grounds of vicarious liability.

ACTIVITY QUESTION 14.2

Parveen, a chemistry teacher, is employed by her local authority. Would the local authority be liable for the following?

(a) During a laboratory experiment, Parveen overheats some chemicals and causes a small explosion which injures several students.
(b) She injures a pedestrian when reversing out of the school car park to visit a student on work experience.
(c) She injures a pedestrian when reversing out of the school car park to go home at the end of her school day.
(d) Noticing that there is no electricity in the laboratory, she switches on the supply at the main fuse box. This causes injury to an electrician who had cut off the supply so that he could check the wiring. All of the teachers had been warned that the electrician would need to disconnect the electricity but Parveen had forgotten.

Further activity question 14.2

John, a building labourer, is employed by a building company. Would the company be liable for the following?

(a) John moves a JCB, which he is not authorised to drive, so that he can continue digging a trench. He does not notice that the JCB is in reverse and injures a colleague.
(b) John habitually drives a JCB on site, even though the foreman knows that he has no licence to do this. While driving the JCB he knocks over a colleague.
(c) John and his colleagues sometimes play a game whereby they deliberately drive as close to each other as they can. While doing this John injures a work mate.
(d) On his birthday John drives the JCB down the main road to the pub. On the way he crashes into a car, severely injuring its occupants.

Strict and fault based liability

As we have already seen, criminal liability and liability in tort are generally fault based. If a person is blameless then he usually incurs no liability. Already though we have noticed one or two minor exceptions. In *Rylands* v *Fletcher* (page 184) the defendant was liable even though it was not his fault that the water escaped from his land. In *Smedleys Ltd* v *Breed* (page 286) Smedleys were liable for the caterpillar in their peas even though they had taken all reasonable care. Strict liability is far more likely to be imposed on businesses than on individuals. In this chapter we examine important statutes which impose strict civil liability and strict criminal liability on businesses.

Strict civil liability

The Consumer Protection Act 1987 Part I

In 1985 a European Community Directive ordered all member states to pass legislation to introduce the concept of **product liability**. The United Kingdom passed the Consumer Protection Act 1987 to comply with this Directive.

Under Part I of the Act, a plaintiff who is injured by an unsafe product will be able to sue the manufacturer of the product (and possibly others) without having to prove the tort of negligence.

When we considered negligence we saw that manufacturers owe a duty of care to their customers. In *Donoghue* v *Stevenson* (page 287), the manufacturers of the ginger beer were liable to Mrs Donoghue because they broke the duty of care which they owed her. However, negligence is a difficult tort to establish. The manufacturers of the ginger beer would not have been liable if they could have proved that they had taken all reasonable care.

Under the Consumer Protection Act liability is strict. This means that, in the absence of one of the defences listed in the Act, injured consumers will always win if they are injured by a product which was less safe than could reasonably be expected. The defences available, as we shall see, are narrow and specific.

Who may sue?

The Act gives the right to sue to any person who is injured by a product, the safety of which was '*not such as persons generally are entitled to expect*'.

For over 100 years the Sale of Goods Acts required that goods sold by a business were of merchantable quality. As we have seen, this requirement has been replaced by a requirement that the goods be of satisfactory quality. If a buyer of goods is injured because goods sold by a business are not of satisfactory quality the Sale of Goods Act 1979 will provide the buyer with a remedy. But privity of contract restricts the remedies offered by the Sale of Goods Act to the buyer of the goods. The Consumer Protection Act now gives a similarly high level of protection to **anyone** injured by the goods.

Who is liable?

The Act places liability on the 'producer' of the product, and sections 1 and 2 define the producer as including:

(a) The **manufacturer** of the product.
(b) The **extractor** of raw materials.
(c) **Processors** of goods.
(d) **'Own branders'** who add their label to products which they did not produce.
(e) Anyone who **imports** the product **into the EC.**

If more than one of these people is liable they are **jointly and severally liable.** This means that the injured person can sue any or all of them.

Defective goods

Section 3 says that products can be regarded as defective if their safety is not such as persons are generally entitled to expect.

The court will consider all the circumstances when deciding whether or not this **objective** standard has been breached. The Act does, however, mention a number of factors to be considered, including:

(a) The way in which the product was marketed.
(b) Instructions and warnings issued with the product.
(c) What might reasonably be expected to be done with the product.
(d) The time at which the product was supplied.

This last factor is designed to give some protection to manufacturers producing new products. These are not to be considered unsafe just because later products were safer. (This is linked to the controversial 'development risks' defence, which is considered below.)

Damage suffered

Section 5 of the 1987 Act allows a plaintiff to claim for **death or any personal injury** caused by the unsafety of the goods.

Damage to **property** is claimable only if it causes an individual to suffer a loss of at least £275. The loss may be made up of damage to several items. Damage to the goods in question is not recoverable. Nor is damage to other products supplied with the goods.

Example Mr and Mrs A are given a toaster as a wedding present. The toaster catches fire and burns Mr A's hand. The kitchen work surface is damaged and the toaster itself is destroyed. Under the Act damages could be claimed for the injury to Mr A and for all of the damage to the work surface as long as that amounted to more than £275. Damage to the toaster itself could not be claimed under this Act. The buyer of the toaster could claim back the price of the toaster under the Sale of Goods Act 1979.

Compensation for injury, death and damage to goods must be claimed within three years of the loss becoming apparent. In addition, there is an absolute time limit of 10 years after the date when the product was supplied. This means that a person injured by a product more than 10 years after it was bought will have no remedy.

Contributory negligence on the part of the plaintiff can reduce the damages.

Defences

Liability is strict, and this means that the plaintiff does not need to prove fault. Nor can liability be excluded by any contract term. There are, however, certain defences available:

(a) That the defect was caused by **complying with EC or UK legislation**.
(b) That the product was not supplied or manufactured **in the course of a business**. For example, a person who made jam as a hobby would not be liable under this Act if the jam poisoned a person who consumed it.
(c) That the defect in the product did not exist **when the product was put on to the market**.
(d) A **supplier of a component** will have a defence if the lack of safety arose because the manufacturer of the finished product misused the component.
(e) The **development risks defence** gives a defence to a producer if he can show that when he produced the product the state of scientific and technical knowledge was '*not such that a producer of products of the same description as the product in question might be expected to have discovered it [the defect] if it had existed in his products when they were under his control*'.

The development risks defence is controversial. It would have meant that the victims of the drug Thalidomide would not have had a remedy, because when the drug was created scientists were not aware of its danger. (For the same reason the drug manufacturers would not have been liable in negligence.) The Government included the development risk defence because it thought that not to do so would make the manufacture of drugs and certain other products so hazardous as to be economically impractical.

Ultimately the balance to be struck between the interests of drug manufacturers and drug users is a matter of politics.

Strict criminal liability

The Consumer Protection Act 1987 Part II

Part II of the Act (which imposes **criminal liability**) says that a person shall be guilty of an offence if he supplies consumer goods which are not reasonably safe, having regard to all the circumstances. This Part of the Act applies to **anyone who supplies the goods.**

Nobody needs to be injured by the goods.

The maximum penalty is a **£2,000 fine** or **six months' imprisonment**.

The goods must be safe in all the circumstances, which include:

(a) The manner in which the goods were marketed, along with instructions and warnings.

(b) Any published safety standard for the goods.

(c) The means, if any, and the cost of making the goods safe.

The defences to Part II of the Act are as follows:

(a) The supplier took **all reasonable care** to avoid committing the offence.

(b) The goods were **for export outside the UK.**

(c) The goods were **not supplied as new.** Second-hand goods are not covered by Part II of the Act. But hired goods are not regarded as second-hand merely because they have previously been hired to someone else.

(d) Retailers have a defence if they supplied the goods **in the ordinary course of business** and had **no reason to suspect** that they were not safe.

Part II of the Act is enforced by trading standards officers of local authorities. They have considerable powers, including the power to test goods, search premises, issue prohibition notices and have goods forfeited or destroyed.

The Consumer Protection Act 1987 Part III covers misleading prices and says that a person commits an offence if:

'in the course of any business of his, he gives (by any means whatever) to any consumers an indication which is misleading as to the price at which any goods, services, accommodation or facilities are available. . . .'

 ACTIVITY QUESTIONS 14.3

Julie is injured when a hair dryer, which she was bought as a birthday present, catches fire and burns her hand.

(a) Why can Julie not use the Sale of Goods Act to sue the shop which sold the hair dryer?

(b) Why would Julie prefer to sue the manufacturer of the hair dryer under the Consumer Protection Act, rather than in negligence?

The Trade Descriptions Act 1968

This Act imposes strict **criminal liability** on traders who falsely describe their goods. Although there are defences, a trader can be guilty of the crime even if he did not know that he was committing it.

Two main offences are created:

(a) Applying a false trade description to goods.
(b) Applying a false trade description to services.

Applying a false trade description to goods

Section 1 defines the first main offence; applying a false trade description to goods:

'Any person who, in the course of a trade or business –
(a) applies a false trade description to any goods; or
(b) supplies or offers to supply any goods to which a false trade description is applied;
shall, subject to the provisions of this Act, be guilty of an offence.'

This section is perhaps best understood if broken down into its constituent parts.

Any person

This could include a company. Section 20 says that officers of a company can be guilty if the offence was committed *'with their consent and connivance'*. So a company will be guilty if it agrees to the offence being committed or disregards the offence.

In the course of a trade or business

The Act is only intended to penalise dishonest businesses. A private seller cannot commit an offence under the Act because such a seller would not apply the description in the course of a trade or business.

It can be difficult to decide whether or not a business supplied goods in the course of trade or business. The deciding factor seems to be how frequently the business supplies the type of goods in question.

Havering Ltd v Stevenson (1970)

The defendant ran a car hire business. He regularly sold the cars when they were about two years old. One car sold had a false mileage on the odometer.

Held The defendant was guilty. The cars were sold in the course of business because the defendant sold cars fairly regularly.

In other cases the courts have decided that the sale of a car by a taxi driver, and the trading in of a car by a self-employed courier, were not covered by the Act. Both the taxi driver and the courier were of course in business. However, neither sold the car in the course of business because neither of them regularly sold cars.

If a very large taxi-driving firm regularly sold off cars, then these sales would be made in the course of a trade or business and would be covered by the Act.

Applies

Section 4 states that a person applies the false trade description if he:

(a) Marks the goods or their packaging.
(b) Marks anything in which the goods are placed (such as a vending machine).
(c) Uses the trade description in any manner which is likely to be taken as referring to the goods.
(d) Makes oral statements which amount to a false trade description.
(e) Supplies goods which were requested under a description, without revealing that they do not correspond with that description.

For example, if a buyer asked a wholesaler for a hundredweight of English apples, the seller would apply a false trade description if he supplied a hundredweight of French apples, without making it plain that this was what he was doing.

Section 5 makes it clear that **advertisements** can amount to false trade descriptions.

Trade description

Section 2 (1) defines a trade description:

'A trade description is an indication, direct or indirect, and by whatever means given, of any of the following matters . . .
(a) *quantity, size or gauge;*
(b) *method of manufacture, production, processing or reconditioning;*
(c) *composition;*
(d) *fitness for purpose, strength, performance, behaviour or accuracy;*
(e) *any physical characteristics not included in the previous paragraphs;*
(f) *testing by any person and the results thereof;*
(g) *approval by any person or conformity with a type approved by any person;*
(h) *place or date of manufacture, production, processing or reconditioning;*
(i) *person by whom manufactured, produced, processed or reconditioned;*
(j) *other history including previous ownership or use.'*

According to section 2(3): *'In this section quantity includes length, width, height, area, volume, capacity, weight and number.'*

ACTIVITY QUESTIONS 14.4

1 We have seen that a person can only be guilty under section 1 of the Trade Descriptions Act if the goods are supplied in the course of a trade or business. Would the Act apply to the landlord of a pub who made the following false descriptions before selling the goods in question to a customer?

(a) The landlord described his keg beer as 'real ale'.

(b) He described his sandwiches as 'English beef' when the beef they contain is imported.

(c) He sold his car with a false odometer reading.

(d) He sold his snooker cue saying that it was made of ash when in fact it is made of maple.

2 Which of the following could amount to the application of a false trade description?

(a) The markings on a soft drink can.

(b) The markings on the machine from which the drink was sold.

(c) Packaging on supermarket vegetables.

(d) A sign outside a shop.

(e) An advertisement in the local newspaper.

Further activity question 14.4

Section 2(1), on page 311, lists 10 matters which can amount to a false trade description. Try to make examples of each of these in relation to either a car bought from a garage or food bought in a supermarket. For instance, an example of section 2(1)(a) might be that a packet of fish fingers contained only eight fish fingers, not 10 as described on the packet. An example of section 2(1)(b) might be that a car was described as fully reconditioned by expert mechanics, when it was not. Try to make similar examples for section 2(1)(c)–(j).

Applying false or misleading statements as to services

Section 14 of the 1968 Act defines the second main offence by saying that it shall be an offence to knowingly or recklessly make a false statement as to any of the following matters:

'(i)   the provision in the course of any trade or business of any service, accommodation or facilities;

(ii)   the nature of any services, accommodation or facilities provided;

(iii) the time at which, manner in which or persons by whom any services, accommodation or facilities are provided;

(iv) the examination, approval or evaluation by any person of any services, accommodation or facilities so provided;

(v)   the location or amenities of any accommodation so provided.'

Defences

Section 24(1): 'Another person'

Section 24(1) of the Act provides a defence to both of the main offences. To establish the defence the defendant must prove:

> '(a) that the commission of the offence was due to a mistake or to reliance on information supplied to him or to the act or default of another person, an accident or some other cause beyond his control; and
>
> (b) that he took all reasonable precautions and exercised all due diligence to avoid the commission of such an offence by himself or any person under his control.'

Section 24 allows a defence if the offence was caused by another person. Whether or not company employees can be regarded as 'another person', rather than as the company itself, will depend upon the seniority of the employees in question. (Whether the employees were the 'minds of the company' rather than the 'hands of the company' as described on page 64.)

In the following case the House of Lords had to decide whether a branch manager of a Co-op store was sufficiently junior to be regarded as 'another person' rather than as the company:

Tesco Supermarkets Ltd v Nattrass (1972, House of Lords)

Tesco advertised that they were selling a certain brand of washing powder at a reduced price. They ran out of the specially marked cut-price packets. A shop assistant, without the store manager's knowledge, filled the shelves with ordinary, full-price packets. The effect of this was that both types were on the shelves together. A customer bought a full-price packet. The supermarket company were charged under the Act.

Held The company were not guilty because the shop manager was 'another person'. A director of the company would have been regarded as the same person as the company, but a shop manager could be regarded as another person.

Section 24(3): Lack of knowledge

Section 24(3) provides a defence to supplying or offering to supply goods. The defendant is not guilty if he did not know, and could not reasonably have found out, that:

(a) the goods did not conform to the description; or

(b) the description had been applied to the goods.

Section 25: Advertisements

Section 25 protects **advertisers** if they took the order for the advertisement in the ordinary course of business and had no reason to suspect that its publication would amount to an offence.

Further activity questions 14.5

1 Several holiday companies have committed offences under section 14, particularly when describing foreign hotels. Try to make examples of offences which a holiday company might commit under each of the five subsections of section 14. For example, a company might commit an offence under section 14(1) if it said that a hotel had a swimming pool, when in fact it did not.

2 A shopkeeper sells a cardigan described as 'genuine lambswool'. In fact the cardigan is made of synthetic material. Under which sections (if any) might the shopkeeper have a defence if:

   (a) A part-time shop assistant applied the description, without the shopkeeper's knowledge or approval.
   (b) The label on the cardigan said that it was made of lambswool and the shopkeeper had no reason to know that it was not.
   (c) The shopkeeper described the cardigan as lambswool because it closely resembled a cardigan of his own, which he knew to be lambswool.

TASK 14

The Albanian students visiting your college are surprised to hear that a business can be liable both civily and criminally even when the business is not at fault. Write a report, indicating:

a) The basis on which a manufacturer of a hot water bottle could be liable to a consumer who was injured when the hot water bottle burst and badly burnt him.

b) How a holiday company could be liable for falsely describing the amenities provided.

c) How an employer can be civily liable for the torts of his employees.

Case decision

(from p. 300)

Ready Mixed Concrete Ltd v MPNI (1968)

Held The drivers were independent contractors. Having to obey the company rules, having to wear a uniform, and not being able to act as carriers pointed in the direction of their being employees: being able to use substitute drivers and having to buy the lorries themselves pointed in the direction of their being independent contractors. The crucial factor, which made them independent contractors, was that they did not agree to provide their own work and skill.

15 The extent of business liability

Liability in contract

If a business breaks a contract, then the person with whom the contract was made will always have a legal remedy. In this chapter we examine the remedies available and the ways in which businesses seek to limit their liability.

Remedies for breach of contract

Damages

Any breach of contract will always give rise to an action for damages.

The **purpose** of contract damages is to put the injured party in the economic position he would have been in if the breach had not occurred.

If a party suffers no loss as a result of the breach he will be entitled only to **nominal damages** (damages in name only, often 5p or £1).

Remoteness of damage

Although some damages will always be recoverable, a victim of a breach of contract is not necessarily entitled to recover damages for every loss which resulted from the breach. To be recoverable the loss must be **foreseeable**, under one of the two rules in *Hadley* v *Baxendale*. This requirement of forseeability is an important limitation on business liability for breach of contract.

(a) Rule 1: A loss is recoverable if it **arises naturally** from the breach **in the usual course of things**.

(b) Rule 2: Other losses are recoverable if it can reasonably be supposed that **the parties would have contemplated them** as arising from the breach, when they made the contract.

These two rules are vitally important. If a breach of contract causes a loss which is not within one of the two rules, then damages will not be payable to compensate for that loss.

The working of the two rules can be seen in the following case:

Victoria Laundry Ltd v *Newman Industries Ltd* (1949, Court of Appeal)

The defendants agreed to sell the laundry a boiler, knowing that they needed it immediately. The defendants breached the contract by delivering the boiler five months late. The plaintiffs claimed for two losses this breach had caused them. First, they claimed £16 a week for trade they had lost by having to continue with their old, smaller boiler. Second, they claimed £262 a week which the new boiler would have allowed them to make under an exceptionally lucrative dyeing contract with the Ministry of Supply.

Held The first claim was recoverable under Rule 1. It was in the usual course of things that if the laundry had got the bigger boiler they could have taken on more business and made more profit. The second claim was not recoverable under either rule. It was not recoverable under Rule I because it was not in the usual course of things for a laundry to have such a lucrative contract. It was not recoverable under Rule 2 because the defendants did not know about the lucrative dyeing contract when they made their contract to supply the new boiler. If they had known about this, the loss would have been recoverable under Rule 2.

In *Victoria Laundry* the loss of the £16 a week was fairly certain to occur, but this certainty is not necessary as the House of Lords showed in the following case:

The Heron 2 (1969, House of Lords)

The defendant agreed to ship 3,000 tons of sugar to Basrah (Iraq), but delivered the sugar nine days late. The plaintiff, a sugar merchant in Basrah, claimed that this breach had cost him over £4,000. He said that this loss had arisen because he had intended to sell the sugar on the day it was meant to arrive, and that by the time it actually did arrive the price of sugar had fallen by £1.40 a ton. The defendant knew that he was delivering to a sugar merchant, and he knew that there was a sugar market in Basrah. He did not know that the merchant intended to sell the sugar the day it should have arrived.

Held The loss was recoverable under Rule 1 because it was '*quite likely*' or '*not unlikely*' to occur. The House of Lords did not explain exactly what they mean by '*quite likely*' and '*not unlikely*', but Lord Reid did give the following example:

> '*Suppose one takes a well-shuffled pack of cards, it is quite likely or not unlikely that the top card will prove to be a diamond: the odds are only three to one against; but most people would not say that it is quite likely to be the nine of diamonds for the odds are then fifty-one to one against.*'

The Market Rule

Once the courts have decided that a loss was foreseeable enough to be recoverable, they then refer to the market to assess the amount of damages.

If the breach amounted to non-delivery of goods, section 51(3) of the Sale of Goods Act 1979 will apply:

> '*Where there is an available market for the goods in question the measure of damages is . . . the difference between the contract price and the market or current price of the goods . . .*'

Example X agrees to supply Y with 40 tons of coal at £100 a ton. A shortage of coal moves the wholesale price up to £120 a ton. If X does not supply Y with the 40 tons as agreed, Y's damages will be 40 × £20 = £800.

Section 50(3) of the Sale of Goods Act 1979 makes a similar rule if the breach is caused by refusing to accept the goods.

Example Y agreed to buy 40 tons of coal from X at £100 a ton but refuses to take the coal because the price has fallen to £90 a ton. X's damages will be £400. (X will also be able to claim the profit he would have made on the deal, but only if he could not make a similar profit by selling the coal to someone else.)

The market rule is stipulated by the Sale of Goods Act, but it is not restricted to contracts to supply goods. The courts will also use it in contracts to supply services.

Example If X agrees to furnish and decorate Y's office for £2,000 but fails to perform the contract, the court will look to the market to see how much more it would cost to get somebody else to do the job. Such extra cost will be available as damages.

Mitigation

A party who has suffered a loss as a result of a breach of contract is under a duty to mitigate the loss. This means that he must take all reasonable steps to reduce the loss. If he fails to do this he will not be able to claim for losses which he should have mitigated.

Brace v Calder and others (1895, Court of Appeal)

A partnership of four employed the plaintiff as manager on a two-year fixed-term contract. When two of the partners retired this technically dissolved the partnership. However, the other two partners carried on the business and offered to employ the plaintiff on identical terms. The plaintiff refused the offer and sued for breach of contract, claiming damages for the 19 months of the contract which were left to run.

Held There had been a breach of contract. However, the plaintiff was only entitled to nominal damages. He should have mitigated his loss by taking the reasonable step of accepting the offer of alternative employment.

Tax

A person who sues for wrongful dismissal is suing in contract for lost earnings. Such earnings are of course taxable. The plaintiff's liability to tax must therefore be considered when assessing the damages.

British Transport Commission v Gourley (1956, House of Lords)

As a result of the defendants' negligence the plaintiff lost earnings of £37,000. However, after paying tax on these earnings they would have been reduced to £6,000.

Held The plaintiff was entitled to only £6,000.

Although this is a tort case the principle would apply equally well if the plaintiff had been suing in contract. The purpose of contract damages is to put the injured party in the position he would have been in if the contract had not been broken. Although the plaintiff lost earnings of £37,000 he was only £6,000 out of pocket. The amount he would have paid in tax would have given him no benefit at all.

ACTIVITY QUESTIONS 15.1

1 A taxi driver orders a new car, asking the garage to adapt the car for use as a taxi. The garage cannot deliver the car on time. The taxi driver has sold his old car and consequently loses business until he can get another car.

   (a) Will the taxi driver get damages to cover the loss of his normal profits?
   (b) If the taxi driver had won an especially profitable contract to take visiting businessmen to Scotland, would he get damages to cover this loss?

2 A makes a contract to supply B with 10 tons of corn at £200 a ton. A does not deliver the corn.

   (a) What would B's damages be if corn was freely available elsewhere at the same price?
   (b) What would B's damages be if corn was available only at £250 a ton?
   (c) If B could not obtain alternative supplies of corn, and lost £1,000 profit which he would have made by reselling the corn to his regular customers, would this loss be recoverable?
   (d) What if B could have made £10,000 profit under a concession which gave him the right to sell the corn as popcorn at open air concerts?

Further activity questions 15.1

1 In *Anglia Television Ltd* v *Reede* (1972), an actor agreed to play the lead part in a film but then repudiated the contract. The plaintiffs tried hard to find another suitable actor but could not do so. Consequently, they had to abandon the film. It was held that the actor had to pay all the filming costs incurred because he must have known that such costs would have arisen.

In 1994 the actress Kim Basinger agreed to take part in a film, 'Boxing Helena', but then changed her mind. In an American court the film company was awarded $9,000,000 damages against Miss Basinger (reduced on appeal). How would the damages have been assessed by an English court:

   (a) On the basis that no substitute could be found?
   (b) If the only substitute who could be found was a much lesser attraction at the box office?

2 On Grand National day a customer books a taxi to take him from Liverpool to Aintree. The taxi does not turn up. Can the customer claim damages for having missed a day at the races?

Agreed damages

Many business contracts provide exactly what the damages should be in the event of breach. These agreed damages may be one of two things: liquidated damages, or penalties:

(a) **Liquidated damages** are a **'genuine pre-estimate of the loss'** and will be applied no matter what the actual loss.

(b) **Penalties** are not a genuine pre-estimate of the loss, but are designed **to terrorise** a party into performing his contract. The courts will ignore penalties completely and calculate damages in the usual way.

An example will show how penalties and liquidated damages operate:

Example   A builder agrees to build a new shop, and a term of the contract provides that if the shop is not ready on time the builder will pay £1,000 damages for every week that it is late.

If the court considered that this sum of £1,000 a week was what the parties genuinely thought the loss to the shop owner would be, when the contract was made, then the term would be liquidated damages and the builder would have to pay at the rate of £1,000 a week. (The £1,000 a week was a 'genuine pre-estimate of the loss'.)

If the court considered that the £1,000 a week stipulated was not what the parties thought the loss would be, then the term would be a penalty and would be ignored. Damages would be calculated in the usual way, using the market rule.

It is not always possible to say which of the parties will be arguing for liquidated damages and which against. Suppose that in the above example the builder finished six weeks late and during those weeks the shop could not have opened anyway because specialist staff were unavailable. If that were the case, then the shop would be arguing for the liquidated damages of £1,000 a week because their ordinary damages would be minimal. But now suppose that in the six weeks the shop would have made excessive profits of £1,500 a week because rival shops had closed for repairs. If that were the case, then the builder would be the one arguing for the liquidated damages of £1,000 a week because that would be considerably less than the amount he might otherwise have to pay in damages.

Dunlop Ltd v *New Garage Ltd* (1915, House of Lords) laid down five rules for distinguishing penalties and liquidated damages:

(a) If the damages are greater than could conceivably flow from the breach then the clause was a penalty.
(b) '*It is no obstacle to the sum stipulated being a genuine pre-estimate of damage, that the consequences of breach are such as to make precise pre-estimation almost an impossibility. On the contrary, that is just the situation where it is probable that pre-estimated damage was the true bargain between the parties.*'
(c) The clause will be presumed to be a penalty if it makes the same sum payable as damages for several different breaches which are likely to cause different amounts of loss.
(d) If the breach of contract consists solely of not paying a fixed sum of money, and the clause provides that in the event of breach a greater sum shall be payable as damages, this will invariably be a penalty.
(e) Calling the clause a 'penalty' or 'liquidated damages' is relevant but not decisive.

Further activity question 15.2

A agreed to refit two butchers shops for B. One was a big, city centre shop. The other was a small, back street shop. The prices for the work were £50,000 and £5,000 respectively.

It is possible to use the five rules in *Dunlop Ltd* v *New Garage Ltd* to decide whether or not the following clauses are likely to be penalties or liquidated damages. Decide which of the five rules applies to each clause, and whether the clauses would be held to be penalties or liquidated damages:

(a) The contract states that if B does not pay the £55,000 contract price on the day due, then damages of £70,000 should be payable instead of the contract price.
(b) The contract states that if either shop is not able to open on time the damages should be £1,500 per week.
(c) The contract states that if the city centre shop is not able to open on time the damages shall be £2,000 a day.
(d) The builder knows that he is refitting the smaller shop so that it will sell nothing but bacon. If the bacon sells well the butcher will make £1,000 a week: if it sells poorly he will make a loss. As no specialist bacon shop has ever been tried in this area, no one knows how well the bacon will sell. The

contract states that for every week that the shop cannot open the damages shall be £600.

(e) The contract states that if the smaller shop is not open on time the damages shall be £10,000 a week. This term is specifically called liquidated damages.

Equitable remedies

In certain circumstances the common law remedy of damages does not adequately achieve justice. The branch of law called equity therefore developed the remedies of rescission, specific performance and injunction to cater for these situations. We considered rescission in Chapter 6; specific performance and injunction are considered here.

Specific performance

This is a **court order** requiring a person to perform his contract. If the party disobeys this order he will be in contempt of court. For example, if A agrees to sell a painting to B but then refuses to hand it over, a decree of specific performance would order A to hand the painting over.

Specific performance is never ordered where damages would be an adequate remedy. Therefore it will not normally be ordered where a seller refuses to deliver mass-produced goods, because generally the buyer will be able to use his damages to buy similar goods elsewhere.

However, damages would not be an adequate remedy if the goods were unique. If a person agreed to sell a painting by Picasso, and then went back on his contract, it is quite likely that specific performance would be ordered.

All plots of land are regarded as unique, and if a seller of land refuses to go through with the sale specific performance will always be ordered.

The courts of equity thought it only fair that if specific performance could be ordered in favour of one party it should also be available to the other party. Therefore, if a buyer of land refuses to complete, specific performance will be ordered against him.

Equitable nature of the remedy

Because specific performance is an equitable remedy it will be awarded only in favour of a party who has behaved fairly.

An old rule of equity has it that '*He who comes to Equity must come with clean hands*'. In the following case the plaintiff did not have 'clean hands' and so equity would not help him.

Falcke v *Gray* (1859)

An antique dealer agreed to buy two china vases from a widow for £20 each. The two vases were worth at least £200. When the widow discovered the value of the vases she refused to honour the contract. The dealer sued for specific performance.

Held The dealer could not have specific performance because the contract was grossly unfair. (If the dealer had been suing for the common law remedy of damages he would have been successful.)

Nor will the court order specific performance where to do so would cause undue hardship to the defendant. It would not therefore order a party to repair a house if it would be cheaper to knock the place down and rebuild it from scratch.

However, a party who makes a bad contract will not be protected against specific performance, as long as the other party has behaved fairly.

Mountford v *Scott* (1975, Court of Appeal)

In December 1971 the defendant sold an option for £1. The option gave the plaintiff the right to buy the defendant's house for £10,000, if he so wished. In January 1972 the defendant tried to call the option off. In March the plaintiff exercised the option. The defendant refused to vacate the house, saying that with the £10,000 he could not find another suitable house. The plaintiff sued for specific performance.

Held Specific performance was granted.

> Russell LJ '*If the owner of a house contracts with his eyes open . . . it cannot in my eyes be right to deny specific performance to the purchaser because the vendor then finds it difficult to find a house to buy that suits him and his family . . .*'

Continuous contracts

Specific performance will not be ordered for on-going contracts which require constant supervision because of the rule '*Equity does nothing in vain*'. It will not therefore be ordered in contracts of employment. To order specific performance of employment contracts would be in vain, because the court would find it impossible to check that the employer and employee were fulfilling their respective duties.

It should be noted that despite this an employer can be ordered to reinstate an unfairly dismissed employee under the Employment Protection (Consolidation)

Act 1978. This is not specific performance, it is merely a statutory provision. If the employer refuses to obey the order he will not be in contempt of court but will have to pay greater compensation.

Injunction

An injunction is a court order requiring a person to do or not to do a certain thing. If the person refuses to obey the injunction he will be in contempt of court.

An injunction can be used to prevent an action which would deliberately cause a breach of contract, as the following case shows:

Lumley v *Wagner* (1851)

The defendant agreed that she would sing at the plaintiff's theatres twice a week for three months, and that she would not perform elsewhere during this period. She decided to break the contract and sing elsewhere.

Held. An injunction was granted, ordering her not to perform elsewhere until the three months were up.

An injunction cannot be used to obtain specific performance indirectly.

Page One Records Ltd v *Britton* (1968)

A pop group, The Troggs, made a written agreement with the plaintiff in 1966. The agreement provided that the plaintiff should be the group's manager for a five-year period, and that they would not appoint anyone else as manager during that period. The Troggs became very successful, particularly with their hit record 'Wild Thing'. They did not attribute this success to the plaintiff, and wanted to replace him as their manager. The plaintiff could not have asked for specific performance because this will not be ordered to enforce personal service contracts. Nor could he have asked for an injunction ordering The Troggs to employ him as manager (because in effect this would have amounted to specific performance). Instead the plaintiff asked for an injunction to prevent The Troggs from employing anyone else as their manager.

Held This injunction could not be granted. It would amount to specific performance. The Troggs definitely needed a manager. If they could not employ anyone else they would be compelled to employ the plaintiff.

However, an injunction can be ordered if it merely persuades, rather than compels, a person to honour a contract of employment.

Warner Bros Pictures Inc v Nelson (1936)

The defendant, better known as the actress Bette Davis, made a two-year contract with the plaintiffs. Under this contract she agreed to act for the plaintiffs and not to act for anyone else. Having become very famous, she wanted to take up a more highly paid offer to act for another film company. The plaintiffs sought an injunction to prevent her from doing this.

Held The injunction was granted. It did not compel the defendant to act for the plaintiffs because she could earn a living performing other jobs. It was, however, very likely to persuade her to act for the plaintiffs as this paid far more than any other types of non-acting work she might obtain.

Time limits on remedies

The Limitation Act 1980 laid down the times within which a contract must be sued upon.

A **simple contract** cannot be sued upon six years after the right to sue arose.

A **contract made by deed** has a time limit of 12 years.

An action for damages for **personal injuries** must be begun within three years of the injury.

These time limits do not run against minors until they become 18. Nor do the rules apply to **equitable remedies**, which are always at the court's discretion. However, equity has always refused a remedy to someone who delayed too long under the doctrine of **laches**. (In general equitable rights are lost far more quickly.)

ACTIVITY QUESTION 15.3

Which of the following contacts do you think would be specifically enforceable?

(a) A has agreed to sell his house to B, but no longer wishes to sell.
(b) A has agreed to sell his house to B, but B no longer wishes to buy it.
(c) C, having agreed to sell an oil painting to D, no longer wishes to sell it.
(d) E has agreed to sell a three-year-old Volvo to F, but no longer wishes to sell.
(e) G has agreed to sell a 24-year-old Rolls Royce to H, but no longer wishes to sell.
(f) I has agreed to sing a concert at J's theatre, but has been offered a more lucrative concert elsewhere.
(g) K has agreed to sell his antique Persian rug, worth £13,000, to a dealer for £3,500.

In each case consider what other remedies would be available to the injured party.

Further activity question 15.3

Last year Cafeco made a contract to buy 10,000 tons of coffee beans from a coffee wholesaler. Due to a terrible frost in South America, there is a world shortage of coffee. The wholesaler has managed to get only 10,000 tons of coffee beans, rather than the 50,000 tons he was expecting. The price of coffee beans has increased fourfold.

(a) Can Cafeco force the wholesaler to deliver the 10,000 tons of beans as agreed?
(b) Can Cafeco prevent the wholesaler from selling the beans to someone else?
(c) If Cafeco do not get the beans they will have to close their factory and will also be in breach of several contracts to supply supermarkets. Assuming that they do not get the beans, would they be able to claim damages for:
  (i) The cost of closing their factory?
  (ii) The damages which they themselves will have to pay to the supermarkets?
  (iii) Profits they would lose by not making and selling coffee?
  (iv) Health care required by the managing director, who had a heart attack when he heard that the contract had been broken?

Exclusion clauses

Exclusion clauses, or exemption clauses as they are sometimes known, are clauses which try to exclude one party's liability. Usually the liability in question will have arisen as a result of an express or implied term of the contract. However, exclusion clauses can go further and can exclude other types of liability, such as liability arising in tort.

Before Parliament limited their effect, exclusion clauses could operate very unfairly. Although the judges often expressed their dislike of exclusion clauses, they were reluctant to strike out such clauses. Most judges were firmly attached to the idea of freedom of contract, which insisted that people should be able to make any contract they wished. To tell a contracting party that he could not agree to a clause which deprived him of his rights was to interfere with that party's freedom to do as he pleased, and was therefore to be avoided.

It is, of course, businesses rather than private individuals who tend to insert exclusion clauses into contracts. Often the business will not deal with a customer unless the customer agrees to the exclusion clause. The customer's 'freedom' to agree to a clause which does away with all his rights is a strange kind of freedom indeed.

L'Estrange v Graucob (1934)

A cafe owner bought a cigarette vending machine and signed a sales agreement which she did not read. This sales agreement contained several terms, one of which said '*in regrettably small print but quite legible,*' that the machine did not need to work. The machine did not work. The cafe owner sued to get her money back.

Held The cafe owner failed. She had signed the agreement and so she was bound by it.

> Scutton LJ '*When a document containing contractual terms is signed . . . the party signing it is bound, and it is wholly immaterial whether he has read the document or not. . . . The plaintiff, having put her signature to the document . . . cannot be heard to say that she is not bound by the terms of the document because she has not read them.*'

Eventually Parliament felt the necessity to intervene, and in 1977 it passed the Unfair Contract Terms Act. We shall examine the Act later in this chapter. But before the Act is considered it is necessary to make sure that the exclusion clause was a term of the contract. If the clause was not agreed to as a term then it would not have any effect anyway, and it would not be necessary to consider the Act.

Is the exclusion clause a term of the contract?

As we saw in *L'Estrange* v *Graucob*, if a person signs a document then he will be bound by its contents. Written, signed documents therefore present little difficulty in deciding whether or not an exclusion clause was a term of the contract.

But in contracts which were not written and signed by the parties it is not so easy to decide. Case law has held that a party will be bound by an exclusion clause if he either **knew** that it was part of the contract or if he **ought to have known**.

If the term is contained in a document, such as a train ticket, which the reasonable man would think was a part of the contract then the term will be binding. If the term was in a mere receipt the term will not be binding. Sometimes what the reasonable man would have thought is obvious enough. In other cases it can be very hard to tell.

Chapelton v Barry UDC (1940, Court of Appeal)

The plaintiff hired a deck chair for 2*d*. When he sat in the chair it collapsed and he was injured. The hirers of the chair relied on an exclusion clause, which said that they were not liable for any accident or damage resulting from the hire of the deck chair. This clause had been printed on a slip of paper which the attendant issued to hirers of the chairs. It was possible to sit on a chair for an hour or two before the attendant took the money and issued the slip.

Held The clause was not a part of the contract because it was contained in a mere receipt. The reasonable man would not have expected the terms of the contract to be contained in such a receipt.

To be effective an exclusion clause must be a term of the contract, and as such it must have been agreed before the contract was made. A term cannot later be incorporated into the contract.

Olley v Marlborough Court Hotel (1949, Court of Appeal)

Mrs Olley booked into a hotel for one week and paid her bill in advance. During her stay at the hotel her fur coat was stolen from her room. The hotel denied liability because a notice in Mrs Olley's room stipulated that the hotel was not liable for lost or stolen property, unless it had been handed in to reception for safe custody.

Held The notice was too late to be effective. The contract was made when Mrs Olley booked into the hotel.

Some judges, particularly Lord Denning, made strenuous efforts to defeat exclusion clauses. In the following case Lord Denning, with typical ingenuity, decided that the clause was ineffective because it was too late to be part of the contract.

Thornton v Shoe Lane Parking Ltd (1971, Court of Appeal)

Thornton drove into the defendants' multi-storey car park which he had never used before. When he parked in front of a barrier an automatic machine issued him with a ticket. This ticket said that the users of the car park did so subject to conditions displayed on notice boards inside the car park. One of the conditions excluded the defendants from liability for injuries to customers. When Thornton returned to his car he was badly injured, partly as a result of the defendants' negligence. He sued the defendants, who relied on the ticket.

Held The ticket was too late to be effective.

> Lord Denning MR *'The customer pays his money and gets a ticket. He cannot refuse it. He cannot get his money back. He may protest to the machine, even swear at it. But it will remain unmoved. He is committed beyond recall. He was committed at the very moment when he put his money into the machine. The contract was concluded at that time.'*

If the court does decide that the exclusion clause was a term of the contract, it will move on to consider the effect of the Unfair Contract Terms Act 1977. Before the Act came into force the courts applied complicated rules of interpretation which occasionally defeated exclusion clauses. These 'mental gymnastics', as Lord Denning described them, have been made redundant by the Act.

ACTIVITY QUESTIONS 15.4

1 In *Kendall* v *Lillico* (see page 161) a 'sold note' containing an exclusion clause was sent the day after the contract was made. Nevertheless the House of Lords held that the note was a term of the contract because in the many previous dealings between the parties an identical sold note had always been sent the following day.

In the light of this decision, would *Olley*'s case have been different if Mrs Olley had regularly stayed at the hotel (assume that the notices have been in the rooms for many years)? How would *Thornton's* case have been different it he had parked in the same car park the day before?

2 At a self-service petrol station, would an exclusion clause be a part of the contract if:
   (a) It was displayed at the entrance to the petrol station?
   (b) It was displayed on the petrol pump?
   (c) It was displayed above the till?

Further activity questions 15.4

1 In *Thornton* v *Shoe Lane Parking*, Lord Denning MR said that the exclusion clause on the ticket did not apply because it came after the contract was made. It follows that the offer and acceptance must have been concluded

before the ticket was issued to the driver. What then was the offer, and what was the acceptance?

2 People make contracts when they buy from automatic vending machines. What will the offer and acceptance be? Would it make a difference if the machine had no coin refund button?

The Unfair Contract Terms Act 1977

Contracts covered by the Act

The sections of the Unfair Contract Terms Act (UCTA) 1977 which concern us apply only to **business liability**. This is defined by section 1 of the Act as liability which arises:

(a) from things done or to be done by a person in the course of a business; or

(b) from the occupation of premises used for the business purposes of the occupier.

The effect of the Act

Section 2: Liability for negligence

Section 2(1) provides that no contract term can exclude liability for **negligence** which results in **death or personal injury**.

Section 2(2) provides that liability for **negligence** which causes **other types of damage**, such as damage to goods, can be excluded if the term was reasonable. (Schedule 2 of the Act and section 11 define what 'reasonable' means, and we will look at these later in this chapter.)

Smith v Eric S Bush (1989, House of Lords)

The plaintiff applied to a building society for a mortgage to buy a house. The building society employed the defendants to make a survey of the house. The plaintiff paid £40 to the building society, who agreed to supply her with a copy of the report. A disclaimer said that neither the building society nor the surveyors would be liable for any inaccuracies. The report, which also contained a similar disclosure of liability, said that the house was worth £16,000 and that no major building work was necessary. Eighteen months later the chimneys fell through the roof because a chimney breast had been removed without proper supports being fitted. The plaintiff sued the defendants for negligence. The defendants relied on the disclaimer.

Held The defendants were liable. The disclaimer which excluded liability had to be reasonable under UCTA 1977, section 2(2). It was not reasonable and so it did not apply.

Section 3: Avoiding liability other than for negligence

Section 3 protects two classes of people:

(a) those who '**deal as a consumer**'; and
(b) those who **deal on the other party's written standard terms**.

Before considering what protection section 3 offers, we should be clear about exactly who is protected.

The Act makes a very important distinction between a person who deals 'as a consumer' and a person who does not. A person deals as a consumer if:

(a) he makes the contract not in the course of business and not holding himself out to be in the course of business,
(b) with a person who does make the contract in the course of business.

A person deals on the other party's **written standard terms** if the contract he makes is the same as the contract made by all the other customers. Matters such as the price and quantity may of course be different. The hire contract printed at the end of Chapter 6 is a standard form contract. All customers must agree to the written standard terms contained in it.

Having decided that a person is either dealing as a consumer or dealing on the other party's written standard terms, the protection given by section 3 is as follows:

(a) An exclusion clause cannot protect a party for breach of contract unless this is reasonable.
(b) An exclusion clause cannot protect a party who fails to perform the contract at all, or who performs in a manner different from what was reasonably expected, unless this is reasonable.

ACTIVITY QUESTIONS 15.5

1 Are the following purchasers dealing as consumers?
   (a) John, a civil servant, buys a car from Mary, a teacher.
   (b) Mary buys a new car from the garage.
   (c) The garage buys 12 new cars from Ford.
   (d) Jack, a self-employed builder, buys a cement mixer from Bill, a retired builder.
   (e) Bill soon regrets having sold his cement mixer. He is bored with retirement and decides to extend his kitchen. He buys a new cement mixer from a builder's merchant, and gets trade discount by pretending that he is still in business.

2 The UCTA 1977 has not outlawed standard form contracts. Such contracts are very commonly used.
   (a) Identify three types of contracts which are usually made by agreeing to a standard form contract.
   (b) Is it only consumers who make such contracts?

Further activity question 15.5

Benjamin, a passenger on a ferry, is injured when the captain of the ferry negligently crashes into a bridge. What would be the effect of:
(a) A clause in the contract which said that the ferry operator was not to be liable for personal injuries?
(b) A clause which said that the operator would not be liable for damage to passenger's luggage?

Section 4: Indemnity clauses

An indemnity clause states that one of the parties to a contract will indemnify the other for any liability which the other may be under. Section 4 provides that a person dealing as a consumer cannot be asked to give any indemnity unless this is reasonable. In non consumer contracts indemnity clauses are not touched by the Act, unless they are covered by one of the other sections. The following case shows how this can happen.

Phillips Products Ltd v Hyland (1987, Court of Appeal)

The plaintiffs, who were in business, hired an excavator and a driver from a hire company. A term of the contract provided that the plaintiffs had to indemnify the hire company for any damage caused by the driver. The driver damaged the plaintiffs' buildings. The plaintiffs sued the hire company, who relied on the indemnity clause.

Held If the plaintiffs had not been in business this would have been a consumer contract and the indemnity clause would not have applied, under section 4, because it was not reasonable. Because the contract was not a consumer contract section 4 did not apply. However, the defendant's negligence had damaged the plaintiff's property. Under section 2(2) a clause can only exclude liability for damage to property caused by negligence if this is reasonable. As the clause was not reasonable, the defendants were not protected by the indemnity clause.

Section 5: Guarantees of consumer goods

A **manufacturer** cannot use a **guarantee** to prevent a person from suing for loss caused by the goods having been negligently manufactured. (If the negligence caused death or physical injury, section 2(1) would not allow the exclusion clause to be effective. Section 5 therefore only covers damage to property caused by the manufacturer's negligence. It does however provide greater protection than section 2(2), in that section 5 applies even if the guarantee's exclusion was reasonable.)

Sections 6 and 7: Exclusion of statutory implied terms

In Chapter 7 we examined the terms implied by the Sale of Goods Act, the Supply of Goods (Implied Terms) Act, and the Supply of Goods and Services Acts. We saw that these Acts require that every good or service sold by a business should be of satisfactory quality. Sections 6 and 7 of the UCTA 1977 say that these terms cannot be excluded in any consumer contract for the supply of goods. The terms can only be excluded in non consumer contracts if this is reasonable.

Section 8: Liability for misrepresentations

No clause can restrict liability for **misrepresentation**, unless the clause was reasonable.

The meaning of 'reasonableness'

Most of the sections we have considered do allow an exclusion clause to be effective if the clause is reasonable.

Section 11 defines 'reasonable' as meaning '*that the term shall have been a fair and reasonable one to be included having regard to the circumstances which were, or ought reasonably to have been, known to or in the contemplation of the parties when the contract was made.'*

Schedule 2 of the Act says that if the contract is to sell or supply any type of goods, regard must be had to the following, in deciding whether or not a term was reasonable:

(a) The relative **strength of the parties' bargaining position**, which will include whether or not the customer **could find another supplier**.
(b) Whether the customer was given **any inducement** to agree to the term, or could have made a similar contract with a different supplier without agreeing to such a term.
(c) Whether the customer **knew** or ought to have known that **the term existed**.
(d) If the term excludes liability unless some condition is complied with, whether or not it was **reasonably practicable to comply** with that condition.
(e) Whether the goods were manufactured, altered or adapted **at the customer's request**.

Although schedule 2 is theoretically only to be used when the contract is to supply goods, the judge considered schedule 2 in the following case which concerned a defective service. It seems that schedule 2 is likely to be extended to all types of contracts.

Woodman v *Photo Trade Processing Ltd* (1981)

The defendants were given a reel of film to develop. Due to their negligence most of the pictures were lost. The defendants relied on a clause: *'All photographic materials are accepted on the basis that their value does not exceed the cost of the material itself. Responsibility is limited to the replacement of the films.'* The plaintiff had taken the pictures at a friend's wedding, where he had been the only photographer.

Held The exclusion clause did not apply because it was not reasonable. In reaching this decision the judge had regard to the fact that the plaintiff had little choice but to agree to such a term, as most commercial film developers insisted on a similar term. Consequently the plaintiff was awarded damages of £75.

ACTIVITY QUESTION 15.6

Assuming in each case that the exclusion clause had been a part of the contract, how would the following cases have been decided under the UCTA 1977? (In each case it would be safe to assume that the Sale of Goods Act, or the Supply of Goods and Services Act, would have given the customer the right to expect that the contract would be performed reasonably well.)
(a) *L'Estrange* v *Graucob* (the cafe owner's vending machine).

(b) *Chapelton* v *Barry UDC* (the collapsing deck chair).

(c) *Thornton* v *Shoe Lane Parking* (the multi-storey car park).

Further activity questions 15.6

1 In *Curtis* v *Chemical Cleaning and Dyeing Co* (1951, Court of Appeal), a woman who took a white satin wedding dress to the dry cleaners was asked to sign a 'receipt'. She asked what it said and was told that it just covered damage to beads and sequins. The woman signed the 'receipt'. In fact the document excluded all liability on the part of the dry cleaners. The wedding dress was stained. The woman sued the dry cleaners, who tried to rely on the exclusion clause. It was held that they could not do so because they had misrepresented the effect of the clause.

(a) How would this case be treated under the UCTA 1977?

(b) How would the case be decided under the Act if the woman had not asked any questions, but just signed the document without reading it?

2 Can an exclusion clause defeat a term implied by the courts? If, in *The Moorcock* (page 123), the jetty owner had prominently displayed a notice, 'All ships moored at their owner's risk', would the court have still implied the term that the jetty owner had taken reasonable care to ensure that the jetty was a safe place to moor a ship?

The EC directive on unfair terms in consumer contracts

This directive came into force on 1 July 1995. The directive will not replace the UCTA 1977, but will run alongside it.

The directive's main provision is that in contracts between 'consumers' and 'sellers or suppliers' the consumers will not be bound by 'unfair' terms which have not been 'individually negotiated'.

Article 3 of the directive states that:

> *'A contractual term which has not been individually negotiated shall be regarded as unfair if, contrary to the requirement of good faith, it causes a significant imbalance in the parties' rights and obligations arising under the contract, to the detriment of the consumer.'*

Terms are to be regarded as not individually negotiated if they are drafted in advance and cannot be changed by the consumer. This is obviously very similar to the UCTA 1977 Act concept of 'written standard terms'.

The directive applies only to contracts made between consumers and sellers or suppliers. Such contracts seem very similar to contracts made by a person who 'deals as a consumer' under the 1977 Act. One difference is that under the directive a company can never be a consumer.

Article 4 of the directive states that when deciding whether or not a term was unfair, regard should be had to the nature of the goods or services supplied and to all the surrounding circumstances. Explanatory notes specify that the parties' bargaining strength, any inducements given to agree to the term, and whether the goods or services were supplied to the special order of the consumer are also relevant. (All of these are contained in schedule 2 of the 1977 Act.)

A term will be binding if the seller or supplier **acted in good faith**. Explanatory notes say that '*The requirement of good faith may be satisfied by the seller or supplier where he deals fairly and equitably with the other party whose legitimate interests he has taken into account*'. The good faith requirement has no equivalent in the UCTA 1977.

At present it is too early to say how, if at all, the directive will increase the protection given by the 1977 Act. The directive does not seem to add a great deal of protection. However, like most directives, the language used is rather broad. The interpretation of this language will be the job of the courts who will not be bound by old cases on the meaning of 'reasonable'. Until cases are decided, the meaning of the directive will not be entirely clear.

The Government has decided that only the Office of Fair Trading should be able to use the directive to bring court actions on behalf of large groups of consumers. Individual consumers can, of course, sue personally.

Liability in tort

In Chapter 13 we considered the tort of negligence, as a means of distinguishing liability in contract from liability in tort. We saw then that tort damages can only be recovered for a foreseeable type of injury which was caused by the tort. These requirements of foreseeability and causation are important limitations on a defendant's liability in tort.

We also considered the defences of contributory negligence and *volenti non fit* injuries. These too are important limitations.

But perhaps the most important limitation is that in England it is a judge who decides the measure of damages and not a jury. As we have seen, this is not the case in America, where juries tend to award absurdly high levels of damages. As a matter of public policy the English judges have tried to keep damages down, and nowhere is this more clearly seen than in the area of damages for nervous shock.

In the leading case, *Alcock* v *The Chief Constable of South Yorkshire*, the House of

Lords had to consider the claims of people made nervously ill by seeing the disaster which unfolded at the Hillsborough football stadium. Some people had witnessed the events in person, others had seen them on television.

The House of Lords ruled that the deciding factors should be:

(a) The closeness of the relationship between the plaintiff and the person injured.
(b) How physically close the plaintiff was to the accident.
(c) Whether the plaintiff needed to witness the accident.

These factors ruled out those who had seen the disaster on television, as well as many others who were either not physically close enough, or not emotionally close enough to those injured.

Criminal liability

Every crime has a maximum sentence. The maximum for theft, for example, is ten years imprisonment. The maximum for false accounting is seven years.

But a person who commits a crime is not usually sentenced to the maximum. A businessman convicted of stealing a few pounds would be most unlikely to be imprisoned at all. However, if a business repeatedly commits the same offence, it must expect the maximum to be imposed and this is particularly true of strict liability offences.

TASK 15

A local dry cleaners deals direct with the public and also does contract work for several hotels. Due to a breakdown of their boiler, the dry cleaners are unable to operate for two weeks. This means that several members of the public are unable to collect their clothes on time. In particular, one customer is unable to pick up a wedding dress in time for the service. A large hotel is also very inconvenienced because their old curtains, due to be used in a new extension, are not available for the opening of the extension.

Write a report, indicating:

a) The extent of the dry cleaner's liability to customers who clothes were not ready in time.

b) The extent of the dry cleaner's liability to the hotel.

c) Whether either type of liability could have been excluded by notices inside the dry cleaners shop, or by small print in the contracts under which the cleaners agreed to do the cleaning.

Answers to activity questions

1.1

1 Both (theft and the tort of conversion).

2 Civil liability only (the tort of defamation).

3 Civil liability only (trespass to land).

4 Both (obtaining by deception and fraudulent misrepresentation).

5 Criminal liability only.

6 Both (arson and conversion).

1.2

1 (a) The company would be entitled to possession of the car for one week.
   (b) The hire firm would own the car.

2 (a) The right to sue in contract.
   (b) The right to sue in tort.

3 (a) The postman would be a consumer. He would not be buying in the course of business and would be buying from a business.
   (b) The cafe owner would not be a consumer as he would be buying the cooker in the course of business.

4 (a) The teacher would have the right to continue living in the house.
   (b) The bank would have the right to repossess and sell the house if the teacher did not pay the mortgage.
   (c) The house is real property, as it cannot be moved.

2.1

(a) Privacy, cheapness, speed, specialist knowledge of the arbitrator, restricted right of appeal.

(b) (i) Small Claims Court. (ii) County Court. (iii) High Court.

(c) (i) Court of Appeal. (ii) Court of Appeal.

3.1

1 The unsecured creditors would have been entitled to the money because Salomon himself would have owed it to them.

2 No. The timber was owned by the company.

3.2

1 No. The concept is that shareholders have limited liability, not that the company itself has limited liability.

2 Any amount of the price of the shares which she has not yet paid. Beyond that she has no liability.

3 Companies are said to have perpetual succession because they can continue in existence indefinitely.

4 (a) Yes.
   (b) Yes.
   (c) Yes.

3.3

1 Salomon was protected by the corporate veil. The veil, the company's artificial legal personality, stood between him and the creditors.

2 No. When Salomon was operating as a sole trader there was no corporation and therefore no corporate veil.

3.4

1 (c)

2 (c)

3 (b)

3.5

1 (a) If Salomon had been carrying on the business as a partnership he and his fellow partners would have had to pay the unsecured creditors in full.
   (b) Yes, they would have been fully liable.

2 (a) As all of the partners are agents of the firm, any of them can make contracts on behalf of the partnership.
   (b) A person who goes into partnership assumes full responsibility for the debts of the partnership.
   (c) The cleaner would not be a partner. The cleaner would be employed by the partnership, not carrying on a business in common with the doctors.

3.6

1 Sole traders are completely liable for the debts of their businesses.

2 Because the definition of a partnership requires that there must be a 'view to profit'.

3 No. One of the members must make the contract.

3.7

	Incorporated? (Yes/No/Maybe)	Profit-Making? (Yes/No)	Government Funded? (Yes/No)
The Body Shop PLC	Yes	Yes	No
Acme Ltd	Yes	Yes	No
Unlimited Company	Yes	Yes	No
Practising barrister	No	Yes	No
Firm of accountants	No	Yes	No
Oxfam	Maybe	No	No
Westminster City Council	Yes	No	Yes
Clarendon College Corporation	Yes	No	Yes
Blagdon Darts Club	No	No	No
Department of Education	Yes	No	Yes
The Civil Service	No	No	Yes

4.1

1   £500. Jane's shares may become worthless and, if she has not already done so, she must pay for them in full. Beyond that, she has no further liability.

2   There is no limit to the amount John could lose.

3   As a majority shareholder, Edwina could vote to appoint herself as sole director. This would give her the right to manage the company's affairs. If Edward and Edwina were in partnership both would have a right to manage.

4   No. Only the directors can make a contract on a company's behalf.

5   Yes. Helen is a partner and would therefore be able to buy items, such as tractors, which would ordinarily be used by the business.

4.2

1 Companies can sell shares or issue debentures, giving the company's assets as security for the loan.

2 Companies pay corporation tax. Partners pay Income tax and National Insurance contributions.

3 (iii) Unlimited liability is not an advantage.

4 (iv)

5

	Ltd Company	Partnership	Sole Trader
Limited Liability (Yes or No)	Yes	No	No
Managed by	Directors	The partners	The trader
Who are agents of the business?	Directors	The partners	The trader
Who owns the assets of the business?	The company (which is owned by the shareholders)	The partners	The sole trader
Methods of raising capital	Borrow money Issue debentures Sell shares	Borrow money Admit new partner	Borrow money
How is the business formed?	By registration	By carrying on business	By commencing business
Liable to which taxes?	Corporation Tax	Income Tax National Insurance	Income Tax National Insurance
Perpetual Succession (Yes or No)	Yes	No	No
Maximum number in the business	No limit	20 in trading firm	1

5.2

(a) Form 10.
(b) The memorandum of association.
(c) The articles of association.
(d) Form 10.
(e) Form 12.
(f) Form 10.
(g) The memorandum of association.

5.4

1 Yes. People become partners as soon as they carry on a business in common with a view to profit. There is no need for any formalities.

2 No.

3 No.

5.5

1 (a) No. The maximum number in a trading partnership is 20.
  (b) The traders could form a company together.

2 Yes. Minors can be partners.

3 As the business carried on together was an illegal one, the law would not regard the traders as partners.

5.6

1 No.

2 No. Generally, they may trade under any name they wish.

3 No, not if the use of their surnames is intended to deceive the public.

6.1

1 The express terms would have been agreed by the parties. Liverpool City Council would have made an offer by asking the tenant to sign the lease. The lease would have contained the express terms and the tenant would have agreed to them by signing. The implied terms were put into the contract by the court.

2 The 'officious bystander' test would have implied a term that the lifts should work because, as Lord Salmon said, if they did not work then the contract would be 'futile and absurd'. When the tenant was about to sign the lease, the officious bystander would have said 'Hadn't you better put in a term that the lifts should work?' and the parties would angrily have said to him 'Of course the lifts have got to work.'

6.2

1 (a) The buyers would have argued that the term was a condition.
  (b) The sellers would have argued that the term was a warranty.
  (c) The court decided that the term was an innominate term. Like the term in the Hong Kong Fir case, this term was very broad and covered both major and minor breaches.

2 Because an absurd result could follow whichever way the term was classified. If the term was classified in advance as a condition, then the whole contract could be called off just because a life belt was missing. If the term was classified in advance as a warranty, then the contract could not be called off no matter how serious the breach.

6.3

1 (a) The contents of the contract will be terms.
  (b) The verbal statements will only be representations.

2 (a) Very strong statements are likely to be terms.
  (b) The party with the greater knowledge is likely to make terms.

6.4

1 A statement of opinion cannot itself amount to a misrepresentation. However, the statement might imply facts which could amount to a misrepresentation, as happened in *Smith* v *Land and House Property Corporation*.

2 No. The statement must induce the other party to make the contract.

3 X's silence will not amount to a misrepresentation.

6.5

1 (a) Fraudulent misrepresentation. The purchaser could have avoided the contract and claimed tort damages.
   (b) Fraudulent misrepresentation. The purchaser could have avoided the contract and claimed tort damages.
   (c) Fraudulent misrepresentation. The employer could have avoided the contract and claimed tort damages.

2 (a) Fraudulent misrepresentation. The plaintiff could avoid the contract and claim tort damages.
   (b) Fraudulent misrepresentation. The plaintiff could avoid the contract and claim tort damages.
   (c) Wholly innocent misrepresentation. The garage might be able to rescind but would have no right to damages.
   (d) Fraudulent misrepresentation. The plaintiff could avoid the contract and claim tort damages.

7.1

(a) No. (b) No. (c) Yes. (d) Yes. (e) No. (f) No. (g) Yes. (h) No. (i) Yes. (j) No. (k) No. (l) No. (m) No. (n) No.

7.2

1 Section 12 (1) says that it is a condition that the seller must have the right to sell the goods. In *Rowland* v *Divall* the defendant thought that he had the right to sell, but this was no defence.

2 No. This is an agreement to sell in the future, and section 12(1) only requires that the seller will have the right to sell at the time when the property is to pass.

3 Because although the buyer had actual possession he never had what he paid for; the right to possession.

7.3

1 (a) Yes. The label will bear a description.
   (b) Yes. The label will bear a description.
   (c) Yes. There are usually descriptions of each type of cheese.
   (d) Yes. The label will usually bear a description saying what type of potatoes they are.
   (e) Usually there will be a sign describing the potatoes.
   (f) If it is packed in cellophane this often contains a description. If the bread is not packed there may be no description.

2 (a) Yes. If no description is made then the customer would not know what was being sold. Mail-order catalogues describe the goods, usually with pictures.

3 Sometimes, but not always. The vegetables are often displayed with no description.

7.4

(a) No. (b) Yes. (c) Yes. (d) Yes. (e) No.

7.6

1   In both cases the buyers would have had a remedy under section 14(3), fitness for purpose, if they had reasonably relied on the seller's skill and judgement.

2   Because the buyer will be given protection under section 14(2) of the Sale of Goods Act 1979, as amended by section 1 of the Sale and Supply of Goods Act 1994. Cars bought from a garage must be of satisfactory quality. Cars bought privately need not be of satisfactory quality, unless an express term provides that they are.

3   Because he will not be protected against defects which he ought to have spotted.

7.7

1   (a)   Likely to be a sale by sample.
     (b)   Likely to be a sale by sample.
     (c)   Likely to be a sale by sample.
     (d)   Likely to be a sale by sample. Usually the sales representative will show the shopkeeper a sample pen and the shopkeeper will then agree to stock some.
     (e)   No. This is a sale by description.

2   Sections 14(2) and 14(3) of the Sale of Goods Act. Now section 1 of the Supply of Goods and Services Act 1994 would amend section 14(2).

3   (a)   The manufacturer.
     (b)   The person who bought from supplier 2 would be the one left without an effective remedy.

7.8

1   Section 14(2) of the Sale of Goods Act 1979, as amended by section 1 of the Sale and Supply of Goods Act 1994.

2   (a)   Section 9 of the Supply of Goods and Services Act 1982.
     (b)   The motorist would have no statutory remedy, unless a description of the car was made, as the car would not have been sold in the course of business.

7.9

1   (a) No. (b) Yes. (c) No. (d) Yes. (e) No. (f) No. (g) Maybe. Yes, if the meal was not bought in the course of business. No, if it was not.

8.1

Tort 1 –Occupier's Liability.

Tort 2 – Trespass to land.

Tort 3 – Private nuisance.

Tort 4 –Negligence.

Tort 5 – Strict liability under *Rylands* v *Fletcher*.

8.2

(a) No. (b) No. (c) Yes. (d) Yes.

9.1

1 (a) A fixed charge might be issued on property which the company does not need to dispose of.
   (b) A floating charge can be issued on all of the company's property, both present and future assets.
   (c) A fixed charge gives greater security. The subject matter of the charge cannot be disposed of without the chargeholder's consent.
   (d) The manufacturer should ensure that he does not grant a fixed charge over anything which he might want to dispose of and that the charge cannot be called in at short notice. The lender should ensure that the assets charged are worth more than the loan, and that no previous charges have been registered on the same assets.

2 (a) Ordinary shares would be the best bet. If the company did prove very successful then the shares should pay good dividends and could become very valuable. However, the articles should be checked to make sure that the shares could be freely sold.
   (b) A debenture would be best. If the company went into liquidation the value of the assets charged would ensure that the loan was repaid.

9.2

(a) Conditional sale.

(b) Hire purchase.

(c) Trade credit.

(d) A contract of hire.

(e) An overdraft.

(f) Loan.

(g) Credit sale.

9.3

(a) No. (b) No. (c) No. (d) Yes. (e) Yes.

9.4

1 Section 75 of the Consumer Credit Act would make the credit card company liable to Shabana for the price of the carpet, but not for the price of the lamp.

2 Sections 94 and 97 of the Consumer Credit Act give Bill a right to find out how much he owes and clear his debts at any time. He might be well advised to use the money in his building society account to do this.

10.1

1 (a) The Sex Discrimination Act.
   (b) The Equal Pay Act.
   (c) The Race Relations Act.

2 Yes, as happened in *Munro* v *Allied Suppliers*.

3 Once a conviction has become spent the offender can deny that the conviction happened, and can claim unfair dismissal if dismissed as a result of the spent conviction.

10.2

1 (a) Yes. (b) No. (c) No. (d) Yes. (e) Yes.

2 (a) £1,800. (b) £3,075.

10.3

1 (a) 3 weeks. (b) 10 weeks. (c) 12 weeks.

2 Unfair dismissal is a statutory remedy giving employees with at least two years continuous employment the right to a payment based on their age and the number of years they have been continuously employed. Employees who are dismissed for a justifiable reason will not be entitled to the payment. Wrongful dismissal is a common law action for breach of contract. The employee will be able to claim damages if he was dismissed, in breach of his contract, without having been given the notice to which his contract entitled him.

10.4

1 (d)

2 (d)

3 (b)

11.1

1 By subscribing for shares when the company is being formed, or by buying or inheriting shares.

2 (a) Over 50% (b) 75% (c) Over 25%

3 Yes. A contract is formed between each member and the company and between each member and every other member.

4 The company secretary is concerned with the company's administration.

11.2

1 Any director can be removed from office at any time by an ordinary resolution of which the members have been given special notice.

2 No. Directors have no automatic right to a salary.

3 If a person is 'held out' to be a director then the company would allow outsiders to believe that the person was a director. The consequences would be that the person could bind the company as if he really was a director.

11.3

1 The contracts were *ultra vires* because they were beyond the capacity of the company, as stated in the objects clause.

2 The *ultra vires* rule protected shareholders in that when they invested in the company they knew the limits of the type of contracts which the company could make.

11.4

1 Yes, as was explained by Harman LJ in *Bamford v Bamford*.

2 The rule is that if a wrong is done to a company then only the company can sue in respect of that wrong.

3 Because certain wrongs done to the company might benefit the majority, who control the company, while causing loss to the minority.

12.1

1 Yes. Every partner is an agent of the firm and his other partners for the purpose of the business of the partnership.

2 No. The supplier of the chair would have known that the partner had no authority to buy the chair on behalf of the partnership.

3 No. It is not in the ordinary course of business for a dental partnership to buy a new fur coat.

12.2

1 Yes. As the tort (negligence) was committed in the ordinary course of the firm's business, the partnership would be liable.

2 No. The partner would not have committed the tort (negligence) in the ordinary course of the partnership's business.

3 A person who 'holds himself out' to be a partner will be as liable as if he really was a partner, as regards people who acted on the strength of the holding out.

12.3

1 No. All the partners must agree to any change in the partnership agreement.

2 The profits will be shared equally between the partners unless there is an agreement to the contrary.

3 Yes. The partner who incurred the expenses can claim an indemnity from the partnership.

4 No. A partner is not entitled to a salary unless this has been agreed.

5 The partner will have to pay to the partnership all of the profit personally made.

12.4

1 No. Shareholders in a limited company have limited liability. A partnership cannot have limited liability.

2 Yes. If the person is registered as a limited partner.

3 No. Even if there are limited partners, there must be at least one general partner with unlimited liability.

13.1

1 (a) The *actus reus* is the guilty act.
  (b) The *mens rea* is the guilty mind.
  (c) The prosecution must prove beyond a reasonable doubt that the accused committed the *actus reus* while having the *mens rea* of the same crime.

2 (a) A plaintiff must prove that the facts he alleges are true, and that these facts give rise to liability.
  (b) The plaintiff must prove both of these things on a balance of probabilities.

13.3

1 Contractual liability is undertaken voluntarily. Tortious liability is imposed by the courts.

2 To establish the tort of negligence the plaintiff must prove that the defendant owed him a duty of care, that the defendant broke that duty, and that a foreseeable type of damage resulted.

14.1

1 The concept of vicarious liability is that an employer will be liable for torts of employees which were committed during the course of their employment.

2 The injured person would generally prefer to sue the employer because he should be insured, and is more likely to be able to pay compensation.

14.2

(a) Yes. Parveen is an employee of the local authority and injured the students while acting in the course of her employment.

(b) Yes. Parveen injured the students while acting in the course of her employment.

(c) No. Parveen was not acting in the course of her employment when she committed the tort.

(d) Yes. Parveen was acting in the course of her employment when she caused the accident.

14.3

(a) Because there was no contract between Julie and the shop.

(b) Because liability under the Act is strict and liability in negligence is based on fault, and it might be very hard to prove that the manufacturer was negligent.

14.4

1 (a) Yes. (b) Yes. (c) No. (d) No.

2 (a) Yes. (b) Yes. (c) Yes. (d) Yes. (e) Yes.

15.1

1 (a) The driver's normal business profits would be recoverable under *Hadley* v *Baxendale* Rule 1.

   (b) These exceptional profits would not be recoverable under either rule in *Hadley* v *Baxendale*, unless the taxi driver had told the supplier of the car about them before the contract was made.

2 (a) B would only be entitled to the cost of arranging the delivery of corn from another supplier.

   (b) In addition to the damages in (a), B would be entitled to the extra £50 per ton.

   (c) This forseeable loss would be recoverable under *Hadley* v *Baxendale* Rule 1.

   (d) This unforeseeable loss would not be recoverable under either rule in *Hadley* v *Baxendale*, unless B had told A about it before the contract was made.

15.3

1 (a) Specific performance would be available. Damages would also be available.

   (b) Specific performance would be available. Damages would also be available.

   (c) Specific performance would be available. Damages would also be available.

   (d) Specific performance would not be available, damages would.

   (e) Specific performance would be available. Damages would also be available.

   (f) Specific performance would not be available. An injunction might however order Y not to sing elsewhere. Damages would be available.

   (g) Specific performance would not be available. Damages would.

15.4

1 If Mrs Olley had stayed at the hotel regularly she should have been aware of the notice when she made recent contracts. Consequently the notice would have been a part of the contract. If Thornton had parked his car in the same car park the day before, and if the warning notice boards had been visible, then the notice boards might have been a part of the contract when he parked in the car park the following day.

2 At a self-service petrol station the contract must have been completed by the time the customer puts petrol into his tank, because by then he is irrevocably committed to the contract. It follows that:

   (a) The clause would be a part of the contract.

   (b) The clause would be a part of the contract.

   (c) The clause would be too late to be a part of the contract. The contract would have been completed before the customer would have seen the exclusion clause.

15.5

1 (a) No. Neither party is making the contract in the course of business.

   (b) Yes.

   (c) No. Both parties are acting in the course of business.

   (d) No. Bill is no longer selling in the course of business.

   (e) No. Bill is holding himself out to be acting in the course of business.

2 (a) There are too many to try and list. Students might include hire of goods, holidays, installation of telephones etc.

   (b) No. They are commonly used when one business is dealing with another, as for example in *Kendall* v *Lillico*, and *L'Estrange* v *Graucob*.

15.6

(a) The cafe owner would not have been a consumer. However, she would not have lost her rights under the Sale of Goods Act unless this was reasonable. It seems unlikely that it would have been reasonable for her to lose her rights.

(b) No term could have excluded liability for the plaintiff's injury caused by the defendant's negligence. In addition, any rights conferred by statute could not be lost, as the hirer of the deck chair was a consumer.

(c) No term could exclude liability for the injuries suffered because the injuries were caused by negligence.

Appendix: *Partridge* v *Crittenden* [1968] 1 WLR 1204

[QUEEN'S BENCH DIVISION]
PARTRIDGE *v.* CRITTENDEN

Animal — Bird — Protection — "Offers for sale" — Advertisement under "classified advertisements" — "bramblefinch cocks, bramblefinch hens, 25s. each" — Whether offer for sale — Whether invitation to treat — Bird with easily removable ring — Whether "close ringed" — protection of Birds Act, 1954 (2 & 3 Eliz. 2, c.30), s. 6(1)(a).

The appellant inserted an advertisement in a periodical, "Cage and Aviary Birds" for April 13, 1967, containing the words "Quality British A.B.C.R. . . . bramblefinch cocks, bramblefinch hens . . . 25s. each," which appeared under the general heading "classified advertisements." In no place was there any direct use of the words "offers for sale." In answer to the advertisement, T. wrote, enclosing a cheque for 25s., and asked that a hen be sent to him. The hen arrived wearing a closed ring which could be removed without injury to the bird.

The appellant was charged with unlawfully offering for sale a bramblefinch hen contrary to section 6(1) of the Protection of Birds Act, 1954.[1] The justices were of the opinion that the hen, being a bird included in schedule 4 to the Act of 1954, was not a closed-ringed specimen bred in captivity because it was possible to remove the ring, convicted him.

On appeal, the appellant contending that his advertisement was merely an invitation to treat and not an offer for sale, and that the mere fact that it was possible to remove the ring from the bird's leg did not mean that it was not of a closed-ring specimen:—

Held, allowing the appeal, that while "close-ringed" in section 6(1)(*a*) of the Act meant ringed by a complete ring which was not capable of being forced apart or broken except by damaging it, so that the bird in question was not a closed-ring specimen (post, p. 1208c); the advertisement inserted by the appellant under the title "classified advertisements" was not an offer for sale but merely an invitation to treat; and that, accordingly, the appellant was not guilty of the offence charged.

Fisher v. Bell [1961] 1 Q.B. 394; [1960] 3 W.L.R. 919; [1960] 3 All E.R. 731, D.C. and dicta of Lord Herschell in *Grainger & Son* v. *Gough* [1896] A.C. 325, 334, H.L.(E.), applied.

Per Lord Parker C.J.: There is business sense in construing advertisements and circulars, unless they come from manufacturers, as invitations to treat and not offers for sale (post p. 1209G).

CASE STATED by Chester Justices.
On June 19, 1967, an information was preferred by the prosecutor, Anthony Ian Crittenden, on behalf of the R.S.P.C.A., against the appellant, Arthur Robert Partridge, that he did unlawfully offer for sale a certain live wild bird, a brambling, being a bird

---

[1] Protection of Birds Act, 1954, s. 6(1): "If, save as may be authorised by a licence granted under section 10 of this Act, any person sells, offers for sale or has in his possession for sale—(*a*) any live wild bird, being a bird included in schedule 4 to this Act of a species which is resident in or visits the British Isles in wild state, other than a close-ringed specimen bred in captivity . . . he shall be guilty of an offence against this Act."

included in schedule 4 to the Protection of Birds Act, 1954, of a species which is resident in or visits the British Isles in a wild state, other than a close-ringed specimen bred in captivity, contrary to section 6(1) of the Act of 1954.

The justices heard the information on July 19, 1967, and found the following facts. On April 13, 1967, there appeared in the periodical "Cage and Aviary Birds" an advertisement inserted by the appellant containing, inter alia, the words "Quality British A.B.C.R. . . . bramblefinch cocks, bramblefinch hens, 25s. each." By letter to the appellant dated April 22, 1967, Thomas Shaw Thompson of Hoole, Chester, requested the dispatch to himself of an A.B.C.R. bramblefinch hen as advertised in "Cage and Aviary Birds" and enclosed a cheque for 30s. On May 1, 1967, the appellant dispatched a bramblefinch hen which was wearing a closed ring to Mr. Thompson in a box by British Rail. Mr. Thompson received the bird on May 2, 1967.

The box was opened by Mr. Thompson in the presence of the prosecutor. Mr. Thompson attempted to and was, in fact, able to remove the ring without injury to the bird. Even taking into account that the bird had travelled from Leicester in a box on British Rail its condition was rough, it was extremely nervous, had no perching sense at all and its plumage was rough.

A bramblefinch or brambling, as it is also called, was a bird included in schedule 4 to the Act of 1954. The expression "close-ringed" was nowhere defined nor was there any universally recommended size ring for a bramblefinch. The ring was placed on the bird's leg at the age of three to 10 days at which time it was not possible to determine what the eventual girth of the bird's leg would be.

It was contended by the appellant that there was no offer for sale in the county of Chester as alleged since the advertisement in "Cage and Aviary Birds" was merely an invitation to treat; and that an offence was not committed under section 6(1) of the Act of 1954 merely because it was possible to remove the ring from the bird's leg.

It was contended on behalf of the prosecutor that the advertisement was an offer for sale in Chester; and that a bird was not a close-ringed specimen bred in captivity if it was possible to remove the ring from its leg.

The justices were of opinion that the advertisement was an offer for sale in Chester on April 22, 1967, and that the brambling so offered for sale by the appellant was not a close-ringed specimen bred in captivity because it was possible to remove its ring. They accordingly found the case proved and fined the appellant £5, and ordered him to pay £5 5s. advocate's fee and £4 9s. 6d. witnesses' expenses.

The question for the opinion of the court was whether the justices were right in law in holding that the advertisement was an offer for sale in Chester on May 1, 1967, and that a bird was not a close-ringed specimen bred in captivity within the meaning of the Act of 1954 if it was possible to remove the ring from its leg.

C.J. Pitchers for the appellant.
Michael Havers Q.C. and *D.T. Lloyd-Jones* for the prosecutor.

The following cases, in addition to those referred to in the judgment, were cited in argument: *Rooke* v. *Dawson* [1895] 1 Ch. 480; *Harris* v. *Nickerson* (1873) L.R. 8 Q.B. 286; *Carlill* v. *Carbolic Smoke Ball Co.* [1892] 2 Q.B. 484; [1893] 1, Q.B. 256, C.A.; and *Spencer* v. *Harding* (1870) L.R. 5 C.P. 561.

LORD PARKER C.J. Ashworth J. will give the first judgment.

ASHWORTH J.: This is an appeal by way of case stated from a decision of Chester justices. On July 19, 1967, they heard an information preferred by the prosecutor on behalf of the R.S.P.C.A. alleging against the appellant that he did unlawfully offer for sale a certain live wild bird, to wit a brambling, being a bird included in schedule 4 to the Protection of Birds Act, 1954, of a species which is resident in or visits the British Isles in a wild state, other than a close-ringed specimen bred in captivity, contrary to section 6, subsection (1) of the Act.

The case arose because in a periodical known as "Cage and Aviary Birds," the issue for April 13, 1967, there appeared an advertisement inserted by the appellant containing, inter alia, the words "Quality British A.B.C.R. . . . bramblefinch cocks, bramblefinch hens, 25s. each." In the case stated the full advertisement is not set out, but by the agreement of counsel this court has seen a copy of the issue in question, and what is perhaps to be noted in passing is that on the page there is a whole list of different birds under the general heading of "Classified Advertisements." In no place, so far as I can see, is there any direct use of the words "Offers for sale." I ought to say I am not for my part deciding that that would have the result of making this judgment any different, but at least it strengthens the case for the appellant that there is no such expression on the page. Having seen that advertisement, Mr. Thompson wrote to the appellant and asked for a hen and enclosed a cheque for 30s. A hen, according to the case, was sent to him on May 1, 1967, which was wearing a closed-ring, and he received it on May 2. The box was opened by Mr. Thompson in the presence of the prosecutor, and the case finds that Mr. Thompson was able to remove the ring without injury to the bird, and even taking into account that the bird had travelled from Leicester in a box on the railway, its condition was rough, it was extremely nervous, it had no perching sense at all and its plumage was rough.

Stopping there, the inference from that finding is that the justices were taking the view, or could take the view, that from its appearance, at any rate, this was not such a bird as a person can legitimately sell within the Act of 1954. The case goes on to find:

> "The expression 'close-ringed' is nowhere defined nor is there any universally recommended size ring for a bramblefinch.
> "(g) The ring is placed on the bird's leg at the age of three to 10 days at which time it is not possible to determine what the eventual girth of the bird's leg will be."

Having been referred to the decision of this court in *Fisher* v. *Bell* [1961] 1 Q.B. 394; [1960] 3 W.L.R. 919; [1960] 3 All E.R. 731, D.C. the justices nonetheless took the view that the advertisement did constitute an offer for sale; they went on further to find that the bird was not a close-ringed specimen bred in captivity, because it was possible to remove the ring. Before this court Mr. Pitchers for the appellant, has taken two points, first, this was not an offer for sale and, secondly, that the justices' reason for finding that it was not a close-ringed bird was plainly wrong because the fact that one could remove the ring did not render it a non-close-ringed bird.

It is convenient, perhaps, to deal with the question of the ring first. For my part I confess I was in ignorance, and in some state of confusion, as to the real meaning and effect of this particular phrase in the section, and I express my indebtedness to Mr. Havers, for the prosecutor, for having made the matter, as far as I am concerned, perfectly clear. I would say if one was looking for a definition of the phrase "close-ringed" it means ringed by a complete ring, which is not capable of being forced apart of broken except, of course, with the intention of damaging it. I contrast a closed-ring of that sort—it might take the form, I suppose, of an elastic band or of a metal circle ring—with the type of ring which sometimes exists which is made into a ring when a tongue is placed through a slot and then drawn back; that is a ring which can be undone and is not close-ringed. In this case what is contemplated, according to Mr. Havers, and I accept it, is that with a young bird of this sort between three and ten days after hatching a closed-ring of the type described is forced over its claws, which are obviously brought together so as to admit the passage of the ring, and it is then permanently on or around the bird's leg, and as it grows, it would be impossible to take that ring off because the claws and the like would have rendered a repetition of the earlier manoeuvre impossible.

Therefore, approaching the matter this way, I can well understand how the justices came to the conclusion that this was not a close-ringed specimen, because they could take the ring off. If that were the only issue, I should not find any difficulty in upholding their decision. But the real point of substance in this case arose from the words "offer for sale," and it is to be noted in section 6 of the Act of 1954 that the operative words are "any person sells, offers for sale or has in his possession for sale." For some reason which Mr. Havers for the prosecutor has not been able to explain, those responsible for the prosecution in this case chose, out of the trio of possible offences, the one which could not succeed. There was a sale here, in my view, because Mr. Thompson sent his cheque and the bird was sent in reply; and a completed sale. On the evidence there was also a plain case of the appellant having in possession for sale this particular bird. But they chose to prosecute him for offering for sale, and they relied on the advertisement.

A similar point arose before this court in 1960 dealing, it is true, with a different statute but with the same words, in *Fisher* v. *Bell* [1961] 1 Q.B. 394. The relevant words of section 1(1) of the Restriction of Offensive Weapons Act, 1959, in that case were: "Any person who . . . offers for sale. . . . (a) any knife. . . ." Lord Parker C.J., in giving judgment said Ibid. 399:

> "The sole question is whether the exhibition of that knife in the window with the ticket constituted an offer for sale within the statute. I confess that I think that most lay people and, indeed, I myself when I first read the papers, would be inclined to the view that to say that if a knife was displayed in a window like that with a price attached to it was not offering it for sale was just nonsense. In ordinary language it is there inviting people to buy it, and it is for sale; but any statute must of course be looked at in the light of the general law of the country."

The words are the same here "offer for sale," and in my judgment the law of the country is equally plain as it was in regard to articles in a shop window, namely that the insertion of an advertisement in the form adopted here under the title "Classified Advertisements" is simply an invitation to treat.

That is really sufficient to dispose of this case. I should perhaps in passing observe that the editors of the publication Criminal Law Review had an article dealing with *Fisher* v. *Bell* [1961] 1 Q.B. 394 in which a way round that decision was at least contemplated, suggesting that while there might be one meaning of the phrase "offer for sale" in the law of contract, a criminal court might take a stricter view, particularly having in mind the purpose of the Act, in *Fisher* v. *Bell* [1961] 1 Q.B. 394 the stocking of flick knives, and in this case the selling of wild birds. But for my part that is met entirely by the quotation which appears in Lord Parker's judgment in *Fisher* v. *Bell*, that Ibid. 400 "It appears to me to be a naked usurpation of the legislative function under the thin disguise of interpretation."

I would allow this appeal and quash the conviction.

BLAIN J. I agree.

LORD PARKER C.J. I agree and with less reluctance than in *Fisher* v. *Bell* [1961] 1 Q.B. 394, and *Mella* v. *Monahan* [1961] Crim.L.R. 175, D.C. I say "with less reluctance" because I think when one is dealing with advertisements and circulars, unless they indeed come from manufacturers, there is business sense in their being construed as invitations to treat and not offers for sale. In a very different context in *Grainger & Son* v. *Gough* [1896] A.C. 325, H.L.(E.) Lord Herschell said dealing with a price-list Ibid. 334:

> "The transmission of such a price-list does not amount to an offer to supply an unlimited quantity of the wine described at the price named, so that as soon as an order is given there is a binding contract to supply that quantity. If it were so, the merchant might find himself involved in any number of contractual obligations to supply wine of a particular description which he would be quite unable to carry out his stock of wine of that description being necessarily limited."

It seems to me accordingly that not only is it the law but common sense supports it.

Appeal allowed with costs.

Solicitors: *R.G. Frisby & Small, Leicester; Rex Taylor & Meadows, West Kirby.*

Source: *The Weekly Law Reports*, 26 July 1968

Company registration forms

COMPANIES HOUSE

10

*Please complete in typescript,
or in bold black capitals.*

Notes on completion appear on final page

First directors and secretary and intended situation of registered office

Company Name in full

F010001H

Proposed Registered Office

(PO Box numbers only, are not acceptable)

Post town

County / Region

Postcode

If the memorandum is delivered by an agent for the subscriber(s) of the memorandum mark the box opposite and give the agent's name and address.

Agent's Name

Address

Post town

County / Region

Postcode

Number of continuation sheets attached

Please give the name, address, telephone number and, if available, a DX number and Exchange of the person Companies House should contact if there is any query.

Tel

DX number   DX exchange

When you have completed and signed the form please send it to the Registrar of Companies at:

Companies House, Crown Way, Cardiff, CF4 3UZ   DX 33050 Cardiff
for companies registered in England and Wales
or
Companies House, 37 Castle Terrace, Edinburgh, EH1 2EB
for companies registered in Scotland   **DX 235 Edinburgh**

Form revised March 1995

Company Secretary (see notes 1-5)

Company name

NAME   *Style / Title   *Honours etc

* Voluntary details

Forename(s)

Surname

Previous forename(s)

Previous surname(s)

Address

Usual residential address
For a corporation, give the
registered or principal office
address.

Post town

County / Region   Postcode

Country

I consent to act as secretary of the company named on page 1

Consent signature   **Date**

Directors (see notes 1-5)

Please list directors in alphabetical order

NAME   *Style / Title   *Honours etc

Forename(s)

Surname

Previous forename(s)

Previous surname(s)

Address

Usual residential address
For a corporation, give the
registered or principal office
address.

Post town

County / Region   Postcode

Country

Day   Month   Year

Date of birth   **Nationality**

Business occupation

Other directorships

I consent to act as director of the company named on page 1

Consent signature   **Date**

Directors (continued) (see notes 1-5)

NAME   *Style / Title [   ] *Honours etc [   ]

* Voluntary details

Forename(s) [   ]

Surname [   ]

Previous forename(s) [   ]

Previous surname(s) [   ]

Address

Usual residential address
For a corporation, give the
registered or principal office
address.

[   ]

[   ]

Post town [   ]

County / Region [   ]   Postcode [   ]

Country [   ]

Day   Month   Year

Date of birth [   ] [   ] [   ]   **Nationality** [   ]

Business occupation [   ]

Other directorships [   ]

[   ]

I consent to act as director of the company named on page 1

Consent signature [   ]   **Date** [   ]

This section must be signed by
Either

an agent on behalf
of all subscribers   **Signed** [   ]   **Date** [   ]

Or the subscribers   **Signed** [   ]   **Date** [   ]

(*i.e those who signed
as members on the*   **Signed** [   ]   **Date** [   ]
*memorandum of
association).*   **Signed** [   ]   **Date** [   ]

Signed [   ]   **Date** [   ]

Signed [   ]   **Date** [   ]

Signed [   ]   **Date** [   ]

Notes

1. Show for an individual the full forename(s) NOT INITIALS and surname together with any previous forename(s) or surname(s).

   If the director or secretary is a corporation or Scottish firm - show the corporate or firm name on the surname line.

   Give previous forename(s) or surname(s) except that:

   - for a married woman, the name by which she was known before marriage need not be given,

   - names not used since the age of 18 or for at least 20 years need not be given.

   A peer, or an individual known by a title, may state the title instead of or in addition to the forename(s) and surname and need not give the name by which that person was known before he or she adopted the title or succeeded to it.

   Address:

   Give the usual residential address.

   In the case of a corporation or Scottish firm give the registered or principal office.

   Subscribers:

   The form must be signed personally either by the subscriber(s) or by a person or persons authorised to sign on behalf of the subscriber(s).

2. Directors known by another description:

   - A director includes any person who occupies that position even if called by a different name, for example, governor, member of council.

3. Directors details:

   - Show for each individual director the director's date of birth, business occupation and nationality. **The date of birth must be given for every individual director.**

4. Other directorships:

   - Give the name of every company of which the person concerned is a director or has been a director at any time in the past 5 years. You may exclude a company which either **is** or at **all times during the past 5 years,** when the person was a director, **was:**

   - dormant,

   - a parent company which wholly owned the company making the return,

   - a wholly owned subsidiary of the company making the return, or

   - another wholly owned subsidiary of the same parent company.

   If there is insufficient space on the form for other directorships you may use a separate sheet of paper, which should include the company's number and the full name of the director.

5. Use Form 10 continuation sheets or photocopies of page 2 to provide details of joint secretaries or additional directors and include the company's number.

COMPANIES HOUSE

Please complete in typescript,
or in bold black capitals.

12

Declaration on application for registration

Company Name in full

✳F012001J✳

I,

of

do solemnly and sincerely declare that I am a [Solicitor engaged in the formation of the company][person named as director or secretary of the company in the statement delivered to the Registrar under section 10 of the Companies Act 1985]† and that all the requirements of the Companies Act 1985 in respect of the registration of the above company and of matters precedent and incidental to it have been complied with.

And I make this solemn Declaration conscientiously believing the same to be true and by virtue of the Statutory Declarations Act 1835.

† Please delete as appropriate.

Declarant's signature

Declared at

the   day of

One thousand nine hundred and ninety

❶ Please print name.

before me ❶

Signed   **Date**

A Commissioner for Oaths or Notary Public or Justice of the Peace or Solicitor

Please give the name, address, telephone number and, if available, a DX number and Exchange of the person Companies House should contact if there is any query.

Tel

DX number   DX exchange

When you have completed and signed the form please send it to the Registrar of Companies at:
Companies House, Crown Way, Cardiff, CF4 3UZ   **DX 33050 Cardiff**
for companies registered in England and Wales
or
Companies House, 37 Castle Terrace, Edinburgh, EH1 2EB
for companies registered in Scotland   **DX 235 Edinburgh**

Form revised March 1995

Small claims forms

County Court Summons

In the

County Court

The court office is open from 10am to 4pm Monday to Friday

Telephone:

Seal

This summons is only valid if sealed by the court
If it is not sealed it should be sent to the court.

(1)

Plaintiff's
full name
address

(2)

Address for
service (and)
payment
(if not as above)
Ref/Tel no.

(3)

Defendant's
name
address

What the plaintiff claims from you

Brief
description
of type of
claim

Particulars of the plaintiff's claim against you

Amount claimed

Court fee

Solicitor's costs

Total amount

Summons issued on

What to do about this summons

You can

- **dispute the claim**
- **make a claim against the plaintiff**
- **admit the claim in full and offer to pay**
- **pay the total amount shown above**
- **admit only part of the claim**

**For information on what to do or if you
need further advice, please turn over.**

Signed
Plaintiff('s solicitor)
(or see enclosed particulars of claim)

Keep this summons, you may need to refer to it

You have 21 days from the date of the postmark to reply to this summons

(A limited company served at its registered office has 16 days to reply.)

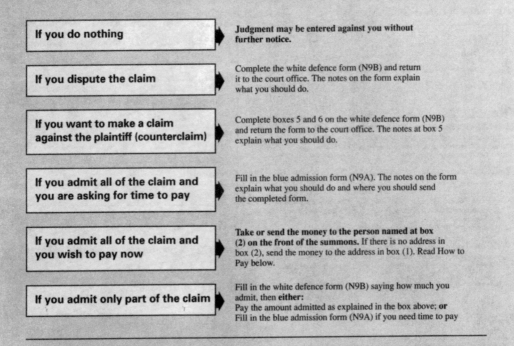

If you do nothing	**Judgment may be entered against you without further notice.**
If you dispute the claim	Complete the white defence form (N9B) and return it to the court office. The notes on the form explain what you should do.
If you want to make a claim against the plaintiff (counterclaim)	Complete boxes 5 and 6 on the white defence form (N9B) and return the form to the court office. The notes at box 5 explain what you should do.
If you admit all of the claim and you are asking for time to pay	Fill in the blue admission form (N9A). The notes on the form explain what you should do and where you should send the completed form.
If you admit all of the claim and you wish to pay now	**Take or send the money to the person named at box (2) on the front of the summons.** If there is no address in box (2), send the money to the address in box (1). Read How to Pay below.
If you admit only part of the claim	Fill in the white defence form (N9B) saying how much you admit, then **either:** Pay the amount admitted as explained in the box above; **or** Fill in the blue admission form (N9A) if you need time to pay

Interest on Judgments

If judgment is entered against you and is for more than £5000, the plaintiff may be entitled to interest on the total amount.

Registration of Judgments

If the summons results in a judgment against you, your name and address may be entered in the Register of County Court Judgments. **This may make it difficult for you to get credit.** A leaflet giving further information can be obtained from the court.

Further Advice

You can get help to complete the reply forms and information about court procedures at any county court office or citizens' advice bureau. The address and telephone number of your local court is listed under "Courts" in the phone book. When corresponding with the court, please address forms or letters to the Chief Clerk. Always quote the whole of the case number which appears at the top right corner on the front of this form; the court is unable to trace your case without it.

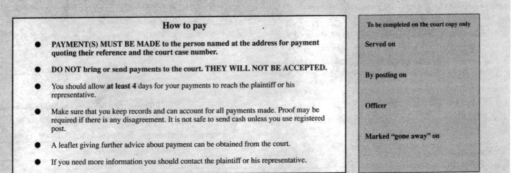

How to pay	To be completed on the court copy only
• **PAYMENT(S) MUST BE MADE to the person named at the address for payment quoting their reference and the court case number.**	Served on
• **DO NOT bring or send payments to the court. THEY WILL NOT BE ACCEPTED.**	
• You should allow **at least 4** days for your payments to reach the plaintiff or his representative.	By posting on
• Make sure that you keep records and can account for all payments made. Proof may be required if there is any disagreement. It is not safe to send cash unless you use registered post.	Officer
• A leaflet giving further advice about payment can be obtained from the court.	Marked "gone away" on
• If you need more information you should contact the plaintiff or his representative.	

Notice of Issue of Default Summons - fixed amount

To the plaintiff ('s solicitor)

Your summons was issued today. The defendant has 14 days from the date of service to reply to the summons. If the date of postal service is not shown on this form you will be sent a separate notice of service (Form N222).

The defendant may either

- **Pay you your total claim.**
- **Dispute the whole claim.** The court will send you a copy of the defence and tell you what to do next.
- **Admit that all the money is owed.** The defendant will send you form of
- admission N9A. You may then ask the court to send the defendant an order to pay you the money owed by completing the request for judgment below and returning it to the court.
- **Admit that only part of your claim is owed.** The court will send you a copy of the reply and tell you what to do next.
- **Not reply at all.** You should wait 14 days from the date of service. You may then ask the court to send the defendant an order to pay you the money owed by completing the request for judgment below and returning it to the court.

In the	
NOTTINGHAM	
	County Court

The court office at
NOTTINGHAM COMBINED COURT
60 CANAL STREET, NOTTINGHAM NG1 7EJ

is open between 10 am & 4 pm Monday to Friday
Tel: 0602 583956

Case Number	*Always quote this*	
Plaintiff *(including ref.)*		
Defendants		
Issue date		
Date of postal service		
Issue fee	£	

For further information please turn over

Request for Judgment

- *Tick and complete either A or B. Make sure that all the case details are given and that the judgment details at C are completed. Remember to sign and date the form. Your signature certifies that the information you have given is correct.*
- *If the defendant has given an address on the form of admission to which correspondence should be sent, which is different from the address shown on the summons, you will need to tell the court.*

A ☐ **The defendant has not replied to my summons**
Complete all the judgment details at C. Decide how and when you want the defendant to pay. You can ask for the judgment to be paid by instalments or in one payment.

B ☐ **The defendant admits that all the money is owed**
Tick only **one** box below and return the completed slip to the court.

☐ **I accept the defendant's proposal for payment**
Complete all the judgment details at C. Say how the defendant intends to pay. The court will send the defendant an order to pay. You will also be sent a copy.

☐ **The defendant has not made any proposal for payment**
Complete all the judgment details at C. Say how you want the defendant to pay. You can ask for the judgment to be paid by instalments or in one payment. The court will send the defendant an order to pay. You will also be sent a copy.

☐ **I do NOT accept the defendant's proposal for payment**
Complete all the judgment details at C and say how you want the defendant to pay. Give your reasons for objecting to the defendant's offer of payment in the section overleaf. Return this slip to the court **together with the defendant's admission N9A** (or a copy). The court will fix a rate of payment and send the defendant an order to pay. You will also be sent a copy.

I certify that the information given is correct

Signed .... Dated ....

In the	**NOTTINGHAM**
	County Court

Case Number	*Always quote this*	
Plaintiff		
Defendant		
Plaintiff's Ref.		

C **Judgment details**

I would like the judgment to be paid

☐ (forthwith) *only tick this box if you intend to enforce the order right away*
☐ (by instalments of £   per month)
☐ (in full by   )

Amount of claim as stated in summons
(including interest at date of issue) ....

Interest since date of summons (if any) ....
Period .... Rate .... %

Court fees shown on summons ....

Solicitor's costs (if any) on issuing summons ......

Sub Total

Solicitor's costs (if any) on entering judgment

Sub Total

Deduct amount (if any) paid since issue ....

Amount payable by defendant

N205A Notice of issue (default summons) and request for judgment (Order 3, rule (2)(d)(1), Order 9 rules 3 and 6)   MCR 601369 8/93 C

368   Small claims forms

Further information

- The summons must be served within 4 months of the date of issue (or 6 months if leave to serve out of the jurisdiction is granted under Order 8, rule 2). In exceptional circumstances you may apply for this time to be extended provided that you do so before the summons expires.

- If the defendant does not reply to the summons or if he delivers an admission without an offer of payment you may ask for judgment. If you do not ask for judgment within 12 months of the date of service the action will be struck out. It cannot be reinstated.

- You may be entitled to interest if judgment is entered against the defendant and your claim is for more than £5000.

- You should keep a record of any payments you receive from the defendant. If there is a hearing or you wish to take steps to enforce the judgment, you will need to satisfy the court about the balance outstanding. You should give the defendant a receipt and payment in cash should always be acknowledged. You should tell the defendant how much he owes if he asks.

- **You must inform the court IMMEDIATELY if you receive any payment before a hearing date or after you have sent a request for enforcement to the court.**

Objections to the defendant's proposal for payment

Case Number

Defence and Counterclaim

In the	NOTTINGHAM
	County Court

Case Number	*Always quote this*	

Plaintiff *(including ref.)*

Defendant

The court office is open from 10am to 4pm Monday to Friday

NOTTINGHAM COMBINED COURT
60 CANAL STREET
NOTTINGHAM
NG1 7EJ

When to fill in this form
- Only fill in this form if you wish to dispute all or part of the claim **and/or** make a claim against the plaintiff (counterclaim).

How to fill in this form
- Please check that the correct case details are shown on this form. You must ensure that all the boxes at the top right of this form are completed. You can obtain the correct names and numbers from the summons. The court cannot trace your case without this information.
- Follow the instructions given in each section. Tick the correct boxes and give the other details asked for.
- If you wish only to make a claim against the plaintiff (counterclaim) go to section 5.
- Complete and sign section 6 before returning this form.

Where to send this form
- Send or take this form immediately to the court office at the address shown above.
- If you admit part of the claim and you are asking for time to pay, you will also need to fill in the blue admission form (N9A) and send **both** reply forms to the court.
- Keep the summons and a copy of this defence; you may need them.

Legal Aid
- You may be entitled to legal aid. Ask about the legal aid scheme at any county court office, citizen's advice bureau, legal advice centre or firm of solicitors displaying this legal aid sign.

What happens next
- If you complete box 3 on this form, the court will ask the plaintiff to confirm that he has received payment. If he tells the court that you have not paid, the court will tell you what you should do.
- If you complete box 4 or 5, the court will tell you what you should do.
- If the summons is not from your local county court, it will automatically be transferred to your local court.

1 How much of the claim do you dispute?

☐ I dispute the full amount claimed *(go to section 2)*

or

☐ I admit the amount of £ [ ] and I dispute the balance

If you dispute only part of the claim you must **either:**

- pay the amount admitted to the person named at the address for payment in box (2) on the front of the summons or if there is no address in box (2), send the money to the address in box (1) (see How to Pay on the back of the summons). Then send this defence to the court.

or

- complete the blue admission form and send it to the court with this defence.

Tick whichever applies

☐ I paid the amount admitted on [ ]

or

☐ I enclose the completed form of admission

(go to section 2)

2 Arbitration under the small claims procedure
How the claim will be dealt with if defended

If the claim is for **£1,000 or less** it will be dealt with by arbitration (small claims procedure) unless the court decides the case is too difficult to be dealt with in this informal way. Costs and the grounds for setting aside an arbitration award are strictly limited. If the claim is for £1,000 or less and is not dealt with by arbitration, costs, including the costs of a legal representative, may be allowed.

If the claim is for **over £1,000** it can still be dealt with by arbitration if either you or the plaintiff asks for it and the court approves. If the claim is dealt with by arbitration in these circumstances, costs may be allowed.

Please tick this box if the claim is worth over £1,000 and you would like it dealt with by arbitration. ☐
(go on to section 3)

3 Do you dispute this claim because you have already paid it? *Tick whichever applies*

☐ No *(go to section 4)*

☐ Yes I paid £ [ ] to the plaintiff

on [ ] *(before the summons was issued)*

Give details of where and how you paid it in the box below *(then go to section 6)*

Case No. [   ]

4 If you dispute the claim for reasons other than payment, what are your reasons?

Use the box below to give full details. *(If you need to continue on a separate sheet, put the case number in the top right hand corner.)*

[   ]

5 If you wish to make a claim against the plaintiff (counterclaim)

If your claim is for a specific sum of money, how much are you claiming?   £ [   ]

- If your claim against the plaintiff is for more than the plaintiff's claim against you, you may have to pay a fee. Ask at your local court office whether a fee is payable.

- You may not be able to make a counterclaim where the plaintiff is the Crown (e.g. a Government Department). Ask at your local county court office for further information.

What are your reasons for making the counterclaim?

- Use the box opposite to give full details.
  (If you need to continue on a separate sheet, put the case number in the top right hand corner.)

  (go on to section 6)

6 Signed
(To be signed by you or by your solicitor)

[   ]

Position
(firm or company)

[   ]

Give an address to which notices about this case can be sent to you

[   ]

Dated

[   ]

Postcode [   ]

Small claims forms   371

Admission

When to fill in this form
- Only fill in this form if you are admitting all or some of the claim **and** you are asking for time to pay
- If you are disputing the claim or you wish to pay the amount claimed, read the back of the summons

How to fill in this form
- Tick the correct boxes and give as much information as you can. **Then sign and date the form.**
- Make your offer of payment in box 11 on the back of this form. **If you make no offer the plaintiff will decide how you should pay.**
- You can get help to complete this form at **any** county court office or citizens' advice bureau.

Where to send this form
- **If you admit the claim in full**
  Send the completed form to the address shown at box (2) on the front of the summons. If there is no address in box (2) send the form to the address in box (1).
- **If you admit only part of the claim**
  Send the form **to the court** at the address given on the summons, together with the white defence form (N9B).

What happens next
- **If you admit the claim in full and offer to pay**
  If the plaintiff accepts your offer, judgement will be entered and you will be sent an order telling you how and when to pay. If the plaintiff does **not** accept your offer, the court will fix a rate of payment based on the details you have given in this form and the plaintiff's comments. Judgement will be entered and you will be sent an order telling you how and when to pay.
- **If you admit only part of the claim**
  The court will tell you what to do next.

How much of the claim do you admit?
- [ ] I admit the full amount claimed as shown on the summons **or**
- [ ] I admit the amount of £ _____

---

1 Personal details

Surname _____

Forename _____

[ ] Mr [ ] Mrs [ ] Miss [ ] Ms

[ ] Married [ ] Single [ ] Other *(specify)* _____

Age _____

Address _____

Postcode _____

In the

NOTTINGHAM County Court

Case Number *Always quote this* _____

Plaintiff *(including ref.)*

Defendant

2 Dependants *(people you look after financially)*

Number of children in each age group

under 11 [ ]   11-15 [ ]   16-17 [ ]   18 & over [ ]

Other dependants *(give details)* _____

3 Employment

- [ ] I am employed as a _____

  My employer is _____

  Jobs other than main job *(give details)* _____

- [ ] I am self employed as a _____

  Annual turnover is...................... £ ____

  - [ ] **I am not** in arrears with my national insurance contributions, income tax and VAT
  - [ ] **I am** in arrears and I owe.......... £ ____

  Give details of:
  (a) contracts and other work in hand _____
  (b) any sums due for work done _____

- [ ] I have been unemployed for ____ years ____ months

- [ ] I am a pensioner

4 Bank account and savings

- [ ] I have a bank account
  - [ ] The account is in credit by .... £ ____
  - [ ] The account is overdrawn by.... £ ____

- [ ] I have a savings or building society account
  The amount in the account is .... £ ____

5 Property

I live in [ ] my own property   [ ] lodgings

[ ] jointly owned property   [ ] council property

[ ] rented property

N9A Form of admission and statement of means to accompany Form N1 (Order 9, rule 2)

MCR 601369 8/93 C

6 Income

My usual take home pay *(including overtime, commission, bonuses etc)*	£	per
Income support	£	per
Child benefit(s)	£	per
Other state benefit(s)	£	per
My pension(s)	£	per
Others living in my home give me	£	per
Other income *(give details below)*		
	£	per
	£	per
	£	per
Total income	**£**	**per**

7 Expenses

(Do not include any payments made by other members of the household out of their own income)

I have regular expenses as follows:

Mortgage *(including second mortgage)*	£	per
Rent	£	per
Community charge	£	per
Gas	£	per
Electricity	£	per
Water charges	£	per
TV rental and licence	£	per
HP repayments	£	per
Mail order	£	per
Housekeeping, food, school meals	£	per
Travelling expenses	£	per
Children's clothing	£	per
Maintenance payments	£	per
Others *(not court orders or credit debts listed in boxes 9 and 10)*		
	£	per
	£	per
	£	per
Total expenses	**£**	**per**

8 Priority debts *(This section is for arrears only. Do not include regular expenses listed in box 7.)*

Rent arrears	£	per
Mortgage arrears	£	per
Community charge arrears	£	per
Water charges arrears	£	per
Fuel debts: Gas	£	per
Electricity	£	per
Other	£	per
Maintenance arrears	£	per
Others *(give details below)*		
	£	per
	£	per
Total priority debts	**£**	**per**

9 Court orders

Court Case No.	£	per
Total court order instalments	**£**	**per**

Of the payments above, I am behind with payments to *(please list)*

10 Credit debts

Loans and credit card debts *(please list)*

	£	per
	£	per
	£	per

Of the payments above, I am behind with payments to *(please list)*

11 Do you wish to make an offer of payment?

- *If you take away the totals of boxes, 7, 8 and 9 and the payments you are making in box 10 from the total in box 6 you will get some idea of the sort of sum you should offer. The offer you make should be one you can afford.*

☐ I can pay the amount admitted on
or
☐ I can pay by monthly instalments of £

12 Declaration   I declare that the details I have given above are true to the best of my knowledge

Signed   **Dated**

Position
(firm or company)

UNIT 15
Business and the Law (Advanced)

Summary of Elements

Element 15.1 Investigate the effect of law on business operations and activities

Element 15.2 Examine the legal status of businesses

Element 15.3 Investigate legal relationships arising from business operations and activities

Introduction to Unit 17

1. In this unit students investigate the business interface with the legal system. The unit will provide an understanding of the legal implications of business activities. Students will identify and investigate a range of legal duties and responsibilities commonly ascribed to a business organisation and gain an understanding of potential liabilities, and the implications and possible outcomes which may follow from non-compliance with the law. The unit raises the student's awareness of the impact of law on a business, rather than providing a detailed knowledge of legal principles.

2. The content of this unit provides opportunities for linking with the **Advanced Mandatory Unit 1: Business in the Economy: Advanced Mandatory Unit 2: Business Organisations and Systems: Advanced Mandatory Unit 3: Marketing and Advanced Mandatory Unit 4: Human Resources.**

3. Element 15.1 is designed to introduce students to the types of law which impact on the way a business can operate. It assumes that students have no previous knowledge of law and will require an explanation of the scope of each area of law in a business context.

4. Element 15.2 concentrates on the reasons for choice of legal status in a particular set of circumstances, the completion of the relevant documentation for company registration and the setting up of a partnership through the drawing up of a partnership deed.

5. Element 15.3 focuses on a business's legal relationships with others rather than its specific rights and duties.

Element
15.1 Investigate the effect of law on business operations and activities

Performance Criteria

A student must:

1. Outline the **types of law** which may affect a business

2. Describe and give examples of the **types of legal duties** arising from business operations and activities

3. Identify and give examples of **legal rights of groups** affected by business operations and activities

4. Explain the **types of legal processes and procedures** which may result from the bringing of legal actions against a business

Range

Types of law:	contract; tort; criminal; consumer; property; employment; finance; company; partnership
Types of legal duties:	criminal; civil; common law, statutory; personal; joint; fault based; strict
Legal Rights:	Consumer Protection; Health and Safety; Employment Law
Groups:	employees; shareholders; consumers; customers; suppliers; creditors; community; state
Types of legal processes and procedures:	criminal; civil; tribunal

Evidence Indicators

A summary of an investigation into the effect of law on business operations and activities; which includes:

● an outline of the types of law which may affect a business

● a description, with examples, of the types of legal duties arising from business activities and operations

● an identification, with examples, of the legal rights of three different groups affected by business operations and activities

● an explanation of the types of legal processes and procedures which may result from the bringing of legal actions against a business

Amplification

Types of law (PC1) teachers and tutors should provide a general introduction to law. It is anticipated that this will be prefaced with a general introduction to legal terminology and classification. Students do not require an in-depth study of the legal principles involved in each type of law stated within the range of this elements but should be able to illustrate the variety of legal areas which a business can be affected by. Examples of the impact of each legal area will suffice, for example, the restrictions on the use of exclusion clauses within a business's standard contractual terms of sale.

Business operations and activities (PC2) in the context of types of legal duties, could be illustrated by such areas as an employer's health and safety duties towards employees, (common law and statutory and civil and criminal duties) liability to customers for defective products (fault based duties as in the common law tort of negligence and strict liability under the Consumer Protection Act 1987).

Legal rights (PC2) for the context of this element this large area has been limited to reflect the specific legal responsibilities of businesses outlined in Element 14.3 PC 1 and PC 2.

Business operations and activities (PC3) in the context of legalists, involve the day-to-day business of the organisation. Examples could include the rights of shareholders exercisable in company meetings or the rights of those in the community surrounding the business exercisable through the tort of nuisance.

Types of legal processes and procedures (PC4) how civil or criminal action may be brought and to which court will depend on the type of legal action.

A series of case studies of business situations could provide a useful opportunity for students to identify relevant types of law, apply principles of law and to suggest potential outcomes of applying that law. These are not intended to be covered in depth, for example, a case study involving an employee stealing from the company, following internal disciplinary action, would involve students in an identification of the area of criminal law, stating the offence committed.

There is some opportunity for linking activities for this Element with activities for Element 1.3 of the **Advanced Mandatory Unit 1: Business in the Economy** and the activities for Element 4.1 of **Advanced Mandatory Unit 4: Human Resources.**

Criminal, civil, tribunal (PC4 range) students should able to identify types of proceedings a particular action may give rise to. For example, unfair dismissal action will be heard by an Industrial Tribunal, a breach of contract on the part of the business will give rise to them being sued in the County or High Court, depending on the amount of claim. Students should be able to describe in simple terms the process of bringing the action to the relevant court, the actual hearing of the case and the outcome. Students should be aware that a situation may give rise to proceedings in more than one court. A health and safety matter for example may result in a business being prosecuted under the Factories Act 1961, whereas an injured employee may sue for compensation for injuries under the tort of negligence in a civil court.

Guidance

Material to focus the activities of students could be given in the form of mini case studies. To show the diversity of the law in this area it is important that any case studies reflect the key areas specified in the range.

Element
15.2 Examine the legal status of businesses

Performance Criteria

A student must:

1. Compare the **legal characteristics** of different types of **businesses**

2. Explain **factors** that can affect the choice of **legal status** for a **business**

3. Outline the **legal process of formation** of different types of **businesses**

Range

Legal characteristics:	legal personality; nature of liability (members, owners)
Businesses:	sole trader; partnership; limited companies
Factors:	implications of legal personality; limited liability; tax position; rights of membership; withdrawal; degree of control; capacity; administrative burden
Legal status:	unincorporated, incorporated
Legal process of formation:	Partnership Act 1890; Companies Acts

Evidence Indicators

A report of an examination of the legal status of businesses, which includes:

● a description of the legal characteristics of each type of business

● an explanation of how factors can affect the choice of legal status for a partnership or company

● an outline of the legal process of formation of each type of business

Amplification

Legal characteristics (PC1) students need to understand the concept of corporate personality, meaning that an organisation is a separate legal 'person' from those who own it and run it. The associated concept of limited liability should be covered. Students should then be able to consider the differences in legal characteristics of unincorporated and incorporated business organisations.

Legal status (PC2) choice may be determined by consideration of a number of factors, for example the extent to which a person wishes to be liable if the business is not successful, or the comparative advantage of Corporation Tax over Income Tax, or the degree to which they wish to remain in control of the business weighed against the need to raise finance. The relative importance of these factors will vary depending on the needs of the individual.

Companies Act (PC3 range) all acts between 1948–1989 have some relevance, but the main legislation is the 1985 Companies Act as amended by subsequent legislation.

Guidance

When considering the choice of a legal status when a business is set up it might be useful for students to carry out a role play exercise where they work in pairs, as client and legal advisor. The client could be given a briefing sheet including actual information on a potential business venture. The legal advisor would then have to elicit the relevant information from the client and advise him/her on the factors that ought to be taken into account when deciding on the legal status of a business. Advice could include the process of formation. The client could receive the advice in the form of a report and would make his/her own decision.

There could be some opportunities for linking the activities for this Element with the activities for Element 2.1 of the **Mandatory Unit: Business Organisations and Systems.**

Element
15.3 Investigate the legal relationships arising from business operations and activities

Performance Criteria

A student must:

1. Identify the nature of **legal responsibilities** of **businesses** towards **key external parties** to the organisation

2. Summarise the **specific legal responsibilities** of **businesses** towards **key internal parties**

3. Describe the ways in which a business's **legal liability** for civil and criminal wrongs committed can be reduced

Range

Specific legal responsibilities key external parties:	Tort (nuisance, negligence); Consumer Protection; Health and Safety Law; disclosure of information; Partnership Act 1890; Companies Acts

Specific legal responsibilities key internal parties:	Tort of negligence; Employment Law; Company Law
Businesses:	sole trader; partnership; limited companies
Key external parties:	consumers; suppliers; community; state; providers of finance
Key external parties:	employees; members; directors
Legal liability:	vicarious; strict; fault based; contractual; common law; statutory

Evidence Indicators

A report of an investigation into legal relationships arising from business operations and activities for one organisation, which includes:

- an identification of the specific legal responsibilities of the business towards key external parties to that organisation

- a summary of the legal responsibilities of the business towards key internal parties

- a description of the specific ways in which the business's legal liability for civil and criminal wrongs committed can be reduced.

Amplification

Specific legal responsibilities (PC1) the responsibilities identified should link with the rights and duties of key parties studied in Element 14.1. The degree to which a business is responsible to others for the consequences of its actions varies. For example responsibility to consumers for goods of unsatisfactory quality or for defective goods is substantial, with minimal defences available to the business. However, where the business is dealing with an organisation with perceived equality of bargaining power, legal responsibilities may become less onerous. Legal responsibilities towards the community or an individual in the area of nuisance may or may not mean that the business is prevented from continuing by the granting of an injunction. The court must choose to exercise its discretion in such a matter, weighing the relative effects of any decision on the business against the community or the individual. Environmental laws may prescribe minimum standards which must be adhered to, taking into account what it is reasonably practical for a business to do and still continue to be profitable. Thus the nature of legal responsibilities can be established through illustrations.

    Consumer Protection (PC1 range) this should focus on the main areas of Consumer Law, that is, Supply of Goods and Services, Sale of Goods Act, (limited to implied terms) provision of Credit for Consumers, Safety of Goods.

    Health and Safety Law (PC1 range) the legal responsibilities in relation to health and safety arise from common law and statute and may be expressed or implied. The main statute is the Health and Safety at Work Act 1974. Students should also be aware of the six sets of regulations introduced in 1993 as a result of a European Directive.

Disclosure of information (PC1 range) refers to the relevant parts of the Data Protection Act.

Partnership Act (PC1 range) refers to section five; the liability of partners for each others' acts.

Specific legal responsibilities of businesses (PC3) are those arising from Employment Law and Company Law requires students to become familiar with the legal responsibilities contained mainly in statute law.

Tort of negligence (PC2 range) refers to the duty of care of employers to employees, for example, health and safety; and the duty of care of directors to members of the company.

Legal liability (PC3) students should be able to ascertain the amount of liability a business may incur and how that varies with the type of wrongful act. Vicarious liability, for example, may mean that the business incurs liability for the wrongful acts of its employees, but this liability can be passed on to an insurance company if the risk is covered and theoretically the insurance company may claim back a contribution towards the compensation paid out if appropriate. In contractual agreements, a company may be able to limit its liability through the use of exclusion clauses. In tort, the amount of damages may, for example be reduced by the extent of the plaintiffs contributory negligence. Strict liability offence under the Health and Safety legislation will mean that a business cannot be permitted to submit defences to the action.

Guidance

For this element it may be useful for students to consider case study material as a useful basis for developing the investigation. Legal responsibilities of businesses in relation to parties external to the organisation could be investigated through the activities of a local business, for example, the effects of factory operations on the surrounding environment.

When considering the legal responsibilities of a business towards key internal parties, students could use a case study scenario of health and safety issues for employers in a manufacturing process. This could link with PC3 where a business may need to consider the implications of not compelling workers to comply with a health and safety requirement.

Liaison with local employers may produce relevant case study material for both of the above.

It would be useful for groups of students to focus on different types of organisations in a variety of sectors and share the information across the whole group. A broader base of information and the differences in legal relationships for different types of businesses in a variety of sectors will then be available to students.

The basic principles of employment law are covered in element 4.1 of **Advanced**

Mandatory Unit 4: Human Resources. The range covering specific legal responsibilities towards key internal parts builds upon these principles.

There are some opportunities for linking the activities for this Element with the activities for Element 3.4 of the **Advanced Mandatory Unit 3: Marketing.** Other opportunities for linkage between activities exist within Element 4.1 of the **Advanced Mandatory Unit 4: Human Resources.**

Index